Literary Taste, Culture and Mass Communication

Volume 7

CONTENT AND TASTE;
RELIGION AND MYTH

Literary Taste, Culture and Mass Communication

Volume 7

CONTENT AND TASTE; RELIGION AND MYTH

edited by

Peter Davison/Rolf Meyersohn/Edward Shils

CHADWYCK-HEALEY CAMBRIDGE
SOMERSET HOUSE TEANECK, NJ

© Chadwyck-Healey Ltd 1978

Chadwyck-Healey Ltd
20 Newmarket Road
Cambridge CB5 8DT
ISBN 0 85964 042 6

Somerset House
417 Maitland Avenue
Teaneck, NJ 07666
ISBN 0 914146 50 5

Library of Congress Cataloging in Publication Data
Main entry under title:

Content and taste.

(Literary taste, culture, and mass communication; v. 7)
Bibliography: p.
1. Mass media — Addresses, essays, lectures.
2. Popular culture — Addresses, essays, lectures.
3. Literature and society — Addresses, essays, lectures.
I. Series.

AC1.L79 vol. 7 [P91.251] 301.16′1s [301.16′1] 77-90615

British Library Cataloguing in Publication Data

Literary taste, culture and mass communication.
    Vol. 7: Content and taste; religion and myth.

    1. Arts and society — Addresses, essays, lectures
    I. Davison, Peter II. Meyersohn, Rolf III. Shils,
    Edward Albert IV. Content and taste; religion and
    myth

    700   NX180.S6

Printed in England

Contents

Introduction

Like volumes 6, 9 or 12, volume 7 is divided into sections for
convenience in use; unlike volume 6, however, although there are some
interests in common (two parts of Usborne's *Clubland Heroes* appearing in
different sections, for example), the sections are discrete and self-defining.
The volume begins with five articles having general implications and
applications for the contributions which deal with specific issues. George
Orwell's 'Good Bad Books' is one of his later essays (it appeared in 1945
five years before he died) and is representative of his work and approach.
The Collected Essays, Journalism and Letters (4 vols, London 1968) contain
a wealth of such material. Orwell took his title from G.K. Chesterton,
responsible for many paradoxes, including 'the two supreme symbolic
assertions of truth' are faith and nonsense, which Orwell might have applied
to *Uncle Tom's Cabin*, his supreme example of the 'good bad' book.

The next three articles are concerned with the nature and effects of
mass media. Possibly no specific technique developed for analyzing the mass
media has proved more valuable and adaptable than content analysis. It may
be said to have come to maturity half a century ago with the publication of
Harold Lasswell's *Propaganda Techniques in the World War*, 1927. This
approach was later developed by him in the 1939—45 war to infer
decisions made by the German High Command. It has been used to analyze
the content of the mass media, and, more recently, as a technique for
encoding materials for retrieval systems. By the time that George Gerbner's
article was published, F.E. Barcus has produced a content analysis of over
1,700 books, articles, and theses concerned with content analysis from 1900
to 1958. Gerbner's article gives a lucid introduction to content analysis and
the literary critic will note how close to the analysis of a play's sub-text are
some aspects of content analysis (e.g. the 'more subtle social relationships
recorded and reflected' in whiskey advertisements, p. 19).

Joseph T. Klapper reviews, in a very fully documented article, what was
known twenty years ago about the effects of mass communications. Elihu
Katz and David Foulkes, five years later, considered the charge that people
'use' mass media to escape, 'to forget their troubles'. Though they find
that this is undoubtedly true for some people, they strongly dissent from the
view that such escapism is 'invariably dysfunctional for the individual and
society' (p. 67). In much the same way, a great deal of Jacobean and
Caroline drama has been said to be 'an escape to cloud cuckooland' and
although it is not difficult to sustain *that* charge, it is also possible to see,
even in the maligned work of Beaumont and Fletcher (e.g. in *Philaster* and

The Maid's Tragedy), and in Massinger's *The Roman Actor*, a reflection of real social and political issues which were themselves only to be resolved in an event outside the range which any dramatist of the time could suggest with a censor breathing hot over his shoulder.

Civil War

Andrew Tolson's article is a revised version of a paper first published in the journal of the Centre for Contemporary Cultural Studies, Birmingham in 1973. This is both a theoretical review and practical exercise (of *Wuthering Heights*) based on a combination of the study of the text itself and the way the novel poses questions to late twentieth-century readers. This paper can be read as an extension of some of the theories argued out in volume 6. The works principally referred to are listed at the end of Further Reading.

Throughout much of the period when the contributions in the second group of articles were first published, Arnold Bennett's *Literary Taste: how to form it*, first published in 1909, went through a number of editions and revisions (including one by Frank Swinnerton in 1937) and appeared as a Penguin just forty years ago. In some ways that book typified an approach to literature – to taste in literature. Bennett also gave 'detailed instructions for collecting a complete library of English literature'. This is characteristic of the age preceding that which begins with such accounts of 'the Great Tradition' as those by Granville Hicks and F.R. Leavis, and which leads to the kind of reading of literature advocated by Andrew Tolson. In this context it can be seen how stout a defence against the alleged depravity of popular taste is Burges Johnson's essay of 1921 (and *Harper's Magazine*, in which it appeared, was one of the first 'popular' journals to realise the *social*, rather than scientific, significance of Heisenberg's *Principle of Uncertainty* – see Further Reading).

Robert Lynd was the literary editor of a London daily from 1908 until two years before his death in 1949. His essay anticipates, in a rather simplified manner, something of the argument to be found in George Steiner's *The Death of Tragedy* (and see Introduction to volume 5, xiii). His urbane style is of the same world of taste and discrimination found in James Wilson's review, which finds I.A. Richards's revolutionary approach to practical criticism, 'an amusing effort'. (See Further Reading for some of Richards's work.)

Laurence Housman, younger brother of the poet and classical scholar, A.E. Housman, was an artist as well as novelist and playwright. His, Lynd's, and Wilson's contributions all suggest 'the exercise of taste' in operation. Ironically, the British censor would not pass one of Housman's most successful works, *Victoria Regina* (1934) – it was performed first of all in America – but it now appears pallid and genteel. A strong sense of propriety dominates his lecture and this is coupled with a determination not to be *too* serious – see the manner in which he makes his proposal for a final appearance by Lady Macbeth and the last paragraph of the lecture, in which he offers this suggestion to any producer, 'free, gratis, for nothing'. It is against a background of such polished, polite essays that the newer literary critics of the thirties had to force a place and find a new language. In such a world was *Scrutiny* born. Nor surprisingly, the tone of this new criticism seemed brusque and the language abrasive to established scholars and critics.

The six groups of articles and extracts that follow draw attention to some of the characteristics of several genres. Long before Marshall McLuhan became a household word, he was, of course, a particularly incisive and witty critic as the review of Viereck's *Dream and Responsibility* makes plain. 'Myth and Mass Media' was published about ten years after *The Mechanical Bride* (New York 1951) and at the beginning of the decade that was to see the publication of *The Gutenberg Galaxy* (Toronto 1962), *Understanding Media* (New York 1964), and *The Medium is the Massage* (New York 1967). McLuhan's insights were combined with a remarkable power of connexion — hence, for example, his noting that those readily offended by Picasso and Joyce were the same people who found no problems in resolving the superficial chaos of the first page of a mass newspaper — which itself, 'a by-product of industrial imagination' had 'led to radical artistic developments' (*The Mechanical Bride*, p. 4). McLuhan stood and still stands, despite such descriptions as 'pop-cult prophet of the electronic age' — Penguin Books in an off-moment — for vigilant awareness of the interaction of media and society, and his approach starts from his own sharp literary critical faculties.

It is rather strange that Howard Roelofs should have to find the need to castigate those involved in a 'Symposium on American Culture' for ignoring Religion and especially 'Religion as Thrill', in the light of the American religious revivalist tradition, and he and Richard Potter, by different means, remind us of the religious elements of cultures, national and popular. Harry Emerson Fosdick was born exactly a hundred years ago and died in 1969. He taught at Union Theological Seminary from 1908 to 1946 and the books mentioned in Potter's article are by no means all he wrote. Two other titles are particularly revealing: *On Being a Real Person* (1943) and *A Faith for Tough Times* (1952). It was as a writer of sermons that he was a 'best seller'.

William Empson's little essay on 'Proletarian Literature' (which first appeared in *Scrutiny* in 1935, about the time that the anthology of American writing called *Proletarian Literature* edited by Granville Hicks *et al.*, was published in London), might seem at first a 'sport'. It could scarcely be more different from Joseph Freeman's introduction to *Proletarian Literature*. The idea of proletarian literature as pastoral, even Covert Pastoral, seems absurd — unless, perhaps, one has seen *Drifters* and in complete silence (although, as Basil Wright points out in *The Rise and Fall of British Documentary* by Elizabeth Sussex, Berkeley 1975, it was originally shown with 'a very good score', p. 7). But still more to the point is the inherent contradiction Empson finds in the concept of proletarian literature.

x

Nothing more suggests the shift in styles and attitudes in literature in the past half-century in Britain (especially popular literature) than Richard Usborne's account of *Clubland Heroes*, not even the delicate urbanity of the essays on taste. The counterpart to the clubland hero in popular literature is the romantic heroine, even if such heroines exist in a different world of books. Beatrice Hofstadter's essay, which considers the heroines of five American best-selling love stories published at approximately twenty-year intervals from 1850 to 1920, may be seen as a parallel to Usborne's chapters and an extension back in time of Ruth Inglis's study in volume 6. *L'Attaque* incidentally, mentioned by Usborne on page 287, still exists — but it is no longer French and, unsurprisingly is called *Attack!* There is even a naval version, but the single 'Espion' is metamorphosed into three submarines.

Laqueur, in his discussion of the interrelation of literature and history considers the suspicious response of professional historians to best-selling histories and their unease with the historical novel. He also argues that history is written, if unconsciously, by the creative writers of the age and their works are essential to understanding its *Zeitgeist*. He also offers a complementary account of the change in the position of the writer after the French Revolution to that given by Martin Turnell in volume 6. Chernischevsky, whom Laqueur mentions on pp. 254 and 256, is referred to in the Introduction to volume 3, p. viii. Chernischevsky's work towards the establishment of Realism had social as well as artistic significance for Realism was to prompt a new awareness (often, indeed, a first awareness) of the nature of society and the condition of life — a fact that those who exiled him to Siberia for twenty-one years fully realised. Joseph Remenyi's 'Psychology of War Literature' serves as a counterpart to Laqueur's article, for he discusses an aspect of history — war — from the novelist's point of view. He offers an explanation of how it is that an event so ghastly, so sad, can, through great literature

> touch the innermost existence of man, and defy the nothingness of human life with a full and rich expression of actions and aims which are organically attached to the will to live and to the will to die

The secret service as it was presented in the popular British novels of the inter-war years gives a romantic view of the world of the spy before the experience of the concentration camp so affected literature (see Albert Votaw in volume 6), whereas Jacques Barzun's article is concerned with the spy 'post-Votaw'. In the world of romantic espionage fiction described by Usborne, there is 'A Code': 'Espionage in peace time is Not Done. When peace breaks out, the brave Englishman, lately an *espion*, must make do with being a *contre-espion*' (p. 288). The absurdities of Sapper are probably less damaging, for all the falseness of the sub-text (content analysis would have a field day here!), than the illusion of reality suggested by a literature which espouses 'love of dishonour' (p. 281), for, 'The great illusion is to believe that all these impulses and enjoyments betoken maturity, worldliness, being "realistic" ' (p. 279). And he goes on to make the social deduction:

> For adult readers to divert themselves with tales of childish fantasy is nothing new and not in itself reprehensible. What is new is for readers to accept the fantasy as wiser than civil government, and what is reprehensible is for the modern world to have made official the dreams and actions of little boys. (p. 279)

One minor point arising from Barzun's article. *The Three Hostages* has recently appeared on the screen — the television screen — in Britain. One cannot tell whether it was 'hooted at by every thirteen-year-old of either sex' (p. 281), but Hannay's attempt to save his deadly enemy was certainly not the least unsatisfactory element in the televised tale.

The last item in this group of articles is part of a paper by Tim Moore called 'Claude Lévi-Strauss and the Cultural Sciences' published as an occasional paper by the Centre for Contemporary Cultural Studies, Birmingham. Moore was then a lecturer in the Birmingham Department of Philosophy and the first part of his paper (pp. 3–31 – not reproduced here) is an introduction to Lévi-Strauss and his structuralism. The second part of the paper consisted of these 'notes towards the analysis of the Bond stories' in which he put into practice a technique designed to read 'myths' in a way that reveals something of the mind of the society to which they pertain. It might be useful to repeat the definitions quoted by Moore from Lévi-Strauss's *Le cru et le cuit* (Paris 1964) p. 205:

> Let us agree to call *armature* a group of properties which remain the same in two or more myths; *code*, the system of functions assigned by each myth to these properties; *message* the content of a particular myth.

The last two contributions are an article on science fiction which was published in *Alta*, an inter-disciplinary journal published by the University of Birmingham for a short period (1966–70), and a very recent review of three books on the fantastic in literature. Peter Miles takes issue with R.W. Irwin's definition of fantasy as 'a story based on and controlled by an overt violation of what is generally acceptable as possibility; it is the narrative result of transforming the condition contrary to fact into "fact" itself' (p. 335). But, even if all readers took a narrative to be 'impossible', that does not mean that read for its social and cultural implications, it might not say a great deal about the society which produces it and for which it is intended. Reading analogously is hardly new! Thus, as Shippey points out, 'end of *our* world' novels are

> a determinedly English phenomenon, for while it would not be quite true to say that all English SF writers write disaster novels, or that all disaster novels are written by Englishmen, neither generalisation is very far wrong (p. 324).

In contrast with English science fiction, however, most writers outside England 'are more concerned with rebirth of any kind than extinction'; 'change is more likely to be *towards* what we can recognise as civilization than away from it'.

Miles's review (which was published after the Prospectus and is additional to the titles listed therein), discusses Eric Rabkin's *The Fantastic in Literature* by setting it against two other recently published critical works with similar concerns. Given broader confines than those of a review, he remarks that, 'Any discussion of fantasy would also have to consider the seminal work of Tzvetan Todorov which has itself been a major influence on Rabkin's arguments. Todorov's *Introduction à la littérature fantastique* (Paris 1970) has been translated by Richard Howes as *The Fantastic: a structural approach to a literary genre* with a foreword by Robert Scholes (Ithaca 1975). Todorov sees the fantastic as signalled by the controlled hesitation of the reader over the status of the events depicted: while the hesitation is unresolved the fantastic is in evidence, but a resolution of that hesitation into an acceptance of natural explanations signals *l'étrange* (the uncanny) as genre, while resolution into acceptance of supernatural explanations signals *le merveilleux* (the marvellous). Todorov's work in poetics, founded in a preoccupation with the text as both literary and linguistic event, figures in Jonathan Culler's survey *Structuralist Poetics: structuralism, linguistics and the study of literature* (London 1975).

Articles concerned with the uses of literacy, with particular reference to the press and magazines, film, radio and television, are brought together in volume 9.

PETER DAVISON

Further Reading

There is a mass of writing on the subjects discussed in this volume.
References to further reading on content analysis and mass communications
are to be found in the bibliographies which conclude Gerbner's and Klapper's
articles. For content analysis, see also:
H.D. Lasswell *Analyzing the Content of Mass Communications: a brief
introduction* Washington 1942; and
G. Gerbner *et al.*, eds. *The Analysis of Communication Content: development
in scientific theories and computer techniques* New York 1969.
For the mass media, in addition to the items listed in volume 2, see:
W.L. Rivers, T. Peterson, and J.W. Jensen *The Mass Media and Modern Society*
San Francisco 1965; 2nd edn., 1971;
Alan Casty, ed. *Mass Media and Mass Man* New York 1968; 2nd edn., 1973.
This consists of over thirty articles in three sections: Mass Media and Society;
Mass Media and Culture; and Mass Media and Information;
J. Curran, M. Gurevitch, and J. Woollacott, eds. *Mass Communication and
Society* London 1977. This is a volume of mainly original materials produced
for students of The Open University.
A. Piepe, S. Crouch, and M. Emerson *Mass Media and Cultural Relationships*
Farnborough 1978. 'The scope of this book is to study the ways in which
social differences connected with class and housing influence community
patterns and uses of mass media' (p. 3). Research is confined to a single
'relatively cohesive community': Portsmouth and its immediate environs
(p. 5).
    Reference is made in the Introduction to Arnold Bennett's *Literary
Taste: how to form it; with detailed instructions for collecting a complete
library of English literature*, first published in 1909. It appeared in an
augmented form as a Penguin in 1938 and it might be said to have been
superseded in 1960 in Penguin's list by *The Reader's Guide*, a 'planned
syllabus for profitable reading' compiled by a 'panel of distinguished
scholars and scientists' (are scientists not scholars?), edited by Sir William
Emrys Williams. Two of Arnold's novels were included in the fiction section,
incidentally: *The Old Wives' Tale* and *Clayhanger*. There is a section on the
social sciences but, even as recently as 1960, little reference to mass culture.
Richard Hoggart's *The Uses of Literacy* (published in the same year as
Bernard Rosenberg's and David Manning White's *Mass Culture* 1957) *is* listed
— under 'Social Class and Social Mobility'. Robert and Helen Lynd's
Middletown (1937) appears under 'Urban Sociology' and Ruth Benedict's
Patterns of Culture (1935) is also recommended.

E.E. Kellett followed *The Whirligig of Taste* (1929), mentioned in Wilson's review, with *Fashion in Literature* London 1931. This concludes with a passage that anticipates Winston Churchill a decade later:

> To quote again a saying that can never be quoted too often, 'all things excellent are as difficult as they are rare'. And I have still sufficient faith in my countrymen to believe that the way to gain their most enthusiastic co-operation is to tell them that the toil of achievement will be great, but that the end is worthy of it (p. 369).

See also, Aldous Huxley *Vulgarity in Literature* London 1930.

Scrutiny was published in nineteen volumes from 1932–1953; a twentieth, index volume, with a Retrospect by F.R. Leavis (reprinted in volume 13 of this series), appeared in 1963. Eric Bentley edited a selection from *Scrutiny*, *The Importance of Scrutiny* New York 1964, and F.R. Leavis compiled his own selection, Cambridge 2 vols. 1968.

A good sample of American proletarian literature (including items from Granville Hicks's *New Masses*) was edited by Granville Hicks, Michael Gold, Isidor Schneider, Joseph North, Paul Peters and Alan Calmer in 1935 or 1936. It was published as *Proletarian Literature in the United States: an anthology*, the undated London edition being the American edition with an English publisher's name on the title-page. There are sections devoted to fiction, poetry, reportage, drama and literary criticism — almost a hundred items in all. For earlier periods, *Popular Literature: a history and guide* by Victor E. Neuburg, Harmondsworth 1977, might very usefully be studied.

Marshall McLuhan's principal studies of the media are listed in the Introduction. *McLuhan Hot and Cool* 1967 ed. G.E. Stern, is 'a primer for the understanding of and a critical symposium with responses by McLuhan'. There are over thirty contributors, including Tom Wolfe, Patrick Hazard, Frank Kermode, Raymond Williams, Harold Rosenberg, Dwight Macdonald, Christopher Ricks, George Steiner, Benjamin DeMott and Susan Sontag. It contains a useful selected bibliography of McLuhan's work. Jonathan Miller's *McLuhan* (Fontana Modern Masters series, London 1971) is also recommended.

The principal Claude Lévi-Strauss texts used by Tim Moore are: *Les structures élémentaires et la parenté* Paris 1949; revised 1967; translated as *The Elementary Structures of Kinship* London 1969; *Anthropologie structurale* Paris 1958; translated as *Structural Anthropology* London 1968; *Le cru et le cuit* Paris 1964 (the first of the four volumes of *Mythologiques*); translated as *The Raw and the Cooked* London 1969.

See also *Myth and Symbol: critical approaches and applications*, edited by Bernice Slote, Lincoln, Nebraska 1963. This reproduces fifteen papers given at an MLA Conference in 1962. Among the contributors are Northrop Frye, L.C. Knights, and Alexander Kern (the last two of whom are contributors to volume 6 of this series).

Reference is made in the Introduction to Heisenberg's Principle of

Uncertainty. This was enunciated in connexion with quantum mechanics in 1927. In the 1949 edition of *Encyclopaedia Britannica*, reference is made to 'an interesting popular article on the philosophical implications of the uncertainty principle'. This was written by P.W. Bridgman and appeared in *Harper's Magazine* 158 (1929) pp. 443—51. It included these two passages (cited in *EB*, vol. 22, p. 680):

> The immediate effect [of the uncertainty principle] will be to let loose a veritable intellectual spree of licentious and debauched thinking . . . One group will find in the failure of the physical law of cause and effect the solution of the age-old problem of the freedom of the will, and, on the other hand, the aetheist will find the justification of his contention that chance rules the universe.

The New Cambridge Bibliography of English Literature iv (Cambridge 1972), gives a selection of titles on various popular genres (columns 123—130) including crime and detection, historical fiction, romance and confession, science fiction, and war. Kingsley Amis's *What Became of Jane Austen? And other questions* London 1970, contains a number of relevant short pieces, including 'A New James Bond', 'Unreal Policemen', and 'Dracula, Frankenstein, Sons & Co.'. Amis is the author of a post-Fleming Bond book *Colonel Sun* London 1968. See also, Les Daniels *Living in Fear* New York 1975, published in Britain as *Fear: a history of horror in the mass media* London 1977.

Finally, among the works referred to by Andrew Tolson are:
Cleanth Brooks *The Well Wrought Urn* New York 1947.
S. Chatman and S.R. Levin *Essays on the Language of Literature* Boston 1967; for M. Riffaterre 'Criteria for style analysis' 412—30.
Noam Chomsky *Language and Mind* New York 1968.
William Empson *Seven Types of Ambiguity* London 1930.
C.C. Fries *Linguistics and Reading* New York 1963.
Northrop Frye *Anatomy of Criticism* Princeton 1957.
Kenneth Goodman ed., *The Psycholinguistic Nature of the Reading Process* Detroit 1968; for Paul A. Kolers 'Reading a temporally and spatially transformed text' pp. 27—48.
Norman Holland *Dynamics of Literary Response* New York 1968.
J. Katz and J. Fodor eds. *The Structure of Language: readings in the philosophy of language* Englewood Cliffs 1964; for their 'The structure of a semantic theory' .
F.R. Leavis *Education and the University* London 1948.
F.R. Leavis *English Literature in our Time and the University* London 1969.
Simon O. Lesser *Fiction and the Unconscious* New York 1957.
Harry Levin and Joanna P. Williams, eds., *Basic Studies in Reading* New York 1970; for Noam Chomsky 'Phonology and reading'; David W. Reed 'Linguistic forms and the process of reading'.
Ulric Neisser *Cognitive Psychology* New York 1967.

Jean Piaget *The Language and Thoughts of the Child* London 3rd edn. 1959.
Jean Piaget *Six Psychological Studies* London 1968.
I.A. Richards *Principles of Literary Criticism* London 1924.
I.A. Richards *The Philosophy of Rhetoric* New York 1936.
I.A. Richards *Speculative Instruments* London 1955. See also an earlier collection of essays *Science and Poetry* London 1925.
Jean-Paul Sartre *Que'est-ce que la littérature?* 1947; translated by Bernard Frechtman as *What is Literature?* London 1950.
Jean-Paul Sartre *Question de méthode* 1960; translated Hazel E. Barnes, 1963 as *The Problem of Method*; in America as *Search for a Method*.
Harry Singer and Robert Ruddell, eds. *Theoretical Models and Processes of Reading* Newark Delaware 1969; for Ruddell's 'Psycholinguistic implications for a systems of communication model' pp. 239—54; John J. Geyer 'Models of perceptual processes in reading' pp. 47—94; David W. Reed 'A theory of language, speech and writing' pp. 219—38; and Kenneth S. Goodman 'Reading: a psycholinguistic guessing game' pp. 259—71.
L.S. Vygotsky *Thought and Language* Cambridge Mass. 1962.
Raymond Williams *The Long Revolution* London 1961.

PETER DAVISON

Literary Taste, Culture and Mass Communication

Good Bad Books
George Orwell

from

Collected Essays, Journalism and Letters of George Orwell, vol. IV, Sonia Orwell and Ian Angus (eds.) Secker and Warburg, London, 1968.

Reprinted by permission of Mrs. Sonia Brownell Orwell and Martin Secker and Warburg Limited.

6. Good Bad Books

Not long ago a publisher commissioned me to write an introduction for a reprint of a novel by Leonard Merrick. This
publishing house, it appears, is going to reissue a long series
of minor and partly-forgotten novels of the twentieth century.
It is a valuable service in these bookless days, and I rather
envy the person whose job it will be to scout round the
threepenny boxes, hunting down copies of his boyhood
favourites.

A type of book which we hardly seem to produce in these
days, but which flowered with great richness in the late nineteenth and early twentieth centuries, is what Chesterton called
the 'good bad book': that is, the kind of book that has no
literary pretensions but which remains readable when more
serious productions have perished. Obviously outstanding
books in this line are *Raffles* and the Sherlock Holmes stories,
which have kept their place when innumerable 'problem
novels', 'human documents' and 'terrible indictments' of this
or that have fallen into deserved oblivion. (Who has worn
better, Conan Doyle or Meredith?) Almost in the same class
as these I put R. Austin Freeman's earlier stories – 'The Singing Bone', 'The Eye of Osiris' and others – Ernest Bramah's
Max Carrados, and, dropping the standard a bit, Guy
Boothby's Tibetan thriller, *Dr Nikola*, a sort of schoolboy version of Huc's *Travels in Tartary* which would probably make
a real visit to Central Asia seem a dismal anticlimax.

But apart from thrillers, there were the minor humorous
writers of the period. For example, Pett Ridge – but I admit
his full-length books no longer seem readable – E. Nesbit (*The
Treasure Seekers*), George Birmingham, who was good so long
as he kept off politics, the pornographic Binstead ('Pitcher'
of the *Pink 'Un*), and, if American books can be included,
Booth Tarkington's Penrod stories. A cut above most of these
was Barry Pain. Some of Pain's humorous writings are, I suppose, still in print, but to anyone who comes across it I recom-
mend what must now be a very rare book – *The Octave of
Claudius*, a brilliant exercise in the macabre. Somewhat later
in time there was Peter Blundell, who wrote in the W. W.
Jacobs vein about Far Eastern seaport towns, and who seems

to be rather unaccountably forgotten, in spite of having been praised in print by H. G. Wells.

However, all the books I have been speaking of are frankly 'escape' literature. They form pleasant patches in one's memory, quiet corners where the mind can browse at odd moments, but they hardly pretend to have anything to do with real life. There is another kind of good bad book which is more seriously intended, and which tells us, I think, something about the nature of the novel and the reasons for its present decadence. During the last fifty years there has been a whole series of writers – some of them are still writing – whom it is quite impossible to call 'good' by any strictly literary standard, but who are natural novelists and who seem to attain sincerity partly because they are not inhibited by good taste. In this class I put Leonard Merrick himself, W. L. George, J. D. Beresford, Ernest Raymond, May Sinclair, and – at a lower level than the others but still essentially similar – A. S. M. Hutchinson.

Most of these have been prolific writers, and their output has naturally varied in quality. I am thinking in each case of one or two outstanding books: for example, Merrick's *Cynthia*, J. D. Beresford's *A Candidate for Truth*, W. L. George's *Caliban*, May Sinclair's *The Combined Maze* and Ernest Raymond's *We, the Accused*. In each of these books the author has been able to identify himself with his imagined characters, to feel with them and invite sympathy on their behalf, with a kind of abandonment that cleverer people would find it difficult to achieve. They bring out the fact that intellectual refinement can be a disadvantage to a story-teller, as it would be to a music-hall comedian.

Take, for example, Ernest Raymond's *We, the Accused* – a peculiarly sordid and convincing murder story, probably based on the Crippen case. I think it gains a great deal from the fact that the author only partly grasps the pathetic vulgarity of the people he is writing about, and therefore does not despise them. Perhaps it even – like Theodore Dreiser's *An American Tragedy* – gains something from the clumsy long-winded manner in which it is written; detail is piled on detail, with almost no attempt at selection, and in the process an effect of terrible, grinding cruelty is slowly built up. So also with *A Candidate for Truth*. Here there is not the same clumsiness, but there is the same ability to take seriously the problems of common-place people. So also with *Cynthia* and at any rate the earlier part of *Caliban*. The greater part of what W. L. George wrote was shoddy rubbish, but in this particular book, based on the career of Northcliffe, he achieved some memorable and truthful pictures of lower-middle-class London life. Parts of this book are probably autobiographical, and one of the advantages of good bad writers is their lack of shame in writing autobiography. Exhibitionism and self-pity are the bane of the novelist, and yet if he is too frightened of them his creative gift may suffer.

The existence of good bad literature – the fact that one can be amused or excited or even moved by a book that one's intellect simply refuses to take seriously – is a reminder that art is not the same thing as cerebration. I imagine that by any test that could be devised, Carlyle would be found to be a more intelligent man than Trollope. Yet Trollope has remained readable and Carlyle has not: with all his cleverness he had not even the wit to write in plain straightforward English. In novelists, almost as much as in poets, the connexion between intelligence and creative power is hard to establish. A good novelist may be a prodigy of self-discipline like Flaubert, or he may be an intellectual sprawl like Dickens. Enough talent to set up dozens of ordinary writers has been poured into Wyndham Lewis's so-called novels, such as *Tarr* or *Snooty Baronet*. Yet it would be a very heavy labour to read one of these books right through. Some indefinable quality, a sort of literary vitamin, which exists even in a book like *If Winter Comes*, is absent from them.

Perhaps the supreme example of the 'good bad' book is *Uncle Tom's Cabin*. It is an unintentionally ludicrous book, full of preposterous melodramatic incidents; it is also deeply moving and essentially true; it is hard to say which quality outweighs the other. But *Uncle Tom's Cabin*, after all, is trying to be serious and to deal with the real world. How about the frankly escapist writers, the purveyors of thrills and 'light' humour? How about *Sherlock Holmes*, *Vice Versa*, *Dracula*, *Helen's Babies* or *King Solomon's Mines*? All of these are definitely absurd books, books which one is more inclined to laugh *at* than *with*, and which were hardly taken seriously even by their authors; yet they have survived, and will probably continue to do so. All one can say is that, while civilization remains such that one needs distraction from time to time, 'light' literature has its appointed place; also that there is such a thing as sheer skill, or native grace, which may have more survival value than erudition or intellectual power. There are music-hall songs which are better poems than three quarters of the stuff that gets into the anthologies:

> Come where the booze is cheaper,
> Come where the pots hold more,
> Come where the boss is a bit of a sport,
> Come to the pub next door!

Or again:

> Two lovely black eyes –
> Oh, what a surprise!
> Only for calling another man wrong,
> Two lovely black eyes!

I would far rather have written either of those than, say, 'The Blessed Damozel' or 'Love in the Valley'. And by the same token I would back *Uncle Tom's Cabin* to outlive the complete works of Virginia Woolf or George Moore, though I know of no strictly literary test which would show where the superiority lies.

Tribune, 2 November 1945; *S.E.*

On Content Analysis and Critical Research in Mass Communication
George Gerbner

from

Audio-Visual Communication Review, 16, 1958.

ON CONTENT ANALYSIS AND CRITICAL RESEARCH IN MASS COMMUNICATION

● GEORGE GERBNER

In this paper George Gerbner has presented an approach to content analysis which raises basic issues regarding its relationship to critical research. The author is assistant professor in the Institute of Communications Research, University of Illinois.

ONTENT IS the coin of the communication exchange. Its nature, functions, and study should be the subject of lively technical and philosophical debate. But they are not. Or perhaps it depends on one's focus; in the broader scope of social and physical sciences the issue of *what* is involved in observation and communication lies at the heart of fundamental controversies. But in the newer specialization that straddles this social-scientific battleground, in content analysis, the outstanding issues appear to have been settled by the authorities.

So one is compelled to tread warily for fear of either adding to the din of battle in the larger context, or of appearing to be bent on disturbing the dignity of established procedures in the specialized field. What prompts us to proceed, nevertheless, is our experience that (a) in both teaching and research it is necessary to raise—and ultimately impossible to avoid—the basic issues of social science within the field of content analysis, and (b) that established procedures tend to limit content analysis to administrative research.

When theory appears to rationalize advances in methodology rather than build a framework for critical discussion of aims, the time is ripe for a consideration of aims without prior commitment as to means. We propose to do that by advancing an approach to content analysis which raises basic issues through tackling them from its own vantage point, and by summarizing the case for critical research.

AN APPROACH TO CONTENT ANALYSIS

Any process may be viewed as a patterned exchange between systems. We make inferences about the nature of processes through observation of stages, or outcomes, or consequences of the exchange. We call these occasions *events;* they make it possible for the observer to infer some things about the states of systems engaged in the exchange, and about their relationships to one another.

If a party to an exchange records, represents, or encodes in conventional (social) forms some aspects of the pattern of the exchange between itself and other systems, an event has been produced which has special qualities. A hot cup of coffee is in the process of exchanging energy with its surroundings. We infer the pattern of this exchange through observation and measurement (or by taking a sip). Coffee cannot produce a formally coded communication event, isolated from that exchange, but encoding the pattern of the exchange, and expressing its own state and relationship in the exchange, such as the words "I am losing heat." We, however, can produce such an event indicative of our relationship in the exchange; we can say, "The coffee is getting cold." From that statement one can make inferences both about the process in the cup, and about the process that gave rise to the statement, i.e., our relationship to the coffee.

A *communication* is, then, a specialized, formally coded or representative social event which makes possible inferences about states, relationships, processes not directly observed. The *process* of communication is the transmission of such events and sharing of certain inferences. The *content* of communication is the sum total of warranted inferences that can be made about relationships involved in the communication event.

These inferences can be of two kinds. The first kind is the conventional associations we make when we view the communication as a generalized form or code. This is the conventional, formal meaning, such as we might find in a dictionary.

Underlying the "formal message" with its denotative and connotative associations and differential response capabilities, we see in content the basis for inference about specific functional relations between the communicating agent or agency and other events or systems, and about actual or potential consequences. The conventional face value of a dollar bill is not the same as its actual role value in a specific exchange. The latter will reflect the objective relationships of producer, product, buyer and seller in the exchange, and some consequences of these relationships, whether or not the parties engaged in the exchange are aware of them. Similarly, the statement "It's hot here" is a linguistic type or "form" which can be isolated from its behavioral context, recorded, recoded, etc., with little or no distortion of its formal, conventional meaning. But it is not only that; once uttered—whether pleasant or unpleasant, good or bad, real or fancied—it is also a unique and irreversible event reflecting, perhaps unwittingly, an objective set of underlying relationships which prompted its utterance. The advertising slogan, "Smoke X cigarettes; they're milder," whether valid or invalid, true or false, effective or ineffective, implies a particular set of social and industrial relationships whose expression in that form leads to consequences fully understandable only in terms of these relationships and not of the explicit message alone.[1]

"Micro" and "Macro" Analysis

The "micro" analyst of communication content is interested in gathering information about persons and making predictions about their behavior. In his search for the hidden dynamics of individual behavior he utilizes communication content either as fruitful material expressive in some form of the state of an organism, or as a necessary source when information about a person is restricted to the messages produced by that individual (30).

The analyst who views content as a social event goes beyond individual behavior. His search is for the social determinants and possible consequences of both personal and institutional dynamics reflected in cultural products. His focus may be the autonomous creations of great art—whether mass reproduced or not—or it may be the everyday commodities of cultural industry.

From the former focus comes a clear statement of those tasks of content analysis which have been sidestepped in the preoccupa-

---

[1] It is evident that our distinctions are in contrast with those of the semioticians and "sign theorists" who see content as having reference *only* to semantic and syntactic characteristics of symbols. However, Kaplan (19) recognizes that content analysis "may, and indeed must take account of [pragmatic characteristics] in determining which aspects of content will be analyzed and in what ways."

tion with methodologies. It is from the introduction to Leo Lowenthal's *Literature and the Image of Man* (28) :

Creative literature conveys many levels of meaning, some intended by the author, some quite unintentional. An artist sets out to invent a plot, to describe actions, to depict the interrelationships of characters, to emphasize certain values; wittingly or unwittingly, he stamps his work with uniqueness through an imaginative selection of problems and personages. By this very imaginative selection . . . he presents an explicit or implicit picture of man's orientation to his society: privileges and responsibilities of classes; conceptions of work, love, and friendship, of religion, nature, and art. Through an analysis of [his] works . . . an image may be formed of man's changing relation to himself, to his family, and to his social and natural environment. . . .

. . . . The specific treatment which the creative writer gives to nature or to love, to gestures and moods, to gregariousness or solitude, is a primary source for a study of the penetration of the most intimate spheres of personal life by social forces.

The analyst of literary content, as a social scientist, "has to transform the private equation of themes and stylistic means into social equations," writes Lowenthal. "In fact," he asserts, "most generalized concepts about human nature found in literature prove on close inspection to be related to social and political change." And: "Man is born, strives, loves, suffers, and dies in any society, but it is the portrayal of *how* he reacts to these common experiences that matters, since they almost invariably have a social nexus."

The "macro" analyst of mass media content deals with broad regularities in large systems of mass-produced cultural commodities. As the "micro" analyst assumes that the underlying laws of human dynamics find expression in communicative behavior, the "macro" analyst assumes that institutions, societies, and cultures manifest laws and order beyond that apparent to large numbers of people at any one time, and that systems of artifacts express objective, even if subtle or implicit, manifestations of this order. In his quest for the *system* behind the facts and forms of mass communication, the media analyst regards content as expressive of social relationship and institutional dynamics, and as formative of social patterns.

Some Tasks of the Mass Media Content Analyst

His task, analogous in certain respects to that of the cultural anthropologist, cannot be merely descriptive of his or other people's subjective impressions. For example, the anthropologist does not see an ax handle only as a stick one could put a blade on and start chopping. To him the meaning of a cave painting is not only that it has reference to buffalos, or even that it implies certain technical skills and individual attitudes, desires, or fantasies. The major significance of artifacts is that they reflect historical human approaches to certain events; that they signify and regulate social relationships in ways their users or creators may not consciously recognize.

Egyptian mythology of a certain period may be traced to reflect the conquest of the upper Nile Valley by the people of the Delta who superimposed upon the water-gods the theological primacy of their Sun. Ancient Mesopotamian culture and religion may be seen to record and facilitate in symbolic forms a system of social relations based on the need for elaborate irrigation networks. Movable type was made possible by a long chain of technological and social revolutions; the printing of the Gutenberg Bible was a social event reflecting cultural relationships and paving the way for future revolutions.

Communications media can be regarded as historical systems of social control, conferring monopolies of knowledge through built-in "biases" (18). Some go even further in claiming that new media are inherently revolutionary in their implications, "each codifying reality differently, each concealing a unique metaphysics" (8). Distinguished analysts of mass media content cite a legal historian to the effect that, "The greatest and most far-reaching revolutions in history are not consciously observed at the time of their occurrence" (23). Be that as it may, it prompts the analysts to remark, "It is by the investigation of style that we may gain more insight into the currents of history which are usually below the threshold of consciousness."

Our contention is not so much that inherent physical characteristics of media as such, or that formal elements of style, vocabulary, syntax, are themselves of profound and direct significance. Rather it is that the nature and consequences of these elements and characteristics can be understood best if content is viewed as bearing the imprint of social needs and uses.

In the words of Leo Lowenthal (27), ". . . objective elements of the social whole are produced and reproduced in the mass media." And: "The stimulus in popular culture is itself a historical phenomenon . . .; the relation between stimulus and response is preformed and prestructured by the historical and social fate of the stimulus as well as of the respondent."

The historical and social fate common to large bodies of mass media content is that they are selected and designed to be mass produced for a market. They spring from complex technological production and market relationships; they are products of an exchange between systems in which the decisive communicating agent is a modern business enterprise. Van Den Haag (38) writes:

> Unlike any other type of culture, popular culture—a full fledged style of living with a distinct pattern of feeling, thinking, believing and acting—was made possible and in the end necessary by mass production. Unless the requirements and effects of industrialization are fully grasped, popular culture does not become intelligible.

Even more specifically, unless the requirements and effects of a specific system of industrial and market relationships (such as the corporate structure) are fully grasped, mass media content analysis remains superficial. Their intimate ties to the specific industrial marketing system from which they arise give mass media materials their institutional autonomy, their implicit role-value or consequential meaning, and their underlying frame of reference.

Aside from the formal, conventional "message," mass media content bears the imprint of concrete circumstances of its creation. This includes such things as external outlook and the internal dynamics of the producing industry; its relationship to competitors; its control over resources, facilities of production, and distribution; the position of its decision makers in the industrial structure; their relationships to audiences, markets, advertising sponsors. Out of these come a set of managerial assumptions— both implicit and rationalized—reflected in large systems of content, and preforming some aspects of its perception. The social determinants of cultural industry thus find their way into the consequential meaning of the material. They are expressed not so much in conventional forms and "messages" as through patterns of selection, omission, juxtaposition, through just the way things are "looked at."

Of course, it is necessary to classify and clarify conventional meanings and widely recognized consistencies in formal content. But the full meaning of such analysis emerges through procedures which combine investigation of the objective social origin and role of the stimulus with that of the response; which search for manifestations of processes whose consequences do not depend on conscious intentions and perceptions. The primary tasks of the mass media content analyst lie in his attempts to *scientifically gather and test* inferences about content that may involve generally unrecognized or unanticipated consequences, to isolate and investigate consequential properties of content which escape ordinary awareness or casual scrutiny, to bring to awareness those hidden regularities of content which record and reflect objective mechanisms of a social order. The classical role of cultural scholarship as a testing ground of critical social theory is to be strengthened, broadened, and deepened—not abolished—in the analysis of mass media content through the newer, more systematic and refined methodologies.

SOME THEORETICAL CONSIDERATIONS

Berelson (5) defines communication content as "that body of meanings through symbols (verbal, musical, pictorial, plastic, gestural) which makes up the communication itself. In the classic sentence identifying the process of communication—*'who* says *what* to *whom, how,* with *what effect'*—communication content is the *what."* His definition of content analysis is "a research technique for the objective, systematic, and quantitative description of the manifest content of communication." Lasswell, Lerner, and Pool (23) speak of "symbol" as a technical term for words that "stand for (symbolize) the attitudes of those who use them, as distinguished, for example, from 'signs,' which are words that point to (signalize) objects external to their user." In their "symbol studies" they define content analysis as "quantitative semantics" which aims at achieving objectivity, precision, and generality through the use of statistical methods.

This approach has stimulated a growing volume of output and increasing recognition. Our purpose here is not to attempt a detailed critique. The "straw man" elements in the restrictive use of quantitative versus qualitative and manifest versus latent dichotomies have been challenged elsewhere (22, 33) as resulting neither in objectivity nor necessarily in precision but quite possibly in fundamentally uncritical "scientism." The present task is to extend the theoretical underpinnings of this approach beyond the limitations of its phenomenalistic framework, to harness its methodological insights to more critical social uses, and to amplify the role of the content analyst in a broader conception of the communication process.

The Lasswellian formula, "who says what to whom, how, and with what effect" proved useful for many practical purposes. But it is too restrictive and too one-directional for a general theoretical communications model, or for a framework for critical research. For example, it places content (the "what") in a severely limited sequence. It has been amply demonstrated that *what* is said by the *who* depends also on his role as a *whom*; i.e., the communicator builds into his statement consciously and unconsciously his terms of perception as a receiver of communications, which, in turn, reflect his relationships with events of his world. Even symbols stand for attitudes, feelings, inner experiences *about* (or expressed in terms of sensory experiences of) events of an objective world. This causal thread from systems of subject-object relations to systems of content and consequences leads through the communicating agent or agency, but not necessarily through his awareness, or that of the receiver. When it comes to measuring "effects," the criterion of effectiveness in the light of conscious intentions or explicit objectives becomes insufficient except for administrative purposes. From the point of view of critical research, more interested in understanding normative aspects of the communication exchange than in appraising effectiveness on behalf of taken-for-granted objectives, a model of communication should be broadened to include certain additional features.

A General Model of Communication

The construction and some uses of such a general model was the subject of a previous *AV Communication Review* article (13). It is summarized here for the purpose of facilitating discussion in that framework. The model makes provision for (a) portraying the communicating agent in a dynamic role as both sender and receiver; (b) designating his relation with the world of events as the ultimate source of his perceptions and statements; (c) making the distinction between formal properties of the communication product, and other inferences about content; and (d) specifically designating the study of consequences (aside from effectiveness in terms of overt intentions or objectives) as an area of research.

The model has 10 basic components, some of which can be illustrated graphically. The 10 components, forming a sentence identifying the essential aspects of a communication act or sequence, appear in capital letters below, accompanied by a brief description. The graphic model (Figure I) illustrates appropriate aspects of the verbal description.

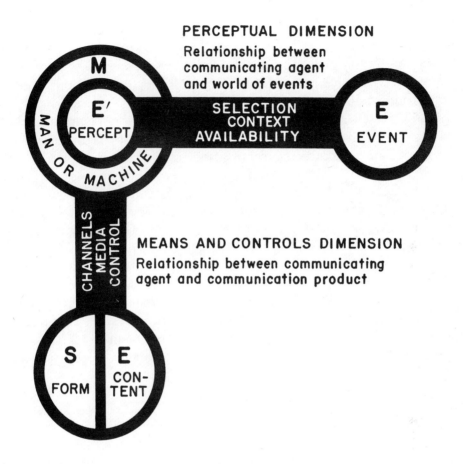

Figure I
The graphic model, illustrating certain aspects of the verbal model

(1) SOMEONE (the communicating agent or agency M engaged in an exchange with events of his world)

(2) PERCEIVES AN EVENT (the exchange—for our purposes primarily perceptual—between systems M and E; horizontal dimension of the graphic model leading from "event" E to "event as perceived" E'; including such critical consideration as M's *selection* in a certain *context* from what is *available* for perception either directly or through the mediation of communication events)

(3) AND REACTS (M's general response, not on graphic model)

(4) IN A SITUATION (social and physical setting, not on graphic model)

(5) THROUGH SOME MEANS (communicative facilities, vehicles, controls, used to produce communication event; vertical dimension of the graphic model)

(6) TO MAKE AVAILABLE MATERIALS (part of the horizontal dimension)

(7) IN SOME FORM (formal state of the communication event; signal system created by nonrandom use of means; conventionalized structure, representative or syntactic patterns; designated as the S—signal—portion of the communication events SE)

(8) AND CONTEXT (field or sequence in which a communication event is perceived; part of horizontal dimension)

(9) CONVEYING CONTENT (the social event portion of the communication SE; those inferences from content which reflect objective relationships independent of intentions, conventional meanings, conscious perceptions)

(10) WITH SOME CONSEQUENCE (the actual role of the communication event in its further exchanges with other M's; objective outcomes as measured by criteria independent from intentions, overt perception, or "effectiveness" in terms of objectives of the communication; not represented on graphic model).

Investigation of Content

The investigation of content focuses attention on SE, the communication product. It proceeds as a relational analysis on two levels. Both "formal" and "content" aspects of the communication product are studied with respect to all other elements of the communication sequence of which SE is a part.

Study of the formal continuities traces the flow or configurations of conventional ("arbitrary") systems of signs and symbols through classification and measurement. It relates the state of specific signal-systems to that of others for comparison, or to intentions, desires, behaviors of the source, or to the "effectiveness" of the responses they elicit, or to technical use of communicative means.

Study of the consequential continuities represented in content includes the above, but is not limited to it. Here the communication product is viewed as a specific social event whose consequential meaning may be constant through variation in form, or may vary when form is held constant.

What we are discussing here is *not* the fact that words have different denotative or connotative meanings; that the sounds "horse" may refer to an animal, or to a condition of the vocal cords; that situation and context alter conventional meanings; that individual responses vary; or even that words (or other signals) may be used for strategic reasons to mask rather than reveal intentions. Rather, we are discussing the fact that a communication event may reveal something about the systematic exchange that produced it, quite apart from what we think it means, or what we intend it to mean.

We may analyze a photograph not to get responses to its conventional forms, but to determine the position of the camera or angle of lighting recorded in it. We may study a series of whiskey advertisements, not to determine their effects on sales, or on ideas about whisky, but to make some inferences about more subtle social relationships recorded and reflected in them (such as the frequency with which their image of the "good life" involves the services of Negro waiters or Philippino busboys).

Content as an expression of objective relationships may be implicit in selection, omission, context, juxtaposition, point of view, etc., or it may be inferred through circumstantial or situational association. In that sense, consequential meaning is far from being an "arbitrary" convention. It is the property of a specific event or system of events. Every utterance of the English word "horse" (animal) is a unique event, socially determined through a long chain of associations in certain cultural context with a certain type of animal which became domesticated at a certain point in history, and has continued to be one of the events people communicate about. In doing so they express an objective historical relationship toward it. Semanticists and semioticians notwithstanding, there is, in this sense, something "horsy" about the word "horse." The "map" is not the "territory" but a map does involve a mapmaker's relationship to territory, determined socially and historically in terms of the territory as well as of the individual mapmaker.

Consider the study of a system of mass media products, e.g., male adventure magazine covers. Suppose formal analysis has indicated that the patterns of violent struggle with nature in juxtaposition with sex fears dominate most covers. Significant questions of content analysis might then be derived from our model by relating this communication event (SE) to the other aspects (see also Figure II) :

In what ways does this material reflect *physical and social qualities* of communicating agencies (publishers), and their relationships to other systems such as markets, advertisers, audiences,

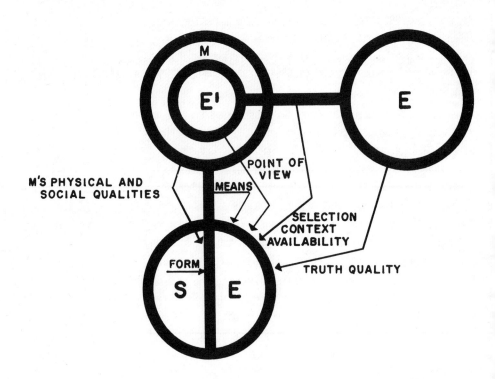

Figure II
Illustration of some of the relationships involved in content analysis

and their world of events? What *points of view* about life and the world as M sees them are implied and facilitated? What social arrangements of ownership and control of communicative *means* and facilities are revealed by the prevalence of this material? What patterns of *selection, context,* and *availability* are inferable from this body of content? How valid, adequate, and coherent is the correspondence of these representations to any actual system of events *(truth quality)*? What might be the *consequences* (aside from sales, likes and dislikes, conventional meanings, or "effectiveness" in terms of conscious objectives) of social relationships and points of view mediated through this content as a social event system? And so on. Each of these questions represents a way of relating the communication event system to other elements or relationships in the model; some of these can be illustrated on the graphic model as shown in Figure II.

The Role of the Content Analyst

Let us sketch the role of the analyst in our scheme, and contrast it with that in some form-oriented approaches for the purpose of highlighting some distinctions. Systematic classification of units of material into categories for the purpose of description and measurement is a pivotal phase of the analyst's work. Form and conventional-meaning oriented analysis begins with the setting up of units and categories on the basis of explicit signal characteristics. This makes coding and classification a semiclerical task of relatively high face validity and reliability. It places the burden of analysis on design for measurement and on the precision of the means employed for testing the nature and significance of differences.

Consequential meaning-oriented content analysis begins elsewhere and in a different perspective. It begins by defining the position of the analyst in relation to the communication system with which he is to deal.

In terms of our diagram, the analyst may be viewed as communicating agent M_2 whose approach to the communication product SE, as analyst, is different from that of an M_1 producing it, or of an M_2 receiving it, or even from his own casual perceptions. The analyst as scientist must be distinguished from the analyst as subject. This requires the development of some philosophical awareness. As Hans Speier (34) has pointed out, "All theories of the relation between ideas and the world we call social have philosophical implications." The analyst is forced into the philosophical area at least twice. When he formulates his hypotheses, "he in fact formulates a tentative philosophy which provides him with a frame of reference for his research. . . . Again, when he comes to develop generalizations on the basis of his findings, he is taking a philosophical stand." The crucial issue is whether or not he is *aware* of the stand he is taking.

Awareness of one's own stand means that we react to our "naive" perceptions of explicit manifestations in terms of a qualitatively different (more "objective") consciousness. As subjects we laugh when the hapless comic slips on the banana peel; as analysts we react to our own (and other subjects') laughter by tracing our own position (spatial, temporal, cultural, personal) in the exchange with that communication event, and by tracing the social history of the product. Our awareness of the known relationships in these two dimensions (along the horizonal and vertical axes of our model) suggests some of the most pertinent and least apparent questions to ask about unknown relationships in content.

Tentative answers to these questions may be thought of as the hypotheses of the analyst, usually stated in the form of content elements, categories, systematic functional relationships which may escape ordinary scrutiny.

Self-conscious hypothesis-making brings into content analysis a concern with the correctness of the analyst's entire approach to his material, with his philosophical stand, with his appraisal of the process out of which the material emerged—in other words, with the validity of a critical social theory implied in his hypotheses. Few of these hazards—and rewards—confront formal or administrative research in which ultimate goals and values are either given or assumed, and are not at stake in the research.

If the development of hypotheses through a scientific self-consciousness and critical value orientation is the first task of the content analyst, the second is the testing of his inferences through the un-self-conscious method and self-critical temper of science. Here critical, formal, and administrative researchers join in common concern over the development of research design and methodology sensitive to functional relationships of different types.

But before we advocate this union in methodology, it is necessary to explore further some crucial distinctions in aims and scope.

CRITICAL RESEARCH IN MASS COMMUNICATION

Paul Lazarsfeld (24) gave a lucid description of the distinctions between administrative and critical research in communication in an article written in 1941.

During the last two decades, he wrote, the media of mass communication have become some of the best known and best documented spheres of modern society. The reason for the rapid rise of communications research, he felt, was the notion that modern media of communication are tools handled by people or agencies for given purposes. As the communications investment of these agencies—both commercial and governmental—grew in size, and as the competitive stakes became higher, empirical research was called upon to help make administrative choices in communications strategy and method.

The objection of critical research is not directed against administrative tasks as such, but against limiting the theoretical scope of communications research to the aims which prevail in the majority of current studies, Lazarsfeld wrote. He summarized as a basic notion of critical research the contention that:

... one cannot pursue a single purpose and study the means of its realization isolated from the total historical situation in which such planning and study goes on. Modern media of communication have become such complex instruments that wherever they are used they do much more to people than those who administer them mean to do, and they may have a momentum of their own which leaves the administrative agencies much less choice than they believe they have. The idea of *critical research* is posed against the practice of administrative research, requiring that, prior and in addition to whatever special purpose is to be served, the general role of our media of communication in the present social system is to be studied.

Some Questions and Hypotheses

Lazarsfeld sketched the approach of the critical student. He will ask such questions as: "How are these media organized and controlled? How, in their institutional set-up, is the trend toward centralization, standardization, and promotional pressure expressed? In what form, however disguised, are they threatening human values?" He will feel that the prime task of research is "to uncover the unintentional (for the most part) and often very subtle ways in which these media contribute to living habits and social attitudes. . . ."

Lazarsfeld then indicated some steps in the formation of critical research hypotheses "by visualizing how a student would be trained to make observations in everyday life and to try to interpret them in terms of their social meaning." Note how these examples distinguish the role of the analyst as social scientist from his role as a subject:

You sit in a movie and look at an old newsreel showing fashions of ten years ago. Many people laugh. Why do those things which we admired just a little while ago seem so ridiculous now? . . . Could it be that by laughing at past submissions, we gather strength to submit to the present pressure upon us? Thus, what looks to an ordinary observer like an incident in a movie theater, becomes, from this point of view, a symptom of great social significance.

Or you find that a large brewery advertises its beer by showing a man disgustedly throwing aside a newspaper full of European war horrors while the caption says that in times like these the only place to find peace, strength, and courage is at your own fireside drinking beer. What will be the result if symbols referring to such basic human wants as that for peace become falsified into expressions of private comfort and are rendered habitual to millions of magazine readers as merchandising slogans? Why should people settle their social problems by action and sacrifice if they can serve the same ends by drinking a new brand of beer? To the casual observer the advertisement is nothing but a more or less clever sales trick. From the aspect of more critical analysis, it becomes a dangerous sign of what a promotional culture might end up with.

Could it be that the mass-produced portrayal of violent means for their own sake reflects social alienation and facilitates cynicism and apathy; that the "evil scientist" is an image of the hired intellectual, "neutral" in matters of human concern; that, as has been suggested, "Peeping Tomism" is a "form of protest literature in prosperity"; that, as has also been suggested, conventional news values and front pages mirror market-orientation, a loss of historical perspective, and discontinuity of experience harmonious with positivistic science and philosophy? Neither administrative nor purely formal analysis will provide the answers to these and other questions striking at the roots of our uneasiness about popular culture in an age of mass production.

Content and Social Reality

Franklin Fearing (12) expressed this view: "The hypothesis that the mass media reflect value-systems, satisfy needs of society, whether consciously or unconsciously held, furnishes the theoretical basis for extensive research in which the content of films and other mass media are analyzed in order to discover what the value-belief patterns of a given society are." But one cannot fully "discover" value-belief patterns without tracing them to their existential bases in the world of objective events, and without shedding some light on *what* and *whose* needs they really satisfy. Prewar German films, seen as reflecting "not so much explicit credos as psychological disposition—those deep layers of collective mentality which extend more or less below the dimensions of consciousness" (20), also reflect a system of concrete social and cultural operations which gave rise to Nazism. "Hollywood's Terror Films" can be seen not only in terms of their creating an "all-pervasive fear that threatens the psychic integrity of the average person. . . ." (21) but also in terms of a broader setting in which market-oriented social mechanisms of cultural industry shape this implicit function, and "need" such psychic consequences. In the last analysis no "state of mind" can be fully understood until its "discovery" is driven through to the objective social determinants that produce and require it.

Inner and external reality share common ground in content. Individual and institutional "perceptual frameworks" with their implicit assumptions, need-value systems, experientially and historically developed vantage points, represent one side of the subject-object relation, structured in systematic unity and opposition with the other side—the events talked about, the social circumstances that shape our experience of meanings. Content arises out of the dialectical relation of subject and event. The nature of this relation depends on the realities of man's existence in, and struggle with, society and nature. Implicitly recorded in content, this relation becomes the property of a social event on whose terms the exchange continues.

Science is the penetration of human consciousness into the realities of existence. Content analysis can share in this enterprise through a critical awareness of social processes that shape both communication products and their perceptions and uses. Its hypotheses arise from the background of awareness of prevailing trends in cultural mass production. Specific studies focus on how content systems express these trends, and how they contribute or run counter to them. They culminate in the investigation of the range of implied consequences, in Lazarsfeld's words, "stamping human personalities in modern industrial society . . . , scrutinized from the viewpoint of more or less explicit ideas of what endangers and what preserves the dignity, freedom, and cultural values of human beings."

*Education, Mass Media, and the Challenge of
Critical Content Analysis*

In the analysis of consequential meanings, educational research and content analysis have joint responsibilities. These responsibilities involve bringing to awareness mechanisms of psychic management masked in righteous overt forms; increasing conscious insight into tensions generated by the exposition of correct "facts" in an implicit structure which serves as an extension of the social process the "facts" purport to illuminate.

World War II Army orientation films come to mind as a fruitful subject for research from that point of view. There is already some evidence suggesting that perhaps the notable "boomerang effect" of some educational material was not so much a "failure" of communication as the implicit communication of built-in relationships superimposed upon formal content, expressing assumptions, points of view, etc., running counter to the explicit message.

A study of the home-front propaganda film, "Don't Be a Sucker" (9), found, for example, that despite the "learning" of specific points by specific target audiences, the majority of the viewers identified with the German Hans rather than with the American Mike. A closer examination of the implicit content of the film revealed under the rather pedantic presentation of an anti-Nazi, pro-tolerance "message," the subtle imprint of a point of view from which fascism appeared dynamic, and democracy an invitation to weakness.

Another anti-bias film entitled "No Way Out" was subjected to searching content analysis (39). It was found that while on the level of verbal argument the film appeared to be a moving document, on a deeper level the producers could not escape the approach of an operationally racist society. The analysts wrote:

> There is of course no doubt of the good intentions of the makers of this film. But in order to show how wrong race hatred is, the film makers had to create a plot and characters and elaborate upon them in detailed images; here their fantasies from a less conscious level come to the surface: the Negro becomes a terrible burden that we must carry on our backs; a sacrifice of white corpses is required for his preservation; the image of the violated white woman forces its way to the screen; and so on. There is an effort to deny these unacknowledged nightmares about the Negro by locating race hatred exclusively in an exceptional, pathological character, but this attempt at denial remains, at bottom, ineffectual. The very title of the film, extremely puzzling in terms of the plot, expresses the basic ambiguity; though the Negro-hater is supposed to be defeated and the falsely accused Negro saved and vindicated, the title seems to state a deeper belief and draw a contrary "moral": there is no way out.

The Payne Fund studies of the early thirties represented the first concerted attack by a group of investigators on broad social problems involved in cultural mass production. "Perhaps the most important conclusion concerning these data," wrote Edgar Dale (11) in his summary of the content analysis portion of that project, "is the fact that in large measure the characters, the problems, and the settings are removed from the lives of the persons who view [motion pictures]." And perhaps the most significant statement revealing the social implications of the "escapist" trend of overt themes was Dale's conclusion, "The good life is no longer a dream which can only be wished for. We now have at hand the machinery for making it a reality. This machinery for changing our current civilization is not commonly shown in the movies. . . ."

Social Relations in Mass Media Content

In the absence of continuing large-scale investigations the evidence concerning the implicit consequential meanings of mass media content is necessarily fragmentary. Berelson and Salter's (6) analysis of magazine fiction involving minority groups finds, under the overtly egalitarian "messages," the expression of stereotyped relationships and views of life that "serve to activate the predispositions of a hostile or even an indifferent audience." Smythe (34) observes similar implicit patterns in his study of television drama.

Head (17) concludes his study of television drama with the additional observation that as a conserver of the status quo television may be a prime contributor to growing cultural inertia. Lowenthal (26) notes in his study of magazine biographies an emphasis upon the private lives of "idols of consumption," indicating a shift from concern with social problems of production to uniformly individualized pressures of consumption. Implicit class bias is observed in the Bush and Bullock study of "Names in the News" (7) ; in Sussman's analysis of "Labor in the Radio News" (37) ; in Auster's "Content Analysis of 'Little Orphan Annie' " (4) ; and in the Spiegelman, Terwilliger, Fearing research on comic strips (36). An audit (10) of 995 movies reviewed in *Variety* between 1953 and 1957 finds four of the five films dealing with organized labor presenting an unsavory view of unions (with the fifth banned from major theaters across the country).

Hamilton (16) traces the rise of pessimism in widely-circulated Protestant sermons, especially in regard to the solution of social problems. Albig (3) finds similar value judgments implicit even in the current trend of opinion research, reflecting a "denigration of the average individual, a belaboring of his obvious lack of knowledge and information, and therefore, a skepticism concerning many aspects of political democracy."

Saenger (31) finds the undercurrent of hostility a dominant note in "Male and Female Relations in the American Comic Strip," and suggests the implicit message, "Love is dangerous because it leads to marriage in which . . . men lose their strength." Legman (25) wonders "whether the maniacal fixation on violence and death in all our mass-produced fantasies is a substitution for a censored sexuality, or is, to a greater degree, intended to siphon off—into avenues of perversion opened up by the censorship of sex—the aggression felt by children and adults against the social and economic structure. . . ."

Adorno (1) sees popular music joining in a response "manipulated not only by its promoters, but, as it were, by the inherent nature of the music itself, into a system of response-mechanisms wholly antagonistic to the ideal of individuality in a free, liberal society. . . ." In another connection (2) he writes: "Mass media . . . consist of various layers of meaning superimposed on one another. . . . As a matter of fact, the hidden message may be more important than the overt since this hidden message will escape the controls of consciousness, will not be 'looked through,' will not be warded off by sales resistance, but is likely to sink into the spectator's mind." He finds that the underlying " 'message' of adjustment and unreflecting obedience seems to be dominant and all-pervasive today." His analysis of popular fiction concludes that:

. . . . The ideals of conformity and conventionalism were inherent in popular novels from the very beginning. Now, however, these ideals have been translated into rather clear-cut prescriptions of what to do and what not to do. . . . True, conflicts of the nineteenth century type—such as women running away from their husbands, the drabness of provincial life, and daily chores— occur frequently in today's magazine stories. However, with a regularity which challenges quantitative treatment, these conflicts are decided in favor of the very same conditions from which these women want to break away. The stories teach their readers that one has to be "realistic," that one has to adjust oneself at any price. . . .

Schramm's (32) quantitative analysis of the "World of the Confession Magazine" substantiates the observation of a punitive, puritanical code hidden in overtly rebellious themes. "It is very interesting," he notes, "to see how 'romance' magazines basically advise young women to shake the dew out of their eyes and the dreams out of their heads."

Consequential Meaning: From Market Position to Cover Girl

A recent study by the present author (15) attempted to trace the consequential meaning and social role of the "confession" magazine from industrial structure to content and cover design. The social mission of that magazine was found to be determined from the outset by its competitive position in a wage-earning reader market. This circumstance led to the development of an editorial prescription designed for working class women with presumably middle class pocketbooks, anxieties, and "behavior problems."

The social appeal of the "confession" story pivots on the heroine's human frailties in an inhospitable world she cannot fully understand. The "truth" of this world is brought home through an inevitable encounter with sin, crime, suffering, and the final coming to terms (but never to grips) with the stern code of society. In the context of the unyielding hazards and fears of pseudo-middle class life, the heroine's "sinful" acts become irrelevant as acts of protest. The safety valve of individual adjustment and social unrelatedness furnishes the antidote for the social appeal of sympathy for simple human beings facing their brutal world.

The ingredient of unrelatedness seems to be further manifested in the implicit structure of the "confession" cover design. Shaped by both editorial requirements and the pressures of supermarket distribution, the "confession" cover design generally features a wholesome, innocent-looking, radiantly carefree cover girl, wholly unrelated to the fear-and-sin-ridden world of verbal titles surrounding her on the cover.

An experimental study (14) of subject responses to the image of the cover girl seemed to indicate that her unrelated juxtaposition serves well the requirements of the "confession" market and distribution. While the cover girl's involvement with the social issues of her verbal context is outwardly as unconscious as that of the heroine is inwardly unreflecting, her implicit association with the verbal context of the cover safely enhances, as if by contrast, some of the perceived attractions of her image.

The Challenge for Critical Analysis

"The knowledgeable man in the genuine public is able to turn his personal troubles into social issues, to see their relevance for his community and his community's relevance for them," wrote Mills (29) in comparing the individual in a community of publics with members of audiences created as markets for cultural mass production. "The individual," he wrote,

understands that what he thinks and feels as personal troubles are very often not only that but problems shared by others and indeed not subject to solution by one individual but only by modifications of the structure of the groups in which he lives and sometimes the structure of the entire society.

Men in masses are gripped by personal troubles, but they are not aware of their true meaning and source. Men in public confront issues, and they are aware of their terms. It is the task of the liberal institution, as of liberally educated man, continually to translate troubles into issues and issues into the terms of their human meaning for the individual. . . .

The case for self-government is predicated upon a community of publics. The dissolution of publics into markets for mass media conceived and conducted in the increasingly demanding framework of commodity merchandising is the cultural (and political) specter of our age. This fear is now joined by a growing concern over the trend of social science research, especially in the field of communications. More and more of this research is seen to succumb to the fate of mass media content itself in being implicitly tailored to the specifications of industrial and market operations. Concern "with questions of ethics in relation to the formation and effects of public opinion," wrote William Albig (3) in his review of the research of two decades, ". . . was largely absent, or at least unexpressed, in the writings of . . . contributors to opinion research in the past 20 years." Albig continued:

Since 1920 a large professional class has developed to man the expanding activities of press, film, radio, television. At the same time, commercial and academic analysts of the communication process have proliferated. To a marked extent these professionals discuss this vast communications activity in terms of process, technique, stimuli, impact, effects, and semantic analysis, but not in terms of the ethical and value problems of communications content and effect.

It is, then, in this context of fragmentary evidence about the consequential meaning of mass media content, and of growing public and professional concern about its implications for a community of publics (including social scientists) that the challenge emerges. The challenge for mass communications research is this: to combine the empirical methods with the critical aims of social science, to join rigorous practice with value-conscious theory, and thus to gather the insight the knowledgeable individual in a genuine public must have if he is to come to grips (and not unconsciously to terms) with the sweeping undercurrents of his culture.

REFERENCES

1. ADORNO, T. W. "On Popular Music." *Studies in Philosophy and Social Science* 9:17-47; 1941.

2. ADORNO, T. W. "How to Look at Television." *The Quarterly of Film, Radio, and Television* 8:213-36; 1954.

3. ALBIG, WILLIAM. "Two Decades of Opinion Study: 1936-1956." *Public Opinion Quarterly* 21:14-22; 1957.

4. AUSTER, DONALD. "A Content Analysis of 'Little Orphan Annie.'" *Social Problems* 2:26-33; July 1954.

5. BERELSON, BERNARD. *Content Analysis in Communication Research.* Glencoe, Illinois: The Free Press, 1952.

6. BERELSON, BERNARD and SALTER, PATRICIA. "Majority and Minority Americans: An Analysis of Magazine Fiction." *Public Opinion Quarterly* 10:168-90; 1946.

7. BUSH, CHILTON R. and BULLOCK, ROBERT K. "Names in the News: A Study of Two Dailies." *Journalism Quarterly* 29:148-57; 1952.

8. CARPENTER, E. "The New Languages." *Explorations* 7; March 1957.

9. COOPER, EUNICE and DINERMAN, HELEN. "Analysis of the Film 'Don't Be a Sucker': A Study in Communication." *Public Opinion Quarterly* 15:243-64; 1951.

10. COX, CAROL A. "Labor in Motion Pictures." Unpublished research paper. Urbana: University of Illinois, College of Journalism and Communications, 1957.

11. DALE, EDGAR. *The Content of Motion Pictures.* New York: The Macmillan Co., 1935.

12. FEARING, FRANKLIN. "Social Impact of the Mass Media of Communication." *Mass Media and Education.* Fifty-Third Yearbook of the National Society for the Study of Education, Part II. Chicago: The University of Chicago Press, 1954. Chapter VIII, p. 165-92.

13. GERBNER, GEORGE. "Toward a General Model of Communication." *Audio-Visual Communication Review* 4:171-99; Summer 1956.

14. GERBNER, GEORGE. "The Social Anatomy of the Romance-Confession Cover Girl." *Journalism Quarterly* (in press).

15. GERBNER, GEORGE. "The Social Role of the Confession Magazine." *Social Problems* (in press).

16. HAMILTON, THOMAS. "Social Optimism in American Protestantism." *Public Opinion Quarterly* 6:280-83; 1942.

17. HEAD, SIDNEY W. "Content Analysis of Television Drama Programs." *The Quarterly of Film, Radio, and Television* 9:175-94; 1954.

18. INNIS, H. A. *The Bias of Communication.* Toronto: University of Toronto Press, 1951.

19. KAPLAN, A. "Content Analysis and the Theory of Signs." *Philosophy of Science* 10:230-47; 1943.

20. KRACAUER, SIEGFRIED. *From Caligari to Hitler: A Psychological History of the German Film.* Princeton, New Jersey: Princeton University Press, 1947.

21. KRACAUER, SIEGFRIED. "Hollywood's Terror Films; Do They Reflect an American State of Mind?" *Commentary* 2:132-36; 1946.

22. KRACAUER, SIEGFRIED. "The Challenge of Qualitative Content Analysis." *Public Opinion Quarterly* 16:631-41; Winter 1952-53.

23. LASSWELL, H. D.; LERNER, D.; and POOL, I. DE SOLA. *The Comparative Study of Symbols.* Stanford, Calif.: Stanford University Press, 1952.

24. LAZARSFELD, PAUL. "Remarks on Administrative and Critical Communications Research." *Studies in Philosophy and Social Science* 9:2-16; 1941.

25. LEGMAN, GERSON. *Love and Death.* New York: Breaking Point, 1949.

26. LOWENTHAL, LEO. "Biographies in Popular Magazines." *Radio Research, 1942-43.* New York: Harper and Brothers, 1944.

27. LOWENTHAL, LEO. "Historical Perspectives in Popular Culture." *American Journal of Sociology* 55:323-33; 1950.

28. LOWENTHAL, LEO. *Literature and the Image of Man.* Boston: The Beacon Press, 1957.

29. MILLS, C. W. *The Power Elite.* New York: Oxford University Press, 1956.

30. OSGOOD, C. E. "The Representational Model and Relevant Research Methods." *Content Analysis Today* (In press).

31. SAENGER, GERHARDT. "Male and Female Relations to the American Comic Strip." *Public Opinion Quarterly* 19:195-205; 1955.

32. SCHRAMM, WILBUR. "World of the Confession Magazine." Urbana: University of Illinois, Institute of Communications Research, 1955. (Mimeographed)

33. SMYTHE, D. W. "Some Observations on Communication Theory." *Audio-Visual Communication Review* 2:24-37; Winter 1954.

34. SMYTHE, D. W. "Reality as Presented by Television." *Public Opinion Quarterly* 18:143-56; 1954.

35. SPEIER, HANS. "The Social Determination of Ideas." *Social Research* 5:182-205; 1938.

36. SPIEGELMAN, MARVIN; TERWILLIGER, CARL; and FEARING, FRANKLIN. "The Content of Comic Strips: A Study of a Mass Medium of Communication," and "The Content of Comics: Goals and Means to Goals of Comic Strip Characters." In *The Journal of Social Psychology* 35:37-57; 1952, and 37:189-203; 1953, respectively.

37. SUSSMAN, LEILA. "Labor in the Radio News: An Analysis of Content." *Journalism Quarterly.* September 1945.

38. VAN DEN HAAG, E. "Of Happiness and of Despair We Have No Measure." *Mass Culture, The Popular Arts in America.* (Edited by B. Rosenberg and D. M. White.) Glencoe, Ill.: The Free Press, 1957.

39. WOLFENSTEIN, MARTHA and LEITES, NATHAN. "Two Social Scientists View 'No Way Out.'" *Commentary* 10:388-91; 1950.

What We Know About the Effects of Mass Communication
Joseph T. Klapper

from

Public Opinion Quarterly, 21, 1957.

Reprinted by permission of the author and *Public Opinion Quarterly*.

What We Know About the Effects of Mass Communication: The Brink of Hope[*]

By Joseph T. Klapper

The "brink of hope" for research in mass communications, according to this author, lies in a new orientation toward its study and some resulting generalizations which order many of the seemingly diverse and unrelated findings. This article contains a description of the new orientation, of the emerging generalizations, and of the findings which they may mold into a body of organized knowledge.

Joseph T. Klapper is Mass Communication Consultant with General Electric. At the time this article was written, he was Research Associate at the Bureau of Applied Social Research at Columbia University.

T WENTY YEARS ago writers who undertook to discuss mass communication typically felt obliged to define that unfamiliar term. In the intervening years conjecture and research upon the topic, particularly in reference to the effects of mass communication, have burgeoned. The literature has reached that stage of profusion and disarray, characteristic of all burgeoning disciplines, at which researchers and research administrators speak wistfully of establishing centers where the cascading data might be sifted and stored. The field has grown to the point at which its practitioners are periodically asked by other researchers to attempt to assess the cascade, to determine whither we are tumbling, to attempt to assess, in short, "what we know about the effects of mass communication." The present paper is one attempt to partially answer that question.

The author is well aware that the possibility of bringing any order to this field is regarded in some quarters with increasing pessimism. The paper will acknowledge and document this pessimism, but it will neither condone nor share it. It will rather propose that we have come at last to the brink of hope.

THE BASES OF PESSIMISM

The pessimism is, of course, widespread and it exists both among the interested lay public and within the research fraternity.

[*] This paper may be identified as publication A-242 of the Bureau of Applied Social Research, Columbia University. It was originally presented as an address at the National Education Association's Centennial Seminar on Communications, at Dedham, Mass., May 21-22, 1957.

Some degree of pessimism, or even cynicism, is surely to be expected from the lay public, whose questions we have failed to answer. Teachers, preachers, parents, and legislators have asked us a thousand times over these past fifteen years whether violence in the media produces delinquency, whether the media raise or lower public taste, and just what the media can do to the political persuasions of their audiences. To these questions we have not only failed to provide definitive answers, but we have done something worse: we have provided evidence in partial support of every hue of every view. We have on the one hand demonstrated that people's existing tastes govern the way they use media,[1] and on the other hand reported instances in which changed media usage was associated with apparently altered tastes.[2] We have hedged on the crime and violence question, typically saying, "Well, probably there is no causative relationship, but there just might be a triggering effect."[3] In reference to persuasion, we have maintained that the media are after all not so terribly powerful,[4] and yet we have reported their impressive successes in such varied causes as promoting religious intolerance,[5] the sale of war bonds,[6] belief in the American Way,[7] and disenchantment with boy scout activities.[8] It is surely no wonder that a bewildered public should regard with cynicism a research tradition which supplies, instead of definitive answers, a plethora of relevant but inconclusive, and at times seemingly contradictory, findings.

Considerable pessimism, of a different hue, is also to be expected within the research fraternity itself. Such anomalous findings as have been cited above seemed to us at first to betoken merely the need of more penetrating and rigid research. We shaped insights into hypotheses and eagerly set up research designs in quest of the additional variables which we were sure would bring order out of chaos, and enable us to describe the process of effect with sufficient precision to diagnose and predict. But the variables emerged in such a cataract that we almost drowned. The relatively placid waters of

[1] E.g., Lazarsfeld (1940), pp. 21-47; Wiebe (1952), pp. 185 ff. (*For complete bibliographical details, refer to Bibliography.*)

[2] E.g., Lazarsfeld (1940), pp. 126 ff.; Suchman (1941). Both Lazarsfeld and Suchman point out that although media may seem to be causative agents, further research reveals that their influence was energized by other factors. The point is discussed at length below.

[3] This is the typical, if perhaps inevitable conclusion, of surveys of pertinent literature and comment. See, for example, Bogart (1956), pp. 258-274.

[4] E.g., Lazarsfeld and Merton (1949); Klapper (1948). The point is elaborately demonstrated in regard to political conversion in Lazarsfeld, Berelson, and Gaudet (1948), and in Berelson, Lazarsfeld, and McPhee (1954).

[5] Klapper (1949), pp. II-25, IV-47, IV-52.

[6] Merton (1946).

[7] The efficacy, as well as the limitations, of media in this regard, are perhaps most exhaustively documented in the various unclassified evaluation reports of the United States Information Agency.

[8] Kelley and Volkhart (1952).

"*who* says *what* to *whom*" were early seen to be muddied by audience pre-dispositions, "self-selection," and selective perception. More recent studies, both in the laboratory and the social world, have documented the influence of a host of other variables, including various aspects of contextual organization;[9] the audiences' image of the source;[10] the simple passage of time;[11] the group orientation of the audience member and the degree to which he values group membership;[12] the activity of opinion leaders;[13] the social aspects of the situation during and after exposure to the media,[14] and the degree to which the audience member is forced to play a role;[15] the personality pattern of the audience member,[16] his social class, and the level of his frustration;[17] the nature of the media in a free enterprise system,[18] and the availability of "social mechanism[s] for implementing action drives."[19] The list, if not endless, is at least overwhelming, and it continues to grow. Almost every aspect of the life of the audience member and the culture in which the communication occurs seems susceptible of relation to the process of communicational effect. As early as 1948, Berelson, cogitating on what was then known, came to the accurate if perhaps moody conclusion that "some kinds of *communication* on some kinds of *issues,* brought to the attention of some kinds of *people* under some kinds of *conditions* have some kinds of *effects.*"[20] It is surely no wonder that today, after eight more years at the inexhaustible fount of variables, some researchers should feel that the formulation of any systematic description of what effects are how effected, and the predictive application of such principles, is a goal which becomes the more distant as it is the more vigorously pursued.

[9] The effect of such variables as the number of topics mentioned, the order of topics, camera angles, detail of explanation, explicitness vs. implicitness, one side vs. both sides, and a host of other contextual variables has been exhaustively studied in virtually thousands of experiments conducted under the auspices of the U. S. Navy, the U. S. Army, and Pennsylvania State University, as well as by individual investigators. Summaries of several such studies will be found, *passim,* in Hovland, Lumsdaine, and Sheffield (1949) and Hovland, Janis, and Kelley (1953).

[10] E.g., Merton (1946), pp. 61 ff.; Freeman, Weeks and Wertheimer (1955); Hovland, Janis, and Kelley (1953), ch. 2, which summarizes a series of studies by Hovland, Weiss, and Kelman.

[11] Hovland, Lumsdaine, and Sheffield (1949), in re "sleeper effects" and "temporal effects."

[12] E.g., Kelley and Volkhart (1952); Riley and Riley (1951); Ford (1954); Katz and Lazarsfeld (1955) review a vast literature on the subject (pp. 15-133).

[13] Katz (1957) provides an exhaustive review of the topic.

[14] E.g., Friedson (1953). For an early insight, see Cooper and Jahoda (1947).

[15] Janis and King (1954), King and Janis (1953), and Kelman (1953), all of which are summarized and evaluated in Hovland, Janis, and Kelley (1953); also Michael and Maccoby (1953).

[16] E.g., Janis (1954); also Hovland, Janis, and Kelley (1953), ch. 6.

[17] E.g., Maccoby (1954).

[18] E.g., Klapper (1948); Klapper (1949), pp. IV-20-27; Wiebe (1952).

[19] Wiebe (1951-2).

[20] Berelson (1948), p. 172.

This paper, however, takes no such pessimistic view. It rather proposes that we already know a good deal more about communications than we thought we did, and that we are on the verge of being able to proceed toward even more abundant and more fruitful knowledge.

This optimism is based on two phenomena. The first of these is a new orientation toward the study of communication effects which has recently become conspicuous in the literature. And the second phenomenon is the emergence, from this new approach, of a few generalizations. It is proposed that these generalizations can be tied together, and tentatively developed a little further, and that when this is done the resulting set of generalizations can be extremely helpful. More specifically, they seem capable of organizing and relating a good deal of existing knowledge about the processes of communication effect, the factors involved in the process, and the direction which effects typically take. They thus provide some hope that the vast and ill-ordered array of communications research findings may be eventually molded, by these or other generalizations, into a body of organized knowledge.

This paper undertakes to cite the new orientation, to state what seem to be the emerging generalizations, and to at least suggest the extent of findings which they seem capable of ordering. In all of this, the author submits rather than asserts. He hopes to be extremely suggestive, but he cannot yet be conclusive. And if the paper bespeaks optimism, it also bespeaks the tentativeness of exploratory rather than exhaustive thought. Explicit note will in fact be taken of wide areas to which the generalizations do not seem to apply, and warnings will be sounded against the pitfalls of regarding them as all-inclusive or axiomatic.

The Phenomenistic Approach. The new orientation, which has of course been hitherto and variously formulated, can perhaps be described, in a confessedly oversimplified way, as a shift away from the concept of "hypodermic effect"[21] toward an approach which might be called "situational," "phenomenistic," or "functional." It is a shift away from the tendency to regard mass communication as a necessary and sufficient cause of audience effects, toward a view of the media as influences, working amid other influences, in a total situation. The old quest of specific effects stemming directly from the communication has given way to the observation of existing conditions or changes—followed by an inquiry into the factors, including mass communication, which produced those conditions and changes, and the roles which these factors played relative to each other. In short, attempts to assess a stimu-

---

[21] Berelson, Lazarsfeld, and McPhee (1954), p. 234.

lus which was presumed to work alone have given way to an assessment of the role of that stimulus in a total observed phenomen.

Examples of the new approach are fairly numerous, although they still represent only a small proportion of current research. The so-called Elmira[22] and Decatur[23] studies, for example, set out to determine the critical factors in various types of observed decisions, rather than focussing exclusively on whether media did or did not have effects. McPhee, in theoretical vein, proposes that we stop seeking direct media effects on taste and inquire instead into what produces taste and how media affect that.[24] The Rileys and Maccoby focus on the varying functions which media serve for different sorts of children, rather than inquiring whether media do or do not affect them.[25] Some of the more laboratory-oriented researchers, in particular the Hovland school, have been conducting ingeniously designed controlled experiments in which the communicational stimulus is a constant, and various extra-communicational factors are the variables.[26]

This new approach, which views mass media as one among a series of factors, working in patterned ways their wonders to perform, seems to the author to have made possible a series of generalizations which will now be advanced. They are submitted very gingerly. They seem to the author at once extremely generic and quite immature; they seem on the one hand to involve little that has not been said, and on the other hand to be frightfully daring. They do seem, however, to be capable of relating a good deal of data about the processes, factors, and directions of communication effects, and of doing this in such a way that findings hitherto thought anomalous or contradictory begin to look like orderly variations on a few basic themes.

Emerging Generalizations. The entire set of generalizations will first be presented in their bare bones, and without intervening comment. The remainder of this paper will be devoted to justifying their existence and indicating the range of data which they seem able to organize. Without further ado, then, it is proposed that we are as of now justified in making the following tentative generalizations:

1. Mass communication ordinarily does not serve as a necessary and sufficient cause of audience effects, but rather functions among and through a nexus of mediating factors and influences.

2. These mediating factors are such that they typically render mass communication a contributory agent, but not the sole cause, in a process of reinforcing the existing conditions. (Regardless of the condition in question—

[22] *Ibid.*
[23] Katz and Lazarsfeld (1955).
[24] McPhee (1953).
[25] Riley and Riley (1951), and Maccoby (1954).
[26] E.g., the experimental program described in Hovland, Janis, and Kelley (1953).

be it the level of public taste, the tendency of audience members toward or away from delinquent behavior, or their vote intention—and regardless of whether the effect in question be social or individual, the media are more likely to reinforce than to change.)

3. On such occasions as mass communication does function in the service of change, one of two conditions is likely to obtain. Either:

    a. the mediating factors will be found to be inoperative, and the effect of the media direct; or

    b. the mediating factors, which normally favor reinforcement, will be found to be themselves impelling toward change.

4. There are certain residual situations in which mass communication seems to wreak direct effects, or to directly and of itself serve certain psychophysical functions.

5. The efficacy of mass communication, either as contributory agents or as agents of direct effect, is affected by various aspects of the media themselves or of the communication situation (including, for example, aspects of contextual organization, the availability of channels for overt action, etc.).

Therewith the generalizations, and herewith the application. The schemata will be applied first to the field of persuasive communication, and then, much more briefly, to the data dealing with the effects of mass communication on the levels of audience taste. The hope, in each case, is to show that the data support the generalizations, and that the generalizations in turn organize the data and suggest new avenues of logically relevant research.

THE GENERALIZATIONS APPLIED: PERSUASION

Persuasive communication here refers to those communications which are intended to evoke what Katz and Lazarsfeld have called "campaign" effects,[27] i.e., to produce such short term opinion and attitude effects as are typically the goals of campaigns—political, civic, or institutional. Long-range phenomena, such as the building of religious values, are not here a focus of attention, nor are the marketing goals of most advertising.

Reinforcement. It is by now axiomatic that persuasive communication of the sort we are discussing is far more often associated with attitude reinforcement than with conversion. The now classic *People's Choice* found reinforcement, or constancy of opinion, approximately ten times as common as conversion among Erie County respondents exposed to the presidential campaign of 1940,[28] and a nine to one ratio was found in the more elaborate study of Elmira voters in 1948.[29] Various other studies have attested that, in

[27] Katz and Lazarsfeld (1955), pp. 17 ff.
[28] Lazarsfeld, Berelson, and Gaudet (1948).
[29] Berelson, Lazarsfeld, and McPhee (1954).

general, when the media offer fare in support of both sides of given issues, the dominant affect is stasis, or reinforcement, and the least common effect is conversion.

But we are not here proposing merely that the media are more likely to reinforce than to convert. We are also proposing, as some others have proposed before us,[30] and as we have stated in generalization number 1, that the media typically do not wreak direct effects upon their audiences, but rather function among and through other factors or forces. And we are going slightly farther by proposing, in generalization number 2, that it is these very intervening variables themselves which tend to make mass communication a contributing agent of reinforcement as opposed to change. We shall here note only a few such variables, deliberately selecting both from among the long familiar and the newly identified, in order to suggest the extent of findings for which this generalization seems able to account, and which, seen in this light, become logically related manifestations of the same general phenomenon.

Audience predispositions, for example, have been recognized since the very beginnings of communications research as a controlling influence upon the effect of persuasive mass communication. A plethora of studies, some conducted in the laboratory and some in the social world, have demonstrated that such predispositions and their progeny—selective exposure,[31] selective retention, and selective perception—intervene between the supply of available mass communication stimuli and the minds of the audience members.[32] They wrap the audience member in a kind of protective net, which so sifts or deflects or remolds the stimuli as to make reinforcement a far more likely effect than conversion.

Let us turn from these very old friends to newer acquaintances. Communications research has recently "rediscovered" *the group*. Katz and Lazarsfeld, drawing on the literature of small group research, have proposed, with considerable supporting evidence, that primary-type groups to which the audience member belongs may themselves function as reinforcing agents and

[30] For explicit statements, see McPhee (1953) and Meyersohn (1957). Similar orientations are implicit in Katz (1957), in all studies cited in footnotes 22-26 above, and in various other works.

[31] "Selective exposure" seems to the author a somewhat more realistic term than the classic "self-selection." It is in a sense true that a given program "selects its audience before it affects it" (Lazarsfeld, 1940, p. 134), i.e., that it acts like a sieve in screening its particular audience from among the vast potential audience of all media offerings. But the sieve works, after all, only because the people, rather than the program are, consciously or unconsciously, selective.

[32] No attempt can be made to cite here the hundreds of studies which demonstrate one or more of these processes. Summaries of a considerable number which appeared during or before the late 1940's will be found in Klapper (1949), pp. Intro 11-12, I-15-26, and IV-27-33. For a particularly intriguing demonstration of selective exposure, see Geiger (1950), and for an extraordinarily elaborate demonstration of selective perception, see Wilner (1951).

may influence mass communication to do likewise.[33] People tend, for example, to belong to groups whose characteristic opinions are congenial with their own; the opinions themselves seem to be intensified, or at least made more manifest, by intra-group interaction; and the benefits, both psychological and social, of continued membership in good standing act as a deterrent against opinion change. Group-anchored norms thus serve, on a conscious or unconscious level, to mediate the effects of communications. The proposition has been empirically demonstrated by Kelley and Volkart,[34] who found that, in general, persuasive communications were more likely to be rejected if they were not in accord with the norms of groups to which the audience member belonged; there were indications, furthermore, that the tendency was intensified in regard to issues more salient to the group, and among persons who particularly valued their membership. Groups are further likely to supplement the reinforcing effect by providing areas for oral dissemination. Various studies have shown that communications spread most widely among persons of homogeneous opinion, and espically among those who agree with the communication to begin with.[35] The "rediscovered group," in short, intervenes between the media stimuli and the people who are affected, and it does so, other conditions being equal, in favor of reinforcement.

Consider another phenomenon which is now in the limelight of communication research: *opinion leadership,* or, as it is sometimes called, "the two-step flow of communication."[36] The operation of such leadership is by definition interventive. And opinion leaders, it turns out, are usually supernormative members of the same groups to which their followers belong— i.e., persons especially familiar with and loyal to group standards and values.[37] Their influence therefore appears more likely to be exercised in the service of continuity than of change, and it seems therefore a reasonable conjecture—although it has not, to the author's knowledge, been specifically documented—that their role in the process of communication effect is more likely to encourage reinforcement than conversion.

All the intervening phenomena which have thus far been cited pertain, in one way or another, to the audience members—to the element of *whom* in the old Lasswell formula. But the range of mediating influences is not so restricted. *The nature of mass communication* in a free enterprise society, for example, falls under this same rubric. It is surely not necessary to here rehearse in detail the old adage of how the need for holding a massive audi-

---

[33] Katz and Lazarsfeld (1955), pp. 15-133.

[34] Kelley and Volkhart (1952), and Kelley (1955), both of which are summarized in Hovland, Janis, and Kelley (1953), Ch. 5.

[35] E.g., Katz and Lazarsfeld (1955), pp. 82-115; also Katz (1957).

[36] Katz and Lazarsfeld (1955), pp. 309-320, and Katz (1957).

[37] Katz and Lazarsfeld (1955), pp. 82-115, and 219-334 *passim,* especially pp. 321 ff.; also Katz (1957).

ence leads the media, particularly in their entertainment fare, to hew to the accepted, and thus to tend to resanctify the sanctified.[38] But it should here be noted that this is to say that the demands of the socio-economic system mediate the possible effects of mass communication in the direction of social reinforcement.

Such phenomena as these lend some credence to the proposition that the media typically work among and through other forces, and that these intervening forces tend to make the media contributing agents of reinforcement. And the generalization, to which these factors lend credence, in turn serves to organize and relate the factors. Diverse though they may be, they are seen to play essentially similar roles. One is tempted to wonder if they do not constitute a definable class of forces—whether, if the process of communicational effect were reduced to symbolic formulation, they might not be severally represented as, say, Q_1, Q_2, and so forth to Q_n. The author does not propose anything so drastic. He merely notes that the generalization suggests it. It suggests, simultaneously, relevant topics for further research. *Do* opinion leaders actually function, as the generalization suggests, to render mass communication a more likely agent of reinforcement than of change? And what of all those Q's between Q_3 or Q_8 and Q_n? What other phenomena function in a similar manner and toward the same end?

We may note also that this generalization, simple though it is, not only accounts for such factors as provide its life blood. It provides as well a sort of covering shed for various bits and pieces of knowledge which have hitherto stood in discrete isolation.

Consider, for example, the phenomenon of *"monopoly propaganda"*—i.e., propaganda which is vigorously and widely pursued and nowhere opposed. Monopoly propaganda has been long recognized as widely effective, and monopoly position has been cited as a condition which virtually guarantees persuasive success.[39] But monopoly propaganda can exist only in favor of views which already enjoy such wide sanction that no opposition of any significance exists. Viewed in the light of the generalization, monopoly position is seen not as an isolated condition of propaganda success, but as a specific combination of known factors. It is a name for the situation in which both the media and virtually all the factors which intervene between the media and the audience, or which operate co-existently with the media, approach a homogeneity of directional influence. Monopoly position is, as it were, a particular setting of the machine, and its outcome is logically predictable.

Change, with mediators inoperative. Generalization number 3 recognizes that although the media typically function as contributory agents of reinforce-

[38] E.g., Klapper (1948); Klapper (1949), pp. IV-20-27; Wiebe (1952).
[39] E.g., Lazarsfeld and Merton (1949); Klapper (1948) and Klapper (1949), pp. IV-20-27.

ment, they also function as agents of attitude change. In reference to this simple point, there is surely no need for lengthy documentation: the same studies that find reinforcement the predominant effect of campaigns typically reveal as well some small incidence of conversion, and a plethora of controlled experiments attest that media, or laboratory approximations of media, can and often do shift attitudes in the direction intended by the communicator. But the generalization further proposes—and in this it is more daring than its predecessors—that such attitude changes occur when either of two conditions obtain: when the forces which normally make for stasis or reinforcement are inoperative, or when these very same forces themselves make for change.

Let us consider first the proposition that change is likely to occur if the forces for stasis are inoperative. A set of experiments which has already been mentioned above is extremely indicative in reference to this proposition. Kelley and Volkhart, it will be recalled, found that, in general, communications opposed to group norms were likely to be rejected if the issue was particularly salient to the group, and that they were more likely to be rejected by persons who particularly valued their group membership. But there is another side to the Kelley-Volkhart coin, viz., the findings that the communication opposed to group norms was more likely to be *accepted when the issue was not particularly salient* to the group, and that it was more likely to be accepted *by persons who did not particularly value their membership* in the group.[40] Put another way, *changes were more likely to occur in those situations in which the mediating effect of the group was reduced.*

A whole slew of other findings and bits of knowledge, both old and new, and previously existing as more or less discrete axioms, seem susceptible of being viewed as essentially similar manifestations of this same set of conditions. It has long been known, for example, that although the media are relatively ineffectual in conversion, they are quite effective in forming opinions and attitudes in regard to *new issues,* particularly as these issues are the more unrelated to "existing attitude clusters."[41] But it is precisely in reference to such issues that predispositions, selective exposure, and selective perception are least likely to exist, that group norms are least likely to pertain, that opinion leaders are least ready to lead—that the mediating forces of stasis, in short, are least likely to mediate. The intervening forces, in short, are likely to be inoperative, and the media are more likely to directly influence their audience.

Much the same explanation can be offered for the observed ability of the

[40] Kelley and Volkhart (1952), and Kelley (1955), both of which are summarized in Hovland, Janis, and Kelley (1953), Ch. 5. As noted above, the findings are highly indicative, but not absolutely clear cut.
[41] Berelson (1948), p. 176.

media to influence their audience on peripheral issues[42] while simultaneously failing in the major mission of the moment, and the same situation probably obtains in regard to media's ability to *communicate facts or even change opinions on objective matters without producing the attitude changes* that such facts and opinions are intended to engender.[43] It may well be that the facts and opinions are not related to the desired attitude change sufficiently strongly to call the protective mediating forces into play: the communication content is probably not recognized as necessarily relevant to the attitude, as not salient, and mediation does not occur. This interpretation, by the way, could very easily be tested.[44]

The inverse correlation between the capability of the media to wreak attitude change and the degree to which the attitude in question is ego-involved may well be another case in point.[45] But this paper cannot analyze and rehearse, nor has the author wholly explored, the entire range of phenomena which might be explained on the basis of the forces for stasis being inoperative. If the generalization is at all valid, it will gather such phenomena unto itself. Let it be the role of this paper to present it, to germinate as it will.

Changes through Mediators. Let us turn now to the second part of the proposition about the conditions under which media may serve as agents of opinion change. It has been suggested that such an effect is likely when either of two conditions obtain: when the forces for stasis are inoperative— as in the cases which have just been discussed—and, secondly, when the intervening forces themselves favor change.

Let us look again, for example, at the influence of group membership and of group norms. These typically mediate the influences of mass communication in favor of reinforcement, but under certain conditions they may abet communicational influences for change.

[42] E.g., McPhee (1953), pp. 12-13; also Hovland (1954).

[43] Hovland, Lumsdaine, and Sheffield (1949), pp. 42 ff. and elsewhere, *passim;* summarized in Klapper (1949), pp. IV-9-17.

[44] A rather simple controlled experiment might be set up, for example, in which two groups were exposed to communications, one of which merely presented the objective facts, and the other of which explicitly pointed out the implications for attitude change of accepting the objective facts. In line with the interpretation presented above, we would hypothesize that in the latter communication the *objective facts themselves* would be more likely to be rejected. Such an experiment would differ from the numerous studies of the relative efficacy of "implicit" vs. "explicit" conclusions, which have to date been primarily concerned with whether the *conclusions,* rather than the facts themselves, were more or less likely to be accepted.

[45] For what, after all, is an "ego-involved attitude," other than an attitude which is particularly salient to the person who holds it, and thus particularly well protected by predispositions, selective perception and the like? For an amusing statement of a similar view, see "John Crosby's Law," as quoted in Bogart (1956), p. 215. Suggestively relevant studies are numerous and include, e.g., Cooper and Jahoda (1947); Cooper and Dinerman (1951); Wilner (1951); Cannel and MacDonald (1956); and various others,

In an ingeniously designed experiment by McKeachie,[46] for example, communications regarding attitudes toward Negroes, and the discussion which these communications engendered, made some group members aware that they had misperceived the pertinent group norms. The great majority of such individuals showed opinion changes in the direction of the norm, which was also the direction intended by the communication. The *newly perceived norms* impelled the audience toward the communicationally recommended change.

A *switch in group loyalties or in reference groups* may likewise predispose an individual toward consonant opinion changes suggested by mass communication.[47] Studies of satellite defectors, for example, suggest that persons who have lived for years as respected members of Communist society, and then fall from grace, develop a new susceptibility to Western propaganda. As their lot deteriorates, they turn their eyes and minds to the west, and their radio dials to VOA and RFE. By the time they defect they have developed a set of extremely anti-Communist and pro-Western attitudes, quite out of keeping with their previous lives, but in accord with what they regard as normative to their new refugee primary group.[48]

Group norms, or predispositions otherwise engendered, may furthermore become dysfunctional; in learning theory terminology, the response they dictate may cease to be rewarding, or may even lead to punishment. In such situations the individual is impelled to find a new response which does provide reward, and communications recommending such a changed response are more likely to be accepted. Some such phenomenon seems to have occurred, for example, in the case of Nazi and North Korean soldiers who remained immune to American propaganda appeals while their military primary group survived, but became susceptible when the group disintegrated and adherence to its normative attitudes and conduct ceased to have survival value.[49] The accustomed group norms in such instances had not merely become inoperative; they had become positively dysfunctional and had sensitized and predisposed their adherents to changes suggested by the media.

Personality pattern appears to be another variable which may mediate the influence of communications, and particular syndromes seem to abet change. Janis, for example, found in a laboratory study that those of his subjects "who manifested social inadequacy, inhibition of aggression, and depressive tendencies, showed the greatest opinion change" in response to persuasive

[46] McKeachie (1954).
[47] E.g., Katz and Lazarsfeld (1955), pp. 66-81.
[48] The phenomenon has not been explicitly detailed, but is implicit in various studies performed for the United States Information Agency, and in Kracauer and Berkman (1956).
[49] E.g., Shils and Janowitz (1948); also Schramm (1954), pp. 17-18.

communication. They appeared, as Hovland puts it, to be "predisposed to be highly influenced."[50]

In sum, it appears that the generalization is supported by empirical data —that intervening variables which mediate the influence of mass communication, and which typically promote reinforcement, may also work for change. And again, the generalization, in turn, accounts for and orders the data on which it is based. Group membership, dysfunctional norms, and particular personality patterns can be viewed as filling similar roles in the process of communicationally stimulated opinion change. Other similarly operative variables will doubtless be identified by a continued phenomenistic approach, i.e., by the analysis of accomplished opinion changes.

The generalization furthermore serves, as did the others, to relate and explain various discrete findings and isolated bits of knowledge. It would appear to cover, for example, such hitherto unrelated phenomena as the susceptibility to persuasive appeals of persons whose primary group memberships place them under cross-pressures, and the effects of what Hovland has called "role playing."[51]

The first case—*the susceptibility to persuasive communications of persons whose primary group membership places them under cross-pressure*[52]—is fairly obvious. In terms of the generalization, such people can be said to be at the mercy of mediating factors which admit and assist communicational stimuli favoring both sides of the same issue. We may also observe that any attitude shift which such a person may make toward one side of the issue does not necessarily entail any reduction of the forceful mediation toward the other direction. On the basis of the generalization, we would therefore predict not only change, but inconstancy, which has in fact been found to be the case.[52a]

The effects of role playing seem another, if less obvious, example of opinion change occurring as a result of a mediating, or, in this case, a superimposed factor which in turn rendered a communication effective. Hovland reported that if persons opposed to a communication are forced to defend it, i.e., to act in a public situation as though they had accepted the recommended opinion, they become more likely actually to adopt it.[53] The crucial element of role playing is, of course, artificially superimposed. But in any case, the entire phenomenon might be viewed as something very akin to what occurs when an old norm, or an old predisposition, ceases to lead to reward. Successful role playing in fact invests the opposing response with reward. The

[50] Janis (1954), which is summarized in Hovland, Janis, and Kelley (1953), pp. 276 ff. (Quotes are from p. 277.)

[51] Hovland, Janis, and Kelley (1953), Ch. 7.

[52] E.g., Berelson, Lazarsfeld, and McPhee (1954); also Kriesberg (1954).

[52a] Lazarsfeld, Berelson, and Gaudet (1948), p. 70.

[53] Hovland, Janis, and Kelley (1953), Ch. 7.

communication is thus given an assist by the imposition of new factors which favor change. The potentialities of this technique, incidentally, are of course appalling. The Communists have already developed and refined it and we have christened the process "brain-washing."

Various other bits of knowledge about communication effect can be viewed as related manifestations of this same general phenomenon, i.e., the phenomenon of communications inducing attitude change through the assistance of mediating factors which themselves favor change. But it is the goal of this paper to be only suggestive, rather than exhaustive or exhausting, and thus generalization number three may be here left, to suggest whatever it will.

So much, then, for the first three generalizations, which attempt to relate the processes, the factors, and the directions of effect. It is hardly germane, at this juncture, to belabor generalizations four and five. They serve only to recognize residual categories. Thus number four merely points out that some persuasive or quasi-persuasive effects do appear, at least to our present state of knowledge, to be direct. The apparently unmotivated learning of sufficiently repeated facts or slogans is a case in point. And generalization number five merely points out that the persuasive efficacy of the media is known to be affected by numerous variables pertaining to the content, the medium itself, or the communication situation—by such matters, for example, as the number and order of topics, the degree of repetition, the likelihood of distraction, the objective possibilities of action, and the like. The proposed schemata suggests that these variables are of a different and residual order as compared with the kind of *mediating* variables which we have just been discussing.

We have thus far been laboring to make and document three points, viz., (1) the set of generalizations is supported by our knowledge of the effects of persuasive communications; (2) the generalizations organize, or bring into logical relation, or, if you will, "predict" in an *a posteriori* sense, a large portion of that knowledge; and (3) in so ordering the data they simultaneously suggest new and logically related avenues for further research.

It is proposed that the same set of generalizations is similarly applicable to other types of communication effect. To spell this out in detail is beyond the scope of a single paper.[54] It may be well for the sake of the argument, however, to at least suggest the applicability of the generalizations to one other area, the effects of mass communication upon levels of public taste.

---

[54] A forthcoming book by the present author, tentatively scheduled for publication in 1958, will attempt to indicate the degree to which the schemata is applicable to a much wider array of effects.

THE GENERALIZATIONS APPLIED: EFFECTS ON TASTE

Reinforcement. It has been long known that the media do not seem to determine tastes, but rather to be used in accordance with tastes otherwise determined. The typical audience member selects from the media's varied fare those commodities which are in accord with his existing likes, and typically eschews exposure to other kinds of material. His existing likes, in turn, seem largely to derive from his primary, secondary, and reference groups, although they are not uncommonly affected by his special personality needs.[55] Whatever their origin, they intervene between the audience member and the vast array of media fare, and between the specific content and his interpretation of it.[56] The media stimuli are thoroughly sifted and molded, and they serve, typically, as grist for the existing mill. Put in a now familiar way, the effects of mass communication are mediated, and the media serve as contributing agents of reinforcement.

Changes. But the media are also associated with changes in taste. Oddly enough, little attention has been paid to the one change which occurs continually—the changing tastes of growing children. Wolf and Fiske seem to be the only researchers who explicitly noted that the pattern of development in children's comic book preferences precisely parallels the changing needs of their developing personalities,[57] as expressed, for example, in games. And no one, to the author's knowledge, has ever pointed out that the pattern of development in comic book and TV preferences also parallels the previously characteristic patterns of development in regular reading preferences. In short, the development and its integral changes in taste are culturally wholly catholic. In terms of our present set of generalizations, this is to say that such mediating variables as personality, cultural norms, and peer group interests impel the media to function as contributory agents of taste change.

The media have also been observed, although rarely, to play a role in elevating the tastes of adults. Suchman, for example, investigated the previous habits of some 700 persons who regularly listened to classical music broadcasts, and found that in the case of 53 per cent the radio had either "initiated" their interest in music or had "nursed" a mild but previously little exercised interest. But—and here is the essential point—the radio had functioned in almost all of these cases not as a necessary and sufficient cause, but as an "energizing agent" or implementer of tendencies otherwise engendered. The so-called initiates had been urged to listen by friends, or in some cases fiancés, whose tastes they respected and whose good opinion they sought, or by their

[55] E.g., Lazarsfeld (1940), pp. 21-47; Wiebe (1952), pp. 185 ff.; Macoby (1954); Johnstone and Katz (1957).

[56] For a curious demonstration of primary-type groups affecting *interpretation* of content, see Bogart (1955).

[57] Wolf and Fiske (1949).

own belief that a taste for classical music would increase their social prestige.[58] The mediating factors, in short, were at it again.

The literature on taste effects is relatively sparse, and seems to offer no illustration of changes which could be ascribed to the forces of stasis being inoperative. It might be conjectured that such effects occur among extreme isolates, but the possibility seems never to have been investigated.

In any case, our two generalizations which regard both reinforcement and change as essentially products of mediating factors account for virtually all of the hard data on the effect of mass communication on public taste. The generalizations furthermore suggest that the data are neither contradictory nor anomalous, but logically related. Stasis, reinforcement, developmental patterns, and individual change appear as different but understandable and predictable products of the same machines.

Residual Matters. There remains a certain residuum of related data and respectable conjecture for which the generalizations do not account. They do not explain why tastes in the development of which media has played a large role tend to have a sort of pseudo-character—why music lovers whose passions have been largely radio-nurtured, for example, appear to be peculiarly interested in the lives of composers and performers, and to lack real depth of musical understanding.[59] Nor do the generalizations cover the phenomenon of media *created* pseudo-interests, about which much speculation exists. McPhee has noted, for example, that the tremendous availability of newscasts seems to have created in some people an addiction, an ardent hunger which is sated by the five-minute newscast, despite its lack of detail and regardless of its irrelevance to the addict's life and interests. McPhee notes a similar passion for big-league baseball results, even among people who have never been in a ball park nor even seen a game on TV.[60] Meyersohn regards this sort of thing as an indication that media create their own common denominators of national taste.[61]

We know little about this phenomenon. Perhaps it is a direct effect, or perhaps it involves mediators as yet unspotted. In any case, deeper understanding seems likely to come from what we have called the phenomenistic approach—from an inquiry into the functions which such addiction serves

[58] Suchman (1941).

[59] E.g., Suchman (1941), pp. 178 f.; Lazarsfeld (1940), p. 255; Bogart (1949). The generalizations are *relevant* to this phenomenon, in that such extramedia forces as the urging of friends are necessary causes of the changed tastes. But there is nothing in the generalization to *account* for the stoppage. There is no reason to assume that extra-media forces which impel the media toward wreaking particular effects also limit the extent of the effect, and in reference to the Suchman data there is not even any reason to presume that people who urge others to listen to good music are themselves possessed of "pseudo-tastes."

[60] McPhee (1953). The comment in footnote 59 is equally applicable here.

[61] Meyersohn (1957), pp. 352-4.

for the addict, and into the role of the media in creating or serving the addiction.

APPLICATION TO OTHER FIELDS

We have now considered the extent to which the proposed generalizations are applicable to existing data regarding the effects of mass communication on opinions and attitudes, and upon levels of taste. It is proposed that they are equally applicable to questions about the effect of specific types of media fare, such as fantasy or depictions of crime and violence, on the psychological orientations and behavior of the audience. In the interests of brevity, these other areas of effect will not be discussed, except to note that the classic studies, both old and new, seem particularly suggestive. The old studies of soap opera listeners by Warner and Henry[62] and Herzog,[63] for example, and the more recent and differently focused work of the Rileys and of Maccoby,[64] all relate such variables as group orientation and personality needs to media use and media effects. They speak, implicitly and explicitly, of the *functions* served by media, and of the role of the media in effects of which they are not the sole cause.

SUMMATION AND CONCLUSIONS

It is time now to look quickly back over the ground we have covered, and to evaluate the set of generalizations which have been proposed—to inquire into what they have enabled us to do, and to note their weaknesses.

On the positive side, they appear to serve three major functions:

First, as this paper has been at some pains to demonstrate, the generalizations have permitted us in some measure to organize, or to account for, a considerable number of communications research findings which have previously seemed discrete, at times anomalous, and occasionally contradictory. The author submits, tentatively and with due humility, that the schemata has in fact made possible organization of several different orders:

... it has enabled us to relate the *processes* of effect and the *direction* of effect, and to account for the relative incidence of reinforcement and of change.
... it has provided a concept of the process of effect in which both reinforcement and change are seen as related and understandable outcomes of the same general dynamic.
... it has enabled us to view such diverse phenomena as audience predispositions, group membership and group norms, opinion leadership, personality patterns, and the nature of the media in this society, as serving similar functions in the process of effect—as being, if you will, all of a certain order, and distinct from such other factors as the characteristics of media content.

[62] Herzog (1944).
[63] Warner and Henry (1948).
[64] Riley and Riley (1951) and Maccoby (1954).

... it has enabled us to view such other unrelated phenomena as monopoly propaganda, new issues, and role-playing as manifestations of the same general process—as specific combinations of known variables, the outcomes of which were predictable.

So much for the organizational capabilities of the media. But note that this organization of existing data, even within so sketchy a framework as these generalizations provide, permitted us to see gaps—to discover, for example, that certain presumed outcomes have to date been neither documented nor shown not to occur. And thus the second contribution: the generalizations seem capable of indicating avenues of needed research, which are logically related to existing knowledge. Put another way, even this simple schemata seems capable of contributing to the cumulatibility of future research findings. This is in no way to gainsay that future thought and research must inevitably change the generalizations themselves. As presently formulated, they constitute only a single tentative step forward, and their refinement or emendation seems more likely to enlarge than to reduce the area of their applicability.

Finally, it is in the extent of this applicability, coupled with the foetal nature of the generalizations, that the author finds particular bases for hope. Sketchy and imperfect as they are, these propositions regarding the process and direction of effect seem applicable to the effects of persuasive communications, to the effects of mass communication on public taste, and, though it has not here been demonstrated, to the effects of specific media fare upon the psychological orientations and overt behavior patterns of the audience. Furthermore, the mediating variables to which they point—variables such as predisposition, group membership, personality patterns and the like—seem to play essentially similar roles in all these various kinds of effect. Even if these generalizations turn out to be wholly in error—and certainly they are imperfect—they seem nevertheless sufficiently useful and sufficiently applicable to justify the faith that *some* generalizations can in due time be made.

These particular generalizations, however, do not usher in the millenium. They are imperfect, and underdeveloped; they are inadequate in scope, and in some senses they are dangerous.

They do not, for example, cover the residuum of direct effects except to note that such effects exist. They are less easy to apply, and perhaps inapplicable, to certain other broad areas of effect, such as the effect of the existence of the media on patterns of daily life, on each other, and on cultural values as a whole. We have here spoken of cultural values as a mediating factor, which in part determines media content, but certainly some sort of circular relationship must exist, and media content must in turn affect cultural values.

Such concepts suggest what is perhaps the greatest danger inherent both in these generalizations and in the approach to communications research from which they derive. And that is the tendency to go overboard in blindly minimizing the effects and potentialities of mass communication. In reaping the fruits of the discovery that mass media function amid a nexus of other influences, we must not forget that the influences nevertheless differ. Mass media of communication possess various characteristics and capabilities distinct from those of peer groups or opinion leaders. They are, after all, media of *mass* communication, which daily address tremendous cross-sections of the population with a single voice. It is neither sociologically unimportant nor insignificant that the media have rendered it possible, as Wiebe has put it, for Americans from all social strata to laugh at the same joke,[65] nor is it insignificant that total strangers, upon first meeting, may share valid social expectations that small talk about Betty Furness or Elvis Presley will be mutually comprehensible. We must not lose sight of the peculiar characteristics of the media, nor of the likelihood that of this peculiar character there may be engendered peculiar effects.

In any case, the most fruitful path for the future seems clear enough. It is not the path of abstract theorizing, nor is it the path, which so many of us have deserted, of seeking simple and direct effects of which media are the sole and sufficient cause. It appears rather to be the path of the phenomenistic approach, which seeks to account for the known occurrence and to assess the roles of the several influences which produced it, and which attempts to see the respondents not as randomly selected individuals each exchangeable for the other, but rather as persons functioning within particular social contexts. It is likewise the path of the cumulating controlled experiments in which the multifarious extra-media factors being investigated are built into the research design. These are the paths which have brought us to what seems the verge of generalization and empirically documented theory. They are the paths which have brought us to the brink of hope.

[65] Wiebe (1952).

BIBLIOGRAPHY

Note: Groups of works by the same author(s) are arranged *in order of their publication dates, not alphabetically by title.*

1. Bernard Berelson (1948), "Communications and Public Opinion," in Schramm (1948).
2. Bernard R. Berelson, Paul F. Lazarsfeld, and William N. McPhee (1954), *Voting: A Study of Opinion Formation During A Presidential Campaign,* Chicago, University of Chicago Press, 1954.
3. Leo Bogart (1949), "Fan Mail for the Philharmonic," *Public Opinion Quarterly,* 13, 3 (Fall, 1949), pp. 423-434.
4. Leo Bogart (1955), "Adult Talk About Newspaper Comics," *American Journal of Sociology,* 61, 1 (July, 1955), pp. 26-30.

5. Leo Bogart (1956), *The Age of Television*, New York: Frederick Ungar Publishing Co., 1956.
6. Charles F. Cannel and James MacDonald (1956), "The Impact of Health News on Attitudes and Behavior," *Journalism Quarterly*, 1956 (Summer), pp. 315-23.
7. Eunice Cooper and Marie Jahoda (1947), "The Evasion of Propaganda," *Journal of Psychology*, 23 (1947), pp. 15-25.
8. Eunice Cooper and Helen Dinerman (1951), "Analysis of the Film 'Don't Be A Sucker': A Study in Communication," *Public Opinion Quarterly*, 15, 2 (Summer, 1951).
9. Joseph B. Ford (1954), "The Primary Group in Mass Communication," *Sociology and Social Research*, 38, 3 (Jan.-Feb., 1954), pp. 152-8.
10. Howard E. Freeman, H. Ashley Weeks, and Walter I. Wertheimer (1955), "News Commentator Effect: A Study in Knowledge and Opinion Change," *Public Opinion Quarterly*, 19, 2 (Summer, 1955), pp. 209-215.
11. Eliot Friedson (1953), "The Relation of the Social Situation of Contact to the Media of Mass Communication," *Public Opinion Quarterly*, 17, 2 (Summer, 1953), pp. 230-238.
12. Theodore Geiger (1950), "A Radio Test of Musical Taste," *Public Opinion Quarterly*, 14, 3 (Fall, 1950), pp. 453-60.
13. Herta Herzog (1944), "What Do We Really Know About Daytime Serial Listeners," in Lazarsfeld and Stanton (1944).
14. Carl I. Hovland (1954), "Effects of the Mass Media of Communication," in Lindzey, Gardiner, *Handbook of Social Psychology*, Cambridge, Mass.: Addison-Wesley Publishing Co., 1954, Vol. II.
15. Carl I. Hovland, Irving L. Janis, and Harold H. Kelley (1953), *Communication and Persuasion*, New Haven: Yale University Press, 1953.
16. Carl I. Hovland, Arthur A. Lumsdaine, and Fred D. Sheffield (1949), *Experiments in Mass Communications* (Studies in Social Psychology in World War II, Vol. III), Princeton, N. J.: Princeton University Press, 1949.
17. I. L. Janis (1954), "Personality Correlates of Susceptibility to Persuasion," *Journal of Personality*, 22 (1954), pp. 504-518.
18. I. L. Janis and B. T. King (195-), "The Influence of Role Playing on Opinion Change," *Journal of Abnormal and Social Psychology*, 49 (1954), pp. 211-218.
19. John Johnstone and Elihu Katz (1957), "Youth and Popular Music," *American Journal of Sociology*, 62, 6 (May, 1957).
20. Elihu Katz and Paul F. Lazarsfeld (1955), *Personal Influence: The Part Played by People in the Flow of Mass Communications*, Glencoe, Ill.: The Free Press, 1955.
21. Elihu Katz (1957), "The Two-Step Flow of Communication: An Up-to-Date Report on an Hypothesis," *Public Opinion Quarterly*, 21, 1 (Spring, 1957), pp. 61-78.
22. Herbert C. Kelman, (1953), "Attitude Change as a Function of Response Restriction," *Human Relations*, 6, 3 (1953), pp. 185-214.
23. H. H. Kelley (195-), "Salience of Membership and Resistance to Change of Group Anchored Attitudes," *Human Relations*, 8 (1958), pp. 275-289.
24. H. H. Kelley and E. H. Volkhart (1952), "The Resistance to Change of Group-Anchored Attitudes," *American Sociological Review*, 17, (1952), pp. 453-465.
25. B. T. King and I. L. Janis (1953), as reported in Hovland, Janis and Kelley (1953), pp. 222-228.

26. Joseph T. Klapper (1948), "Mass Media and the Engineering of Consent," *The American Scholar*, 17, 4 (Autumn, 1948), pp. 419-429.
27. Joseph T. Klapper (1949), *The Effects of Mass Media*, New York: Bureau of Applied Social Research, Columbia University, 1949.
28. Siegfried Kracauer and Paul L. Berkman (1956), *Satellite Mentality*, New York: Frederick A. Praeger, Inc., 1956.
29. Martin Kriesberg (1949), "Cross-Pressures and Attitudes: A Study of the Influence of Conflicting Propaganda on Opinions Regarding American Soviet Relations," *Public Opinion Quarterly*, 13, 1 (Spring, 1949) pp. 5-16.
30. Paul F. Lazarsfeld (1940), *Radio and the Printed Page*, New York: Duell, Sloan and Pearce, 1940.
31. Paul F. Lazarsfeld, Bernard Berelson, and Hazel Gaudet (1948), *The People's Choice*, New York: Columbia University Press, 1948.
32. Paul F. Lazarsfeld and Robert K. Merton (1949), "Mass Communication, Popular Taste and Organized Social Action," in Schramm (1949), Q.V.
33. Paul F. Lazarsfeld and Frank N. Stanton (1941), *Radio Research, 1941*, New York: Duell, Sloan and Pearce, 1941.
34. Paul F. Lazarsfeld and Frank N. Stanton (1944), *Radio Research, 1942-3*, New York: Duell, Sloan and Pearce, 1944.
35. Paul F. Lazarsfeld and Frank N. Stanton (1949), *Communications Research, 1948-1949*, New York: Harper & Brothers, 1949.
36. Eleanor E. Maccoby (1954), "Why Do Children Watch Television?" *Public Opinion Quarterly*, 18, 3 (Fall, 1954), pp. 239-244.
37. Wilbert J. McKeachie (1954), "Individual Conformity to Attitudes of Classroom Groups," *Journal of Abnormal and Social Psychology*, 49, (1954), pp. 282-9.
38. William N. McPhee (1953), *New Strategies for Research in the Mass Media*. New York: Bureau of Applied Social Research, Columbia University, 1953.
39. Robert K. Merton (1946), *Mass Persuasion*, New York: Harper and Brothers, 1946.
40. Rolf B. Meyersohn (1957), "Social Research in Television," in Rosenberg and White (1957).
41. Donald M. Michael and Nathan Maccoby (1953), "Factors Influencing Verbal Learning under Varying Conditions of Audience Participation," *Journal of Experimental Psychology*, 46 (1953), pp. 411-418.
42. Matilda W. Riley and John W. Riley, Jr. (1951), "A Sociological Approach to Communications Research," *Public Opinion Quarterly*, 15, 3 (Fall, 1951), pp. 444-460.
43. Bernard Rosenberg and David Manning White (1957), *Mass Culture: The Popular Arts in America*, Glencoe, Ill.: The Free Press, 1957.
44. Wilbur Schramm (1948), *Communications in Modern Society*, Urbana, Ill.: U. of Illinois Press, 1948.
45. Wilbur Schramm (1949), *Mass Communications*, Urbana, Ill.: U. of Illinois Press, 1949.
46. Wilbur Schramm (1954), "How Communication Works," in his *The Process and Effects of Mass Communication*, Urbana, Ill.: U. of Illinois Press, 1954.
47. Edward Suchman (1941), "Invitation to Music," in Lazarsfeld and Stanton (1941).
48. Edward A. Shils and Morris Janowitz (1948), "Cohesion and Disintegration in the Wehrmacht in World War II," *Public Opinion Quarterly*, 12, 2 (Summer, 1948), pp. 280-315.
49. W. Lloyd Warner and William E. Henry (1948), *The Radio Day Time Serial: A Symbolic Analysis*, Genetic Psychology Monographs, 37 (1948).

50. Gerhart D. Wiebe (1951-2), "Merchandizing Commodities and Citizenship on Television," *Public Opinion Quarterly*, 15, 4 (Winter, 1951-2), pp. 679-691.

51. Gerhart D. Wiebe (1952), "Mass Communications" in Hartley, Eugene L. and Ruth E. Hartley, *Fundamentals of Social Psychology*, New York: Alfred E. Knopf, 1952.

52. Daniel M. Wilner (1951), *Attitude as a Determinant of Perception in the Mass Media of Communication: Reactions to the Motion Picture "Home of the Brave,"* Unpublished doctoral dissertation, U. of California, Los Angeles, 1951.

53. Katherine Wolf and Marjorie Fiske (1949), "The Children Talk About Comics," in Lazarsfeld and Stanton (1949).

On the Use of the Mass Media as 'Escape': Clarification of a Concept
Elihu Katz and David Foulkes

from

Public Opinion Quarterly, 26, 1962.

ON THE USE OF THE MASS MEDIA AS "ESCAPE": CLARIFICATION OF A CONCEPT

BY ELIHU KATZ AND DAVID FOULKES

It is often argued that the mass media "give the people what they want" and that the viewers, listeners, and readers ultimately determine the content of the media by their choices of what they will read, view, or hear. Whether or not this is a valid characterization of the role of the mass in relation to the media, it is only an arc of circular reasoning unless there is independent evidence of what the people do want. More particularly, there is great need to know what people do with the media, what uses they make of what the media now give them, what satisfactions they enjoy, and, indeed, what part the media play in their personal lives. Here is a discussion of some of the functions the media may perform in the lives of the members of the mass society.

Elihu Katz is Associate Professor of Sociology at the University of Chicago. He is co-author, with Paul Lazarsfeld, of *Personal Influence* and active at the frontiers of communication research. David Foulkes is an Instructor in the Department of Psychology at Lawrence College. This article is a revision of a paper they presented to the American Association for Public Opinion Research at its annual conference in Berkeley, California, in May 1961.

BERELSON'S recent requiem for communication research[1] is probably appropriate to the main, but very narrow, tradition of communication research known as the study of "campaigns" or, in other words, the ability of the mass media to effect dramatic changes in opinions, attitudes, and actions. It is all too clear that mass media "campaigns" do not have the power to brainwash or to induce radical changes. What we have learned from these years of research is how complex the process of mass persuasion really is.

Two viable programs seem open to communication research—viable in the sense that, first of all, they derive from what has been accomplished so far and, second, that the necessary research tools are available to carry them forward.

One of these programs is research on the diffusion of new ideas, products, and practices. This is a direct continuation of the study of mass media "campaigns," with the addition of a more sophisticated frame of reference. The emphasis now is on following the itinerary of social and technical change through a variety of media as well as the formal and informal networks of social relations rather than focusing

[1] Bernard Berelson, "The State of Communication Research," *Public Opinion Quarterly*, Vol. 23, 1959, pp. 1-6.

narrowly on the effects of mass media per se. This approach has been discussed elsewhere at some length.[2]

The second of the two programs is the study of the "uses and gratifications" of mass communications. This approach proceeds from the assumption that the social and psychological attributes of individuals and groups shape their use of the mass media rather than vice versa. This is the approach that asks the question, *not* "What do the media do to people?" but, rather, "What do people do with the media?"

ON USES AND GRATIFICATIONS

Such research has a respectable history, of course. Indeed, some of the earliest media studies focused on problems of uses and gratifications: why women listen to soap operas, the gratifications provided by quiz programs, the functions of newspaper reading, the motives for getting interested in serious music on the radio, are famous examples.[3] And, rather recently, there has been a new crop of studies concerned with the uses children make of television and of its characteristic content: adventure stories and aggressive heroes.[4] But, in between these two periods and in general, such studies have been far outnumbered by the study of "campaigns." It is a most intriguing fact in the intellectual history of social research that the choice was made to study the mass media as agents of persuasion rather than as agents of entertainment.

There is an important difference between the two phases of "use" studies, however. In the forties, a "use" study typically was reported in terms of a list of functions served by a given type of communications content. Thus, soap operas were alleged to be sources of advice, targets of vicarious identification, sources of reassurance that the listener was not alone in her troubles, etc., and newspapers were found to provide ritualistic activity, orientation to everyday living (and dying), conversation starters, and the like. Studies in the fifties, however, proceeded somewhat differently. Typically, they began with a classification of

[2] See Elihu Katz, "Communication Research and the Image of Society: Convergence of Two Traditions," *American Journal of Sociology*, Vol. 65, 1960, pp. 435-440, and "The Social Itinerary of Technical Change: Two Studies in the Diffusion of Innovation," *Human Organization*, Vol. 20, Summer 1961, pp. 70-82.

[3] The series edited by Paul F. Lazarsfeld and Frank Stanton contained many of the best of these studies. See *Radio Research 1941* and *Radio Research 1942-43*, New York, Duell, Sloan & Pearce, 1941 and 1944; and *Communication Research 1948-49*, New York, Harper, 1949.

[4] For a general statement in this area, one which clearly parallels the emphasis of the present paper, see Wilbur Schramm, Jack Lyle, and Edwin B. Parker, *Television in the Lives of Our Children*, Stanford, Calif., Stanford University Press, 1961. Specifically on aggressive content, see R. S. Albert, "The Role of Mass Media and the Effect of Aggressive Film Content upon Children's Aggressive Responses and Identification Choices," *Genetic Psychology Monographs*, Vol. 55, 1957, pp. 221-285, and Lotte Bailyn, "Mass Media and Children: A Study of Exposure Habits and Cognitive Effects," *Psychological Monographs*, Vol. 71, 1959, pp. 1-48.

individuals in terms of some psychological or social attribute—social integration and isolation, for example, or the extent of worrying—and then examined the patterns of mass media behavior of the individuals so classified.

In addition to the obvious fruitfulness of this approach (judging from research so far), the study of uses and gratifications represents a bridge to two major sources of ideas that have remained largely untapped in empirical mass media research. One of these, obviously, is functional theory. Klapper and Wright have illustrated the applicability of Merton's functional paradigm to mass media behavior, and there is little doubt that it will easily overtake the behavioristically oriented, stimulus-response type of theory which has been prevalent heretofore.[5] Second, however, the uses and gratifications approach represents a bridge to the theorists of popular culture—the group of humanists, psychoanalysts, reformers, etc., who have been speculatively analyzing the mass media and mass society. Until very recently, they have been paid no heed by the empirically oriented mass media researcher and have returned the compliment. One reason for the gulf, it may be suggested, is that while the mass media researcher was asking, "What do the media do to people?" the theorist of popular culture—while no less interested in the impact of the media—was asking, among other things, "What do people do with the media?" If empirical mass media research now turns to this latter question, there is some reason to believe that it can draw profitably on the reservoir of hypotheses proposed by the theorists of popular culture.[6]

ON THE USE OF MASS MEDIA AS ESCAPE

The favorite answer of the popular-culture writers to this question, "What do people do with the media?" is that they use it for escape. People are deprived and alienated, it is suggested, and so they turn to the dreamlike world of the mass media for substitute gratifications, the consequence of which is still further withdrawal from the arena of social and political action. This answer appears to suggest that everyday roles in modern society give rise to tensions or *drives* (stemming from alienation or felt deprivation) which lead one to *high exposure* to mass media with its characteristic *context* (e.g. the movie palace)

[5] See Charles R. Wright, "Functional Analysis and Mass Communication," *Public Opinion Quarterly*, Vol. 24, 1960, pp. 603-620, and Joseph T. Klapper, *The Effects of Mass Communication*, Glencoe, Ill., Free Press, 1960, Chap. 1.

[6] For examples of some suggestive hypotheses, see the articles in Bernard Rosenberg and David Manning White, editors, *Mass Culture*, Glencoe, Ill., Free Press, 1958. In this connection, the Committee on Communication at the University of Chicago (recently dissolved) provides an interesting historical footnote. The records of the Committee show that, originally, it was a joint venture of both humanists and social scientists. At the point where the social scientists opted for a program of research on the short-run effects of the media, the humanists dropped out.

and its characteristic *content* (e.g. fantasy) from which, via *psychological processes* such as identification, one can obtain compensatory gratification and, perhaps as an unanticipated *consequence*, "narcotization" of other role obligations. Such use of the mass media, in other words, would have negative feedback to one's everyday roles.

While it is probable that most critics, both humanist and social-scientific, of popular culture, have something like this process in mind, their discussions most often focus upon one or another isolated element in the process. Thus the drives which lead one to mass media exposure, or high exposure itself, or the social context of exposure, or the content of the media, or the psychological process involved in mass media consumption are singled out and labeled "escapist."

This paper will examine these limited applications of the concept of escape, based, as they are, on the often unwarranted assumption that there is a necessary association between the various elements (drive, high exposure, social context of exposure, content, psychological process) and certain dysfunctional consequences. It will be argued that the ultimate referent of the term "escape" should have to do with the consequences of media usage, consequences which cannot be inferred automatically from other elements in the above model of the escape process. The evidence of the necessity for adopting such a position will indicate the usefulness of functional analysis in the study of media behavior. In fact, the entire discussion is an attempt to illustrate the fruitfulness of approaching media behavior via "uses and gratifications."

Drives: deprivation, alienation, etc. The starting point for any study of the uses of the mass media is some particular social or psychological attribute in terms of which a population can be stratified. The theorists of escape suggest alienation. Alienation may mean the feeling of powerlessness or meaninglessness, or the feeling of ideological or social isolation.[7] Alienation produces the desire to escape, a desire which the mass media are presumed to be instrumental in satisfying.

As Klapper has pointed out, there are now a number of studies that support the hypothesis that alienation or deprivation do, indeed, appear to lead to increased exposure to the mass media.[8] One set of data, for example, shows that women who worry more or who report themselves as more anxious than others are more frequent consumers of confessional magazine fiction and of radio soap operas and the like.[9] The Rileys found that children who were relatively isolated from peers

[7] For a very careful typological analysis of the concept of alienation, see Melvin Seeman, "On the Meaning of Alienation," *American Sociological Review*, Vol. 24, 1959, pp. 783-791.

[8] Klapper, *op.cit.*, Chap. 7.

[9] Elihu Katz and Paul F. Lazarsfeld, *Personal Influence*, Glencoe, Ill., Free Press, 1955, p. 378.

were slightly more exposed to adventure stories.[10] Maccoby found that middle-class children who experience difficulty in the parent-child relationship spend more time with TV than other middle-class children,[11] and Pearlin explicitly related high stress and liking for "programs that help us forget our personal problems."[12] More recently, by means of a demographic analysis, Olsen has tried to demonstrate that the extent of in-migration and intra-city mobility in a community is predictive of the extent of movie going.[13] Finally, two very recent studies have major contributions to make in this area. Schramm et al. find that disparities between a child's own aspirations for himself and the perceived aspirations of his peers or parents are related to high use of "fantasy-oriented" media and low use of "reality-oriented" media.[14] The greater the degree of parent-child conflict (where parents' aspirations are higher than the child's), the higher the consumption of television, radio, and movies and the lower the use of magazines and books. Johnstone studied adolescents' use of the media and found, for example, that the lower one's self-esteem the more time one spends with TV; the less one has of whatever it is that one's schoolmates happen to value (grades, athletic prowess, money), the more heavily one is exposed to the media; the more one feels "out in the cold," the more one is likely to be a rock-'n'-roll fan, and so on.[15]

Considered together, these studies present impressive evidence that alienation or deprivation are associated with increased exposure to particular media or particular kinds of media content. However, even if it is true that alienation or deprivation tend to drive people to seek refuge in the mass media, it is not at all self-evident what they find when they get there. If mass media exposure is sought for relief from, or compensation for, inadequacies in certain of an individual's social roles, that does not mean, necessarily, that positive feedback is impossible for the roles in question. It certainly does not mean that such feedback is impossible for *other* of the individual's roles. A drive, in other words, may well be "escapist," but its fulfillment may or may not be. Escape may or may not be the *result* of the operation of such a drive.

[10] Matilda W. Riley and John W. Riley, Jr., "A Sociological Approach to Mass Communications Research," *Public Opinion Quarterly*, Vol. 15, 1951, pp. 444-450.

[11] Eleanor E. Maccoby, "Why Children Watch TV," *Public Opinion Quarterly*, Vol. 15, 1951, pp. 421-444.

[12] Leonard Pearlin, "Social and Personal Stress and Escape Television Viewing," *Public Opinion Quarterly*, Vol. 23, 1959, pp. 255-259.

[13] Marvin E. Olsen, "Motion Picture Attendance and Social Isolation," *Sociological Quarterly*, Vol. 1, 1960, pp. 107-117.

[14] Schramm, Lyle, and Parker, *op.cit.*, pp. 129-131.

[15] John W. C. Johnstone, "Social Structure and Patterns of Mass Media Consumption," University of Chicago, Department of Sociology, 1961, unpublished Ph.D. dissertation.

High exposure. The foregoing evidence suggests that increased media exposure may be sought as a means of escape from everyday role situations. This has led some critics to equate high media exposure itself with escape. Yet it seems quite clear that the media may also be sought for purposes of strengthening one's position in his immediate network of social relations. Eliot Freidson has suggested that children who are attached to their parents use TV to draw themselves more closely to the bosom of the family, while children who are closer to their peers reject TV in favor of movies, the medium of the peer group.[16] Johnstone supports Freidson's hypothesis with much more adequate data and finds, particularly, that sociometric status and feelings of attraction to the peer group are highly predictive of mass media behavior: group listening to popular music, for example, serves the socially integrated adolescent as much as listening alone to popular music, or watching TV, appeases the isolate.[17]

These studies suggest that the media may be both sought and used not only to compensate for abortive or ineffective social relations but also to maintain extant and presumably effective ones. It may also be— although this goes beyond the data reported—that the mass media behavior of the alienated and deprived also contains an element of striving to reestablish effective interpersonal contacts.

Escapist content. "Escapist content," that much-heard epithet, is the next issue to consider. Escapist worlds, for most critics, are made up of unreal or improbable people who are very good or very bad (or very good-bad) and whose successes and failures conveniently cater to the supposed wishes of the audience. Vicarious participation in the lives and adventures of such fictional characters is considered escapism. Others have been concerned not so much with the unreality of this world as with its unrepresentativeness. Working class people are underrepresented, ethnic types are cast in the role of villain, and so on. It is somehow considered escapist for members of the working class to people their fictional world with upper-middle-class characters. Still other critics have focused on the danger of trying to apply the pat wisdom obtained from participation in the mass media world to real life. Taking advice from a soap opera is the classic example.

Content analyses assume the risk of inferring uses or effects from mere examination of content. It is true, of course, that what little we know does give some support to the hypothesis that so-called escapist content is employed wishfully and vicariously. For example, the Rileys demonstrate that children isolated from their peers use adventure stories as a basis for fantasizing.[18] Another illustration of this hypothesis is the

[16] Eliot Freidson, "The Relations of the Social Situation of Contact to the Media in Mass Communication," *Public Opinion Quarterly,* Vol. 17, 1953, pp. 230-238.
[17] Johnstone, *op.cit.*   [18] Riley and Riley, *op.cit.*

worship of movie stars, although this is something we know very little about.[19]

But to emphasize that media content is "escapist" when it is used for vicariousness and make-believe is to avoid serious consideration of the function of fantasy and ignore other probable uses of this very same content. Surely, respite may be obtained, at least in the short run, and this is by no means irrelevant to the performance of one's roles. And who is to say that what goes on inside the spectator's head when exposed to fantasy materials does not feed back, indirectly, to his other roles? Indeed, it has been argued repeatedly (to choose a far-out example) that the old-fashioned black-and-white Western contributes to the resolution of the Oedipus complex, and that it is precisely the ostensible unreality of the story (the apparently "escapist content") that enables one to circumvent one's own inner defenses and to identify.[20] Again, the Rileys have shown that the "escapist" story may be used by socially integrated children in quite unsuspected ways—as a basis for the assignment of roles in group games, for example,[21] and Bogart reports that comic strip characters are used in working class groups as a topic for conversation and as a typology by means of which personalities may be classified.[22]

It is clear that content usually classified as "escapist" may be put to uses that are not at all implied by that label. If one takes advice from a soap opera, however unreal, or uses an adventure story as a basis for group games, or resolves one's Oedipus complex, there is feedback to one's real-life social roles. Moreover, content that generally is not described as "escapist" may serve functionally to promote escape. If one feels alienated from one's role as citizen—if politics is remote and the feeling of personal effectiveness is low—the latest news from Luang Prabang or Ruandi-Urundi may provide as much escape as does a frontier town of the Old West. And, altogether, it is very difficult to infer uses, or effects, from content.

The social context of media exposure. Rather than the specific content of the media, however, there might be some reason to believe that it is the situation in which media exposure occurs which, per se, provides much of the opportunity to escape. It seems plausible to assume

19 The pioneering studies reported in W. W. Charters, *Motion Pictures and Youth*, New York, Macmillan, 1933, and in J. P. Mayer, *The Sociology of Film*, London, Faber and Faber, 1946, report on dreaming about the stars, on fan clubs, etc.

20 A recent formulation of this hypothesis is F. E. Emery, "Psychological Effects of the Western Film: A Study in Television Viewing," *Human Relations*, Vol. 12, 1959, pp. 195-214. Also see Frederick Elkin, "The Psychological Appeal of the Hollywood Western," *Journal of Educational Sociology*, Vol. 24, 1950, pp. 72-86.

21 Riley and Riley, *op.cit.*

22 Leo Bogart, "Adult Talk about Newspaper Comics," *American Journal of Sociology*, Vol. 61, 1955, pp. 26-30.

that certain types of content do serve some purposes better than others, but at least as important may be the fact that *all* content is characteristically received in certain socially defined contexts.

The viewing situation—or, more generally, the situation of attending to the media—is one which society affords a certain amount of protection. "Shh, Daddy is reading the newspaper," or "Can't you see we're trying to watch this program?" imply that exposure to the media is sufficient to justify a degree of insulation or immunity from other pressures. One would be less likely to hear, "Be quiet, Daddy is *thinking*." One may legitimately hide from one's wife behind the newspaper at the breakfast table, or cut oneself off in this way from fellow subway and bus passengers (including female standees). Going to the movies or to the theater absolves one of certain responsibilities: one is permitted, by society, to cut oneself off from other roles.

But if the situation of attending to the mass media may serve as a façade for individual retreat, it may also serve to promote certain kinds of social activities which are less easily, or subtly, accomplished under other circumstances. Freidson shows that the media may be used to keep oneself close to desired others, and it is obvious that the movies are used in this way.[23]

It is very difficult to dismiss these latter functions with the epithet "escape." Moreover, the application of the term seems equally questionable in cases where attending to the mass media seems only to serve the function of social retreat. That the media transport one to the world outside of one's immediate environment is the very essence of their function. The better question to ask would seem to be whether these excursions feed back to one's real-life concerns, personal or social. The use of the newspaper as a shield to protect one from the immediate demands of other roles does not mean that reading the newspaper is therefore merely "escape." The media, of course, may also bring one closer to society and, perhaps, to one's more immediate social environment.

The psychological process. A question that has peered out at several points in the discussion so far has to do with the psychological dimension in the process of escape. Escape, viewed psychologically, appears to imply a kind of checking of one's social roles at the movie-house door. Escape, for most theorists who have thought in these terms, seems to mean identifying with a star or hero to the point that one loses oneself in a dream which cannot possibly have any feedback to real life.

But the fact is that identification with the hero is by no means the only psychological process at work in the mass media exposure situation.

23 Freidson, *op.cit.*

Indeed, radio and television do not so much have stars with whom one identifies as stars whom one plays opposite. Horton and Wohl have given the label "para-social interaction" to the kind of program aimed, they say, at lonely and alienated viewers and offering companionship and inviting "interaction."[24] Such programs, it is suggested, *bolster* the real-life ego rather than overwhelm it. Surely these programs also offer possibilities for escape, but exposure to them involves something quite different from the process of identification or identity loss. It is too facile to pronounce the psychological process involved in attending to media content as "escape," and, furthermore, it tends to obscure the variety of possible consequences that may follow.

Consequences. Ultimately, those concerned with the process of escape are concerned with consequences. They fear the "narcotizing dysfunction" of exposure to the media.[25] In the simplest sense, it is certainly true that the media must affect the performance of one's social roles by virtue of the mere number of hours invested in mass media exposure. But the more subtle problem is to specify exactly the way in which particular patterns of exposure feed back to particular social roles, whether the feedback is functional or not, and whether it is a consequence of exposure per se or exposure to particular content.

Clearly, this is the realm of functional analysis. Much of the discussion, to this point, has focused on the manifest gratifications of the media, but the concern, now, is also with the latent, or unanticipated, consequences of exposure.[26] Some examples of possible dysfunctions at several levels, as a consequence of either specific content or mere exposure, are given in the accompanying table. But it should be clear that an individual operates at many levels and that a given pattern of exposure can contribute functionally at one level and dysfunctionally at another. The same behavior that causes an individual to withdraw from social and political participation may contribute to the success of his performance at work the next day. And what is true within the same individual is also true among individuals: the same usage may have different consequences for different individuals. Thus, Schramm, Lyle, and Parker say that children's use of the mass media for fantasizing may "*either* (a) drain off some of the discontent resulting from the hard blows of socialization; (b) provide insights and analogies that may help an alert viewer see himself better; *or* (c) lead a child into withdrawal from the real world, encourage the confusion of real

[24] Donald Horton and R. Richard Wohl, "Mass Communication and Para-social Interaction," *Psychiatry*, Vol. 19, 1956, pp. 215-229.

[25] See Paul F. Lazarsfeld and Robert K. Merton, "Mass Communication, Popular Taste and Organized Social Action," in Wilbur Schramm, editor, *Mass Communications*, 2nd ed., Urbana, Ill., University of Illinois Press, 1961, pp. 492-513.

[26] See Robert K. Merton, *Social Theory and Social Structure*, Glencoe, Ill., Free Press, 1957.

SOME DOMAINS OF ESCAPE: SELECTED ILLUSTRATIONS

Level Where Dysfunction Is Noted	Origin of Dysfunction	
	Symbolic Dimension (Media Content)	Spatial-Temporal Dimension (Media Exposure or Context)
1. Social, political affairs	A housewife is assured in a soap opera that there is perfect justice in the world and, as a result, is socially unconcerned and politically apathetic.	A man watches TV continually in his spare time and, simply as a result of the time he spends in this behavior, has no time for social causes or political participation.
2. Interpersonal relations (in the family)	A daytime TV "persona" becomes a husband substitute on account of his greater thoughtfulness than the real husband, and there is a consequent impairment in husband-wife relations.	An adolescent goes to the movies, whatever is playing, to get away from his parents, and there is a resulting strain in the child-parent relationship.
3. Intrapsychic	Through identification with a drama character, a person's own impulses are negated or denied, impairing personality integration.	A person carries a transistor radio with him all the time, playing it continually whatever program is on, since its constant distraction means he does not have to think about his inner impulses and thoughts.

situations with fantasy, and thereby cause him more trouble than he should have in learning the rules of the real world; (d) build up aggression, rather than draining it off, so that socially acceptable adjustment becomes more difficult."[27]

CONCLUSIONS

It is probably true that the concept of escape blurs too many distinctions to be genuinely serviceable. Still, given the current shift of research interest from the study of "campaigns" to the study of the functions and effects of "entertainment," the concept is likely to be invoked more and more. Hence this attempt to take seriously some of the loose talk about escape, in order, at least, to clarify the issues involved.

We found that social scientists and students of popular culture have, at one time or another, applied the notion of "escape" to every step in the social-psychological process of attending to the mass media. And the label "escapist" has been used to characterize the psychological drives that motivate exposure, the extent of exposure itself, the contexts

[27] Schramm, Lyle, and Parker, op.cit., pp. 73-74.

in which exposure takes place, the content of the media, the psychological processes involved in attending, and the consequences of all these things.

So long as the exact referent of the terms "escape" or "escapist" is clear, no harm is done, of course; indeed, the concepts may even be useful. There is little doubt that some people *do* go to the movies, for example, "to forget about their troubles" or "to lose themselves." To call this an "escapist" drive is to be faithful to common-sense usage. The label is similarly appropriate for various of the other aspects of the process of mass media exposure.

Our objections are rather different. We object, basically, to the assumption, usually implicit and often unwarranted, that "escapist" drives or "escapist" content or "escapist" patterns of involvement with the media are invariably dysfunctional for the individual and society. Clearly it is an empirical question whether one's escape was actually "successful" or not, or whether escaping from one role or one level of functioning does not lead to active and positive involvement in another role or level. A recent discussion of "regression in the service of the ego," in which it is argued that psychoanalytically derived mechanisms of what might be called "escape" may even have functional consequences, seems to parallel our argument here.[28]

By the same token, we object not only to the assumption of an invariant connection between one or another of these forms of "escapism" and ultimate consequences but to the assumption of an invariant relationship among the elements themselves. Thus "escapist drives" do not invariably lead to "escapist exposure patterns"; indeed, there are routes of escape available in addition to the mass media. Nor does "escapist content" function as escape for all who are exposed; indeed, "nonescapist" content may function for some as escape. And so on. The evidence available to date suggests that these linkages cannot be taken for granted.

OTHER ROUTES OF ESCAPE: AN EXPLORATORY NOTE

It has just been noted that routes of escape other than exposure to the mass media are available in modern society, and it is curious that discussions of the mass media—even functionally oriented ones—so rarely take these into account. Deprivation, alienation, loneliness—the very same drives which are supposed to lead to escape via the mass media—are motives which have been traditionally associated with suicide, alcoholism, drug addiction, spiritualism, etc. It is clear that a theory of the relationship between deprivation and the use of the mass

[28] See Roy Schafer, "Regression in the Service of the Ego," in Gardiner Lindzey, editor, *Assessment of Human Motives*, New York, Rinehart, 1958, pp. 119-148.

media must inquire into the conditions under which individuals choose one route rather than another.

The discussion can only be opened up in this paper. The most obvious difference between the mass media and these other escape routes is the comparative risk involved. Compared with the mass media, one of the major hazards of these other routes is that they not only transport one from the cares of everyday reality but that they often fail to bring one back. The narcotizing dysfunctions are so great, that is, that one is often prevented from performing any of one's roles at all.

Still, the parallel between the uses of the mass media and the uses of alcohol is instructive. Like the mass media, alcohol may be "used" quite differently by different sorts of people: it may be used to withdraw from society, or it may be used to come closer to society. And what shall we say about the musician who performs better under the influence of drugs? Functional feedback to a basic social role surely is not escape.

But because of the lesser hazard involved and perhaps because of some of their manifestly positive functions, the mass media constitute a more legitimate escape route. "Don't disturb Daddy, he's drinking," clearly has a lower priority.

But rather than consider alcohol or drugs or spiritualism or any of the other possible routes of escape in greater detail, it may be worth concluding by turning to the most pervasive route of all—more widespread than the mass media—sleep. In a suggestive analysis, Auber and White catalogue the social and psychological attributes and functions of sleep.[29] Of all types of withdrawal from society, sleep is the most protected: "Be quiet, Daddy is sleeping," has the very highest priority. Sleep time, say Auber and White, is a legitimate façade for a variety of hidden activities, such as deviance, or creativity, or even marital sex relations. The sleeper is not held responsible for his daytime roles; indeed, it is legitimate for him to lose his very identity—not to know who he is—in the course of the night. Dreams in some societies have meaning for the real world: they may be signs, for example, and there are dream books to interpret their meaning. In our society, however, dreams are essentially invalid and unreal as portents for society (though they may be diagnostic of the individual's own inner workings), and, perhaps, suggest Auber and White, this is why the content of dreams in our society is so irrelevant. It is a sobering idea, considering the state of the mass media, to suggest, as do Auber and White, that if we thought that dreams were more meaningful we might have better ones.

[29] Vilhelm Aubert and Harrison White, "Sleep: A Sociological Interpretation," *Acta Sociologica*, Vol. 4, fasc. 2, pp. 46-54, and fasc. 3, pp. 1-15.

Reading Literature as Culture
Andrew Tolson

Revised version of a paper originally published in *Working Papers in Cultural Studies*, 4, 1973.

Reading Literature as Culture

1. For students of contemporary culture, the activity of 'reading' is double-sided. On the one hand, as members of a literate society, we read daily a 'universe' of texts. In this manner everyone 'reads' - newspapers, novels, magazines; and even perhaps the manners, fashions, rituals etc. that make up the 'context' of everyday life. A theory of reading is thus, in the first place, a theory of what we already take for granted.

But on the other hand, in cultural studies, we are concerned with how this daily acquaintance with texts can give rise to some kind of 'knowledge' - to a critical perspective in which our experience is defined. It is necessary for us to account for the 'taken-for-granted'; and to demonstrate how a theory of what we already 'know' can teach us something new.

This article attempts to sketch a theory of the practice of reading, with these two problems in mind. In part, it is a description of the reading process as such; in part, an exploration of the foundations for cultural 'knowledge'. Specifically, it is concerned with 'literature' - especially that which has been selected and preserved as the finest in 'creative art'. This area has a continuing relevance: not only because of the intrinsic fascination of the texts themselves (and the multitude of 'readings' they sustain); but also in the claims of literary criticism to constitute a 'body of knowledge' - or at least a 'discipline' with educative value.

For when we examine the literary-critical inheritance we are immediately struck by the range and diversity of its aspects. There seems to be an unlimited variety of possible approaches - ranging from bibliographical scholarship, through practical criticism, to diverse and eclectic applications of marxism, existentialism and psychoanalysis. In recent years, some critics themselves have be-gun to acknowledge this diversity - as a 'crisis' in the humanities; but trapped in their individual 'positions', in personal 'points of view', they have been unable to suggest a more satisfactory state of affairs.

One possibility, which suggests itself to us, is that the diversity and eclecticism of traditional literary criticism is related to its notion of 'reading'. Or rather, since this is nearer the mark, to its absence of a theory of reading. It is indeed surprising that critical readers, of heightened skill and sensibility, should have neglected the basis

for their practice. But it remains the case that despite its remarkable detail in accounts of textual production (the 'creative process')
and literary form (the 'verbal icon' etc.) - apart from occasional
asides from psychoanalysts (Lesser 1957, Holland 1968) and
existential philosophers (Sartre 1950) - and with one notable exception
(Richards 1936), literary criticism lacks a theory of reading.

We might therefore, with justification, enquire whether the 'crisis'
in the humanities, and the absence of a theory of reading (and, bearing
in mind our second introductory question, the absence of a theory of
knowledge) are in some way interconnected.

2. Ideological Reading.

A perspective on the situation of literary criticism can be gained by
considering, in general outline, its peculiar historical development.
We can recognize here two dominant modes of argument: both concerned to justify, as 'apologies' for poetry, the study of literature as a
university discipline.

The first of these is the humanist argument - founded in a general
social concern which is not specific to literature. Characteristically
this has taken the form of a critique of cultural relativism, and a
corresponding 'decline of standards'. The humanist commitment is
to 'cultural tradition', against the 'standardization' of a 'mass civilization'. From this basis, the further assumption is made that reading works of literature can combat cultural decline. Thus Richards,
in Practical Criticism and elsewhere, proposes the study of 'mis-
readings'. "Rhetoric", he argues, should be the study of "misunder-
standing and its remedies". It should "measure our losses in
communication" (1).

The humanist argument is thus obliged to demonstrate the distinctive
'value' of literary discourse - and in developing this position two factors
are emphasized: (1) the creative qualities of the artistic imagination,
(2) the aesthetic qualities of poetic language. The first factor is formulated as the 'sincerity' of the author - first defined by Richards (1924)
as the psychological transmission of impulses from author to reader
(allowing the reader to simply internalize the author's perception of
life): and later developed by Leavis (1948) and the Scrutiny school, as
a more sophisticated theory of the re-creation of shared 'values' (the
literary 'tradition' in which the great writer is placed). The second

factor (the emphasis on poetic language) becomes a theory of the 'meaning potential' embedded in the literary text. For the later Richards (1936) this dynamic principle is found in the 'interinanimation' of metaphors. Similar notions are developed by Empson (1930) as 'ambiguity', and Brooks (1947) as 'paradox'. The language of poetry liberates 'connotations' - that is, the meaning is not directly 'referential' (denoting objects or concepts). It creates, through a web of hints and suggestions, a formal synthetic pattern.

But the common factor in both these arguments is the lack of consideration for the reader. The first emphasis, on authorial 'experience', either leads to simplistic theories of 'transmission' (which the reader passively receives), or to a more complex, but nevertheless determined notion of 'close reading' (which posits a 'continuous analogical enactment' by the reader of the author's 'values'). The second emphasis, on language, is a little more open-ended - since in so far as the text opens up possibilities for the reader, he or she can be given an active role. Some of Richards's later work especially seems to develop this focus. But more frequently, the source of 'value' located in the structure of the text reduces reading to a process of contemplation, or at best 'following-through' (2).

In so far as the humanist argument does take up the problem of reading, it is to refer to external factors - the author's 'experience', or the language of the text. In neither case is the reader made responsible for his or her own reading. Thus, humanist ideology, which values reading as a 'lived appropriation' of literature, commits a double-sided fallacy. Firstly, it idealises the values of the past, and gives authority to the 'wisdom' of 'great authors'. Secondly, it reifies the medium through which these values are conveyed: poetic language - which is contemplated as containing within itself the principle which is the source of its 'value'. The reader is subservient to, and everywhere encompassed by, a body of literature which assumes mythic status - rather like religious icons which both point beyond themselves to the Absolute, and yet contain within themselves some vestige of magical power.

A second justification for the 'discipline' of literary-criticism is given by the argument of the 'scientist'. Here, the focus is not so much on the communication of 'personal experience', as an attempt to establish literary-criticism as a distinctive 'body of knowledge' - with principles and methods which lay claim to 'scientificity'.

There are again, two dominant tendencies of scientism. The first gives priority to a rigorous description of the language of the text;

the second to a 'totalizing perspective', which 'stands back' from the text itself, and establishes its relation to a wider conceptual frame-work.

To some extent, the growth of precise methods of linguistic analysis is a development of one concern of humanism. The focus on the poem as a 'thing in itself' (in classical practical criticism, with its author-ship excised), and the extraordinarily detailed dissection of poetry which this focus first encouraged (cf. Empson etc.), crystallized in America, as the 'new criticism' of the 1940s and 50s. It was only a short step from the latter to a descriptive stylistics no longer depend-ent on humanist foundations, but seeking a 'value-free', formalist analysis of 'the words on the page' (3).

On the other hand, the totalizing perspective, of which the most influential exponent is Frye (1957), from the outset defines itself against a humanised 'public taste'. Here, the question of scientificity is posed, not as the elaboration of textual complexity, but as the search for "a co-ordinating principle, a central hypothesis... which will see the phenomena it deals with as parts of a whole". In this context, Frye cites as an analogy the theory of evolution in biology. The test for any science is its ability to unify its data around a "central hypo-thesis" (4).

But again, both forms of scientism lack consideration for the reader. From the point of view of stylisticians, such as Riffaterre (1959), the reader is postulated as a system of responses to 'stylistic devices' located in the text. The humanist notion of 'close reading', as 'following-through', here becomes a stimulus-response model, a 'reading competence' of response categories, in which creative expect-ations on the part of the reader are dismissed as irrelevant (5). Alternatively, the emphasis on literature as a self-sufficient 'body of knowledge', looks for its co-ordinating principle in the text themselves (or, in Frye's case, the archetypal structures of mythology). The reader, as critic, makes a 'positive value–judgement', from a 'cath-olic' point of view - which assumes from the outset the coherence of the data. Reading therefore, the foundation for critical knowledge, is no longer an activity of the 'whole man'. Rather it strives towards a "transcendental act of consciousness": "The theorist of literature and the consumer of literature are not the same at all, even when they co-exist in the same man" (6).

Thus, what interests us about scientism, is not its claim to 'break' with humanism, but on the contrary, that with respect to the activity of reading, the two modes of argument are <u>identical</u>. The reader is again, by the scientist, referred to external factors (the linguistic structure, the body of knowledge etc.); and although there is an attempt to 'stand back', and view the act of reading from a theoretical perspective, that perspective is only achieved by denying the validity of reading itself. It is the particular text, as a stylistic unity, that specifies 'reading competence'; and it is a system of texts, in Absolute coherence, that 'de-humanises' the active reader.

We can account for the double inattention of literary criticism to the activity of reading (and thus the absence of a central literary-critical theory) by pointing to the ideological character of the discipline's foundation. Conceived, in the 1920s, as a crusade against 'declining standards', humanist literary criticism explicitly encouraged an attitude of deference to the values of the past. And subsequent re-actions to, or against, this programme (which have not always maintained an explicitly humanist perspective) have continued to reproduce its ideological construction. 'Scientism' is not science, but the fallacy of positivism: it denies the constitutive relation of the reader to the text. It preserves a method of naive induction, of 'innocent' description - which contradicts one of the first premises of cultural studies, that the analyst is part of the culture he or she describes.

And so, to move beyond the circle of ideology we must break with literary-criticism. Our present task is to 'return' readers to their readings - and on this basis to undertake the production of cultural knowledge.

3.   Cultural Knowledge.

We have noted the tendency of conventional literary criticism to 'collapse' the activity of reading - in the service of ideological goals. In this procedure the needs and wishes of critics themselves (for example, the desire for 'community', the myth of 'value-freedom') are projected as necessities - they assume an imperative character. For the ideologist is so immersed in his 'lived situation': his experience is so permeated by dreams and desires - that in his eagerness to build his utopia he distorts both his 'tools' (the texts themselves) and his cultural activity (in this case, reading). The critic thus denies to himself the means to comprehend his practice.

In our attempt therefore, to describe the reading process (and thus the literary text which is its immediate focus), we must first attain theoretically, a certain 'distance from ourselves'. Without 'positively' falling into the trap of scientism (the 'other face' of the humanist crusade), we must recognise that our knowledge of the culture we inhabit is distorted by our experience of it. We are working towards a new conception of the conditions for critical reading, dialectically incorporating the moment of 'response'. To avoid both fallacies, of humanism and scientism, we are obliged to effect an 'epistemological break' with the literary-critical debate.

After Althusser (1969, 1970) we have begun to understand the production of knowledge as a distinctive social practice. Knowledge is a kind of labour, a 'mode of production', which involves the transformation of pre-given 'raw materials' (facts, concepts etc.) via certain 'means of production' (language, discourse), into a new 'product' (a scientific problematic). That problematic enters the life of society as the 're-presentation' (articulation) of a theoretical transformation - and it may serve as the starting point for future transformations (7).

To some extent, the social character of the production of knowledge is guaranteed by its textual appearance - of which there are two main elements. The first element is the resistance to 'pure creativity' dictated by language itself (the "defiles of the signifier" - Lacan 1966). Knowledge does not escape the system of shared conventions, the langue, that sustains all verbal communication. But language as such is not the principal determinant on the text - and the latter cannot be reduced to it. At a second level, the text is discursive (Foucault, 1972): it has a historical character. The text systematizes references and 'traces' which go beyond its immediate location. Some of these traces may be hidden, or even 'absent'; but if that is the case they are part of the discourse by virtue of their 'absence'. All texts, whether or not they explicitly indicate the fact, are produced through discursive practices.

However, the specificity of knowledge is not a function of the text itself. This is apparent (but it needs to be stressed) when we consider that ideologies too are linguistic, discursive, and appear in a textual form. The function of the text is simply to organize discourse, in general: it does not differentiate between levels of discursive practice.

For what defines a knowledge (as distinct from an ideology) is not the text as such, and not discourse in general, but a particular kind of problematic, characterized by 'reflexivity'. That is to say, knowledge is a kind of 'meta-discourse': a discourse about itself. It comprehends the conditions for its own production - in a way that an ideology, trapped in the necessities of 'experience', cannot conceive.

This definition of knowledge, as 'meta-discourse', stresses its 'transcendence' of the situation in which it is formed. Indeed, it might be argued that a specific degree of 'autonomy' is the foundation of the 'knowledge-effect'. Equally however, it is important to recognize that the 'knowledge-effect' (as specified by a scientific problematic) cannot, by itself, simply 'escape' ideology. The 'epistemological break' is never 'clean'. What we are describing is a critical perspective, 'autonomous' to ideology, but nonetheless <u>related</u> to it. For knowledge is generated through a <u>critique</u> of ideology - with which it is perpetually engaged.

Two aspects of the social production of knowledge are especially prone to ideological distortion. First, it is apparent that most texts have individual authors; and that these authors (often) 'identify' with their 'works'. Thus the text of the problematic, on which knowledge is founded, is easily reduced to individual expression - just as, in the humanist argument, poetry 'expresses' personal feeling. But if texts are discursive practices, they are not simply 'created' by 'individuals'; rather, they are subject to <u>social</u> conflicts and concerns. Individual authors may see their 'works' stolen, neutralised, or turned against them by others (cf. Sartre 1950). The totality of these various 'projects' cannot be understood from the individual's point of view - for it constitutes a 'field of operations', an 'ideological domain', which is the <u>social</u> context of textual production.

The second kind of ideological distortion is closely related to the first. For just as the text, in which knowledge appears, may be seen as the 'work' of its author; so (because that person is a member of social groups, class-fractions etc.) it may be claimed to represent a 'collective identity'. Members of class-fractions for example, may see themselves as 'transindividual subjects' (Goldmann, 1955) - a procedure which, although it involves some transcendence of individuality, still remains bound to the fallacy of 'identification'. The production of knowledge is reduced to 'world-vision' (<u>Weltanschauung</u>), a self-enclosed system of beliefs. And from within such a system, it is impossible to comprehend the totality of 'world-visions', which defines the way a class-fraction operates on the 'political terrain'.

So it is against this double risk of ideological contamination (the collapse into an individual or collective 'identity'), that knowledge must insist on its principle of 'reflexivity'. It must comprehend itself, as a social practice, within a complex social formation. In this act of reflexive understanding an important dimension is <u>historical</u>: that is, the scientific problematic must understand the conditions for its own transformation. It cannot be 'absolute science', true for all time: rather it is a particular theoretical practice, lived through a 'present conjuncture' - which relatively autonomously defines that conjuncture's social relations.

These relations are grasped by a double theoretical movement, which is both regressive and progressive (Sartre, 1963). The regressive movement reveals the totality of social and historical relations, through economic, political, and ideological 'domains'. The progressive movement attempts a re-construction of these relations with respect to the 'present conjuncture' (8). At the end of this article I shall try to demonstrate the scope of this 'regressive-progressive' method, in a critical reading of Emily Bronte's Wuthering Heights. I shall argue that this novel may be 'regressively' understood, firstly through the biography of Emily Bronte herself, a study of her immediate locality, family and social milieu (her place as a woman within that milieu, her religious ideology etc.); and secondly through an analysis of class, and the economic and social relations between classes. Something may be thus revealed concerning the novel's character as a protest, not only in the local situation, but also to general social problems (for example, the conflict internalized by some middle class women between values of education and domesticity, which in many respects pertains today). We do not here deny that a society changes. On the contrary we affirm that we change society - often blindly it is true (making predictions highly uncertain), but also reflexively, little by little, to the degree that we understand our own situation. Neither can we deny that at the same time as we make these transformations, we live them through ideologically. There is no simple 'revelation': knowledge is a long battle with experience. But only thus can we understand the place of cultural reading in the epistemological foundation of cultural studies.

4. Cultural Reading

How then, can the reading process be described? We are now in a position to understand this description as a systematic re-tracing of the encounter of the reader with the text - and a corresponding attempt to re-construct that encounter as the foundation for cultural studies. In the first, 'regressive' analysis, we have two major tasks: to describe the psychology of readers, their 'reading competence'; and to formulate the social relations of communication which define the encounter with the text. In both cases, our description may take a metaphorical form, specifying 'levels' which unite to form 'wholes': the 'lower levels' are progressively synthesized to form 'higher levels'. In the second, 'progressive' movement, we can return to our main concern: which is to suggest how a reading of a literary text can produce cultural knowledge.

(i) The Reading Process
The reader brings to the text a number of psycho-linguistic mechanisms which can be scientifically described. At the lower levels of analysis,

these features can be separated, but as we move to higher levels, we begin to posit a unified 'psycholinguistic competence'. From the somewhat scanty and diffuse research in this field (9), we may define four distinct levels:

(a) Perceptual strategy

The analysis begins with an account of perceptual strategy, an area of cognitive psychology (cf. Neisser, 1967). This is a description of processes of perception which firstly centres on the problem of constructing 'visual figures' from discrete elements; and secondly attempts to specify the immediate visual units (such as letters, word shapes etc.) which are established by these processes. However, because both the temporal processes and the spatial units occur simultaneously, as an undifferentiated perceptual act, differentiation can only be made in retrospect, from the point of view of a higher level of reading competence. A description of the perceptual processes of reading must take into account the essential factor of the speed of reading (Kolers, 1968). The adult, in silent reading, may scan at least six hundred words per minute, which (given an arbitrary average of say, five phonemes per word) would require a rate of fifty phonemes per second if each phoneme were processed sequentially. As psychologists are agreed that a formation time of at least 0.3 seconds is required to completely process an input into clear perception, such a rate of one phoneme per 0.02 seconds is plainly impossible. It follows that individual phonemes are not processed sequentially, but in terms of higher order units. In view of this it is likely that perceptual strategy is not a unitary process, but is differentiated (the sensory movement of the eye is not directly tied to processing systems), and selective (words are not perceived as units of letters, but certain significant letters are selected as 'cues'; and predictions are made on the basis of incomplete data - word shape, word length, contextual patterning etc.). Reading thus exploits the high degree of redundancy in written language; not all aspects of the text are of equal importance.

A model for perceptual strategy is an attempt to systematize this differentiated process of selection. In outline, three levels can be postulated (Geyer, 1969) - a sensory input (scanning) system; a cue storage system; and an internal response system. At all levels essential data is being sifted by 'organizational procedures'. Between the scanning and storage systems is posited a procedure which organizes diverse visual sensations; and between the storage and response systems a further procedure identifies significant response material. One way this may be done is by the automatic recognition of grammatically significant material - such as the head word of a nominal group or the main verb of a sentence (Hochberg, 1970).

(b) Sound-letter patterns

One criterion for selection in making a reading response is the sound
pattern of a language, and this has been the focus for a great deal of
pedagogic discussion (regarding the transfer from oral to visual behaviour on learning to read). The relative regularity of phoneme (sound)
-grapheme (letter) correspondences has been demonstrated at a 'morphophonemic' level (Fries, 1963), which suggests the importance of 'phonic
blending ability' (the ability to synthesize different phonemes). It is suggested that combined units, similar to the syllable, and variously described as the 'vocalic-centre group' (Ruddell, 1969) or the 'linguon'
(Reed 1970), form morphophonemic systems mediating short-term perception and long-term response. This is the level of 'lexical representation' (Chomsky, 1970) - the moment at which sensory visual data is
perceived as the 'lexical item', a meaningful part of verbal structure.

(c) Cognitive processes

But the integration of perception with response, and the passage into
long-term memory, requires further selection. Even as 'lexical items'
the reader would not have time to process individual units. Accordingly,
selection must be made on the basis of cognitive expectations, and reading must be seen as an active process of hypothesis-testing and decision
making - a 'psycho-linguistic guessing game' (10). At this level, graphic
data serves as the basis for syntactic and semantic 'predictions', which
utilize the reader's knowledge of sentence structure and narrative form.
If the prediction is wrong, reading is delayed - and the reader must
question, not only the text, but also his or her expectations. The 'working system' is challenged; and to the degree that this is a fundamental
linguistic orientation to the world, a reader is continually threatened by
the act of reading.

(d) Affective factors

As we move into the region of expectation and long-term memory, we
begin to approach a crucial problem: that the psycho-linguistic system
we have here constructed cannot account for reading as a whole. Some-
where between the lexical and contextual levels, a 'break' occurs. A
semantic typology for example, after the manner of Katz and Fodor (1964),
only goes so far (and not very far) in accounting for reading competence.
For in so far as reading is a 'goal-directed' activity, which points beyond
itself to a social experience, it involves the reader's whole personality.

A great deal of psycho-linguistic research adopts the framework of trans-
formational grammar. This is inadequate for an understanding of reading,
because the attempt to account for the structures of the mind on the basis
of linguistic structures (cf. Chomsky, 1968), cannot comprehend the
cultural expectations which the reader brings to the text. In so far as
transformational grammar makes these claims, it is guilty of the collapse

we observed in Riffaterre. We have a projection of linguistic structures as pre-given 'innate ideas' (11).

An alternative to this approach is the theory of language developed by the tradition of 'genetic epistemology', especially by Piaget (1959, 1968) and Vygotsky (1962). Here language is understood as one part of a total process of 'symbolic differentiation' (which includes play activity and techniques of experimentation). The genetic development of language is part of the socio-historical experience of childhood: language is a 'tool', which the child learns to use, to tackle the problems he encounters in his daily life. The foundation of this theory is socio-linguistic, arising from Piaget's own observations of linguistic behaviour in the context of a kindergarten. (12)

Thus, as our analysis moves up the psycho-linguistic scale, from the immediate perception of letters and words, to the long-term formulation of verbal systems and structures, we approach the moment at which this behaviour becomes meaningful. And the starting-point for an account of reading as a meaningful activity is the existential encounter with the text. We can no longer be satisfied with an external, psycho-linguistic description of reading, which treats reading as an object for experimentation. On the contrary, because we recognize the reader's 'freedom' to go beyond mechanical perception, and to structure that perception according to cultural values, we also recognize that the reader is a privileged object - a subject (which we are ourselves). To reduce that privilege to dimensions of 'objectivity' is the fallacy of scientism.

(ii) Communication
An existential analysis is made from within, as our self-conscious description of ourselves. It is primarily an immediate recognition of two factors. First, we can reflect that our activity has become conscious, and that it is possible for us to speak of 'motivations' or 'ends and means'. Secondly, because we are conscious of ourselves, we can recognize others: in so far as the text 'expresses' a consciousness, it is the 'signification' of an author. Because we perceive ourselves, therefore we perceive others - and we have the moment of communication.

In their books writers create worlds for themselves. Having initially perceived reality as 'other' (the differentiated subject/object which is the basis of self consciousness), they have attempted to 'internalize' it, to make it essentially their own. Thus they have approached the external world as the raw material for a 'fiction', and in so far as this project is successful, the world (as it was, external to consciousness) is subsumed in the act of creation. Together with this, there arises a tendency for writers to idealize their activity (or 'praxis') as an end in itself. The 'objective' world is lost in the act of transcendence. So writers always need a new objectivity - they require readers to re-establish their personal worlds.

Readers complete the projects of writers. However, these projects, 'objectified' in books, do not confront readers simply at random – they are objects which signify human consciousness, and thus, in a sense 'direct' them. This is not to say that readers themselves do not 'create', according to their own expectations and ends; but their creation is a peculiar kind of 'directed creation' – which, at the same time as it subsumes the object, also recognizes it as a human signif- ication (13).

Thus the activity of communication, described from within, is an act of human commitment. It is not what one reads that is important, it is the fact that as one reads, one realizes a value – a "perpetually renew- ed choice to believe" (Sartre). Reading is an 'exercise in generosity', an activity which is a giving and taking of 'freedom' – which may be subjectively understood as an expression of 'community'. Aesthetic pleasure might be seen in this way as the identity of reciprocal freedoms, a feeling which arises in the reader of being essential to an essential object. The joy of reading is a utopian vision of communal harmony.

However, though this inter-personal communication is an important feature of reading, and indeed at the very centre of our 'lived experience', it is not as idealists would have it, sufficient in itself. It has long been fashionable to hold this view, whereby the act of reading becomes a kind of 'pure praxis' – a harmonious release of form and content without re- pression or restraint. Thus Romantics have argued for a 'communion of souls', and Freudians for 'substitute gratification'. But such arguments not only deny the reality of reading – they also deny the significance of literature. For even when it seems to construct 'reality' for its own sake, a text provides a perspective – a 'discursive context' – on the immediate situation. And it is through this socio-historical context that the reader is able to 'place' the text – from a 'relatively autonomous' perspective.

To reduce that perspective to immediate communication is the fallacy of humanism.

(iii) Cultural Reading
Reading literature as culture, is not only reading to exercize psycho- linguistic structures, nor even to participate in the affirmation of 'community'. It is both these and more: being a practice which goes be- yond these conditions and retrospectively comprehends them.

For example, a reading of Wuthering Heights will be more than a series of predictions – a psycho-linguistic 'guessing game'. In addition, it will involve a recognition of the importance of certain formal (generic, stylistic) features of the text. We will compare this novel to other novels (eg. use of the retrospective narrator – Nelly Dean – an unusual feature of the genre). We will note the novel's dialectical structure (the antithesis of two houses, the conflict between Heathcliff and Linton, the search for 'resolution' in the marriage of Hareton and Cathy). And we will focus upon aspects of the novel's style (use of symbolic motifs – windows, coffins, fires, storms - and the tight, clinical quality of language). All these 'mediations' in our reading of the text (genre, structure, and language) challenge our expectations: they are resistances to an 'immediate' perception of meanings. Through them, we are encouraged to question the unity of the novel; and we may outline a formal structure, by which to explore its organization.

Furthermore, our reading will be more than a 'catharsis', or release of emotion, important though this may be. In addition, it will recognize a 'structure of feeling' in the text (cf. Williams, 1973) - an interrelation of cultural values and a distinctive 'authorial voice'. We will be impressed by the parochial vision of Wuthering Heights (in which the action seldom moves from the immediate situation); and the extraordinarily detailed description of the local environment (the moors, the interiors of houses). We will encounter the strangeness of characters (particularly the men - Heathcliff, Hindley, Hareton, even Joseph - all are extremes of one sort or another). And we will confront the significance of certain key themes (the supernatural, sexuality, death - which give the novel its Romantic, even Gothic atmosphere). All these aspects of the 'structure of feeling' (point of view, characterization, thematic construction) are discursive mediations to 'immediate' reading. We read the novel in its cultural context (the parochial vision, and disturbed sexuality, are features of provincial isolation) - and on this basis we may construct a discursive problematic, to explore its historical location.

In these respects, our reading of Wuthering Heights is a 'regressive' account of its construction, both as a formal unity and a discursive problematic. In both cases we are referred beyond the text: in determining the originality of its form (means of organization, use of language etc.); and in determining the character of its discourse (within a 'discursive field'). However we are not simply interested in Wuthering Heights as a 'document' of its period, nor do we seek to reduce the novel's specificity. It is necessary to locate the novelist herself, precisely within her family, locality and class position. Our analysis of Wuthering Heights must refer to the life of Emily Bronte: understanding her particular family (its conservative politics - its low-church Anglicanism) in the context of its 'community'; analyzing the lower-middle class family as an institution (its economic 'prudence', its moral 'respectability'). Only in this kind of detail can we account for the tragic vision of the novel - the extremes of conflict in both its form and its discourse - and avoid simply caricaturing its (undoubted) 'petit-bourgeois' ideology. Ambiguously, Emily Bronte was able to transcend her situation, and only by understanding what was unique about her can we do justice to her novel.

Nor can the 'regressive' moment of cultural analysis, by itself, do
justice to our reading. For in so far as the text demands a reciprocal
'directed creation', we are interested in the critique of our own experience which it makes possible. In this 'progressive' account, the novel
poses questions to ourselves as contemporary readers, and to the
'present conjuncture' of our reading. Perhaps fortuitously, the structure
of Wuthering Heights itself encourages a kind of 'reflexivity' - for its
vision is narrated in retrospect, by Nelly Dean. Her presence in the
novel 'positions' our reading: first we listen to Lockwood; then with him
to Nelly Dean; then with her to the characters of her story. In this way
we are made aware of our relation to events - of the pivotal space we
occupy as listeners and readers. Raymond Williams has suggested that
Wuthering Heights "teaches a new feeling" (14). The point is not that the
novel itself 'teaches' us anything; but that it puts us in a position to question our own experience.

In Cathy's choice between Linton and Heathcliff (between, we might say,
socialized affection and elemental passion) Wuthering Heights identifies
a 'lived contradiction'. The strength of the novel is that this contradiction becomes the basis for a 'world vision', which it projects as universal. It is apparent that the formal mediations of the novel are rooted
in Cathy's experience: the antithesis of the houses (the social order of
the Grange vs. the natural chaos of the Heights); and various stylistic
motifs (the window as link between the domestic world and 'beyond', the
juxta-position of bed and coffin in dreams of death/sexual consummation).
Similarly the ideological themes (the woman's choice between types of
men; the absolute choice between social and natural worlds) serve to
'totalize' Cathy's position. These features give the novel its problematic unity - as a Romantic critique of social propriety. Romance and
marriage are irreconcilable; and the ghost of Heathcliff haunts the
'final resolution'.

How we respond to the novel's conclusion will undoubtedly depend on many
contingent factors. We cannot simply reduce its potential to a single
contemporary reading - for different readers will perceive different
qualities in the text (from its formal elegance, to the romance and
mystery of its plot). On the other hand, as we begin to understand the
social and historical context of the novel, so we are able to know the
history of its criticism - and thus the lasting patterns of our cultural
life which the novel calls into question. In this sense Wuthering Heights
is selected for us, as one of the supreme, yet problematic examples
of nineteenth century fiction. It poses questions about the genre as such;
about the position of women (as novelists etc.); and about the 'world-
vision' of the provincial middle-class. Any 'reading' of these questions
is inevitably 'placed', as a historical moment, in a critical 'tradition'.
But it is only by recognizing the horizons of this tradition (and thus the
limitations of our position as critical readers) that we can begin to
develop the 'reflexivity' necessary for cultural knowledge.

Notes

(1) I.A.Richards (1936), pp.3-4

cf. Speculative Instruments (London, 1955):

"Radio, TV. and the screen propagate most successfully the most superficial, the most facile, and the least educating elements of a culture ... In every culture it has been the things which received the most lasting and recurrent attention - the books re-read again and again, the stories and sayings known and familiar from infancy to old age, the rites repeated throughout a lifetime, the perennial monuments, the enduring ideas, the constant aesthetic institutions - which have done the most part of the work of the humanities. Mass media at present replace such continuing shaping forces by an incessantly shifting play of light and confusing impacts. It is not surprising that they are of little help in seeing life steadily and seeing it whole." (p.62)

(2) cf. Brooks (1947):

"The poem communicates so much and communicates it so richly and with such delicate qualifications that the thing communicated is mauled and distorted if we attempt to convey it by any vehicle less subtle than the poem itself." (p.58)

(3) cf. M.A.K.Halliday (1973):

"In The Inheritors, the syntax is part of the story. As readers, we are reacting to the whole of the writer's creative use of 'meaning potential'; and the nature of language is such that he can convey, in a line of print, a complex of simultaneous themes, reflecting the variety of functions that language is required to serve ... In The Inheritors it is the linguistic representation of experience, through the syntactic resources of transitivity, that is especially brought into relief..." (p.135)

(4) Northrop Frye (1957), 'Polemical Introduction', pp.15-16.

(5) cf. Riffaterre (1967):

"Our problem is to transform a fundamentally subjective reaction to style into an objective analytic tool to find the constant (encoded potentialities) beneath the variety of judgements, in short to transform value judgements into judgements of existence." (p.149)

(6) Frye, op.cit. p.20

(7) cf. Louis Althusser (1970):

"A philosophical reading of Capital is only possible as the application of that which is the very object of our investigation, Marxist philosophy. This circle is only epistemologically possible because of the existence of Marx's philosophy in the works of Marxism. It is therefore a question of producing, in the precise sense of the word, which seems to signify making manifest what is latent, but which really means transforming (in order to give a pre-existing raw material the form of an object adapted to an end), something which in a sense already exists. This production, in the double sense which gives the production operation the necessary form of a circle, is the production of a knowledge. To conceive Marx's philosophy in its specificity is therefore to conceive the essence of the very movement with which the knowledge of it is produced, or to conceive knowledge as production." (p.34)

(8) cf. Jean-Paul Sartre (1963):
"Knowing is simply the dialectical movement which explains the act by its terminal signification in terms of its starting conditions... The movement of comprehension is simultaneously progressive (toward the objective result) and regressive (I go back toward the original condition)." (pp.153-4)

(9) See: Goodman, Kenneth, ed. The Psycholinguistic Nature of the Reading Process, (Detroit, 1968).

Levin, Harry, and Williams, Joanna P. eds. Basic Studies in Reading, (New York, 1970).

Singer, Harry, and Ruddell, Robert B. eds. Theoretical Models and Processes of Reading, (Newark, Del. 1969).

(10) cf. Goodman (1969):
"Reading is a selective process. It involves partial use of available language cues selected from perceptual input on the basis of the reader's expectation. As this partial information is processed, tentative decisions are made to be confirmed, rejected or refined as reading progresses." (p.26)

(11) cf. Chomsky (1968):
Chomsky's hypothesis that syntactic structures are reflected in mental structures is methodologically unsound, since it involves reducing the mechanisms concerned with the perception of language (eg. in the process of language acquisition) to the structure of language itself. That is to say, Chomsky works from the 'answer' to the 'question'; from the description of syntactic structure to how that structure is perceived. This procedure is reflected in the character of the description itself - a highly formalized

analysis of anomaly and ambiguity, which <u>supports</u> rather than <u>tests</u> his theory. Chomsky thus falls into the ideological trap of the be-haviourists he criticizes. He fails to treat his data (syntactic struct-ures) <u>in its specificity</u> - rather he generalizes from one set of problems to another.

(12) cf. Piaget (1959). "Genetic epistemology" avoids the fallacies of trans-formational linguistics because it studies the perception of language in the context of the perception of social experience. Language is not given a privileged status, and so it cannot be argued that the structures of language are the structures of the mind. The confrontation of the two (language and mind) is the basis for language acquisition.

(13) cf. Sartre (1950):
"Reading seems, in fact, to be the synthesis of perception and creation. It supposes the essentiality of both the subject and the object. The object is essential because it is strictly transcendent, because it im-poses its own structures, and because one must wait for it and observe it; but the subject is also essential because it is required not only to disclose the object (that is, to make it possible for there to <u>be</u> an ob-ject) but also so that this object might exist absolutely (that is, to pro-duce it)...The reader must invent ... in a continual exceeding of the written thing. To be sure, the author guides him, but all he does is guide him. The landmarks he sets up are separated by the void. The reader must unite them; he must go beyond them. In short, reading is directed creation." (pp.30-1)

(14) cf. Williams (1961):
"Here, at a peak of intensity, the complicated barriers of a system of relationships are broken through, finally, by an absolute human commitment. The commitment is realized through death, and the essential tragedy ...becomes the form of the whole work. The cre-ative elements in the other fiction (of the 1840s) are raised to a wholeness which takes the work right outside the ordinary structure of feeling, and teaches a new feeling." (p86)

Bibliography

Althusser, Louis — *For Marx*, tr. Brewster, Allen Lane, London, 1969.

Reading Capital, tr. Brewster, New Left Books, London, 1970.

Brooks, Cleanth — *The Well Wrought Urn*, New York, 1947.

Chomsky, Noam — *Language and Mind*, Harcourt Brace & World, New York, 1968.

Phonology and Reading, in Levin & Williams, *Basic Studies in Reading*, New York, 1970.

Empson, William — *Seven Types of Ambiguity*, Chatto & Windus, London, 1930.

Foucault, Michel — *The Archaeology of Knowledge*, tr. Sheridan Smith, Tavistock, London, 1972.

Fries, Charles C. — *Linguistics and Reading*, Holt Rinehart & Winston, New York, 1963.

Frye, Northrop — *Anatomy of Criticism*, Princeton University Press, 1970.

Geyer, J.J. — 'Models of Perceptual Processes in Reading' in Singer & Ruddell , *Theoretical Models and Processes of Reading*, Newark, Del, 1969.

Goodman, K.S. — 'Reading: a Psycholinguistic Guessing Game', in Singer & Ruddell, op. cit.

Goldmann, Lucien — *The Hidden God*, (1955) tr. Thody, Routledge & Kegan Paul, London, 1964.

Halliday, M.A.K. — *Explorations in the Functions of Language*, Arnold, London, 1973.

Hochberg, Julien — 'Components of Literacy: Speculations and Exploratory Research', in Levin & Williams, op. cit.

Holland, Norman — *The Dynamics of Literary Response*, New York, 1968.

Katz, J. & Fodor, J. — 'The Structure of a Semantic Theory', in *The Structure of Language: Readings in the Philosophy of Language*, Prentice-Hall, Englewood Cliffs, 1964.

Kolers, Paul — 'Reading a temporally and spatially transformed text', in Goodman, *The Psycholinguistic Nature of the Reading Process*, Detroit, 1968.

Lacan, Jacques — 'The insistence of the letter in the unconscious', pp.112–147, in *Yale French Studies*, 36–37, 1966.

Leavis, F.R. — *Education and The University*, 2nd. edition, Chatto & Windus, London, 1948.

Lesser, Simon O. — *Fiction and the Unconscious*, Boston, 1957.

Neisser, Ulrich — *Cognitive Psychology*, Appleton-Century-Crofts, New York, 1967.

Reed, David W.	'Linguistic forms and the process of reading', in Levin & Williams, op. cit.
Riffeterre, Michael	'Criteria for Style Analysis', in Word XV, 1959, pp.154-74; reprinted in Chatman S. and Levin S.R. eds., Essays on the Language of Literature, Boston, 1967.
Richards, I.A.	Principles of Literary Criticism, Routledge & Kegan Paul, London, 1924.
	The Philosophy of Rhetoric, Oxford University Press, New York, 1936.
Ruddell, Robert B.	'Psycholinguistic implications for a system of communication model', in Singer & Ruddell, op. cit.
Sartre, J-P	What is Literature?, tr. Frechtman, Methuen, London, 1950.
	Search for a Method, tr. Barnes, Knopf, New York, 1963.
Vygotsky, L.S.	Thought and Language, tr. Hanfmann & Vakar, Massachusetts Institute of Technology Press, Cambridge, 1962.
Williams, Raymond	The Long Revolution, Chatto & Windus, London, 1961.
	The Country and the City, Chatto & Windus, London, 1973.

The Alleged Depravity of Popular Taste
Burges Johnson

from

Harper's Magazine, 142, 1921.

THE ALLEGED DEPRAVITY OF POPULAR TASTE

BY BURGES JOHNSON

"THE present vulgarity of the public taste," "the barbarous taste of the public"—these two phrases occur in two separate articles in a recent number of a critical review. In their appraisal of the public taste I wonder whether these writers made any distinction between evidences of popular curiosity and proofs of popular approval! Curiosity is aroused by weeks of skillful advertising, and spends itself in a moment. Curiosity, like suspicion, anger, or amusement, is an emotion easily aroused in the popular breast by the skilled manipulator of crowds, who usually is indifferent to the fact that it is spent in a moment, provided it is spent his way.

"Susie's Double Bed," played night after night in New York to crowded houses. Perhaps even you, gentle reader, helped surreptitiously to swell that crowd. Please analyze frankly your own motives for going. "I wonder," said you, "why everyone keeps talking about that play?" "I wonder," said you again, "how bad it really is!" "Let's break loose and be really wicked," said you to a group of equally respectable pillars of suburban society; "let's have supper in some Italian back yard and then go to that 'Susie' show everyone is talking about"; and by "everyone" you unwittingly meant every billboard, and an army of pen-wielding mongers of stage gossip. So you went and ate small portions of food from soiled dishes and enjoyed it because it was a variation from your routine; and then you went and saw a large portion of "Susie" and came away oddly disappointed. Pause a moment in the lobby as you go out and listen to the comments: "Not much of a show!" "Worn-out plot, but several good laughs." "Daring, wasn't it? Nobody would have stood for that ten years ago!" "Well, now we've seen that, what next?" It is actually the fact that not one of the many comments we overhear indicates that the play has met the approval of popular taste, but rather that popular curiosity has been satisfied.

One would not believe for a moment that the crowds which thronged the Twenty-third Regiment Armory in New York City a few years ago to view the widely advertised exhibition of cubist and futurist paintings were a proof that experiments in these unconventional schools satisfied the popular taste. The exhibiting artists themselves would hasten to disclaim this. The public cannot approve until it has examined, and the chief conclusions to be drawn from the fact that vast numbers did examine are these: that the show had been well advertised, that it was within easy reach of vast numbers, and that the price of admission was not too high.

Let me admit here that I have no settled convictions as to popular taste. My quarrel is with those pronouncements of smug minds which we tend to accept without limiting their application or remeasuring their value. Repeat a statement often enough and people begin to believe you, even though what you say is true. Repeat an aspersion against a person or a public, and if it be epigrammatically expressed at once it becomes currency. "Naturally there's little good in the magazines; their editors have to please the public," says some one or other! "I never read a best seller—you know what popular judgment is worth!" "The play has made a big hit—it must be bad!" It may be worth while to examine these common slurs upon the popular judgment before we pass them along so glibly.

If we are to discuss popular taste in the light of theater-going, it is worth while asking what portion of the public determines the quality of our drama, as well as what kind it actually approves, and we must first of all focus attention on a small section of Manhattan Island. Here a little group of managers—one might almost call it a clique—limits the public's opportunity to see plays. While undoubtedly these dictators are themselves guided by the popular preference so far as they can gauge it, yet the crowds whose tastes they study are the crowds within easy reach.

New York City's theater-going public is *sui generis*. Very largely it is a visiting public. Mr. and Mrs. Public-on-a-holiday are prone to leave better judgment at home to keep house with the babies and the cook. Pew rents or collection plates are temporarily left out of the estimates. Week-enders in New York develop a weakness at the top end. The manager's problem, especially if he be a man without instinctive taste, is to arouse the superficial curiosity of this passing throng.

It is, in fact, the lively curiosity of even healthy-minded America that plays this unimaginative manager's game for him throughout. "One hundred nights in New York" is a catchword that will fetch the gate receipts in Grand Rapids, where very possibly the New York manager has some interlocking claim upon the leading theater, and Mr. and Mrs. Grand-Rapidian say, "Let's go and see why New York went!" It is even whispered that in cases where the manager of limited vision has failed to arouse floating New York's curiosity up to a hundred-night pitch he has played to "papered" houses at a loss, for enough additional days to justify that magic phrase when on the road. This may at least be credited to his business acumen.

Yet, whatever the manager's caliber,

one would assume that current plays on Broadway ought to represent his best effort to *locate* the fixed tastes of his audiences. This might be assumed if each play was a hazard—a gamble on public preferences. If the manager correctly appraises popular taste he wins; if incorrectly, he loses. But it is said on good authority that in not a single Broadway production nowadays is the manager taking any risk. His enterprise is underwritten before it starts. Payments for moving-picture rights, stock rights, and the like, contingent only upon a few days of actual Broadway presentation, are sufficient to protect him against any loss whatever. He is betting on a sure thing. He does not need to educate himself in public taste. He can thrive without such knowledge.

To growl indiscriminately at the theater is not the purpose of this screed, nor would it then fairly represent the attitude of the writer. But in considering common disparagements of the popular taste in drama, it is well to point out that other factors beside general public preference help to determine the character of the most loudly heralded plays. It is possible that the widespread "little theater" movement, the drama leagues and amateur players everywhere are not merely the passing fads of a few "intellectuals." They may be proof of popular unrest over a financial control of the stage that is insufficiently responsive to the common desires. If all butter manufacture on a large scale came under the control of a few men and they marketed a rancid product, we might accuse the public of being weakly acquiescent, but not of preferring rancid butter. And it is a safe guess that little independent sweet-butter factories would spring up here and there over the land and struggle along, despite the difficulties of distribution. It is indeed an acquiescent public, but its conscious preferences will occasionally evidence themselves.

The disparager of popular taste is sure to cite most triumphantly the "movies" of to-day in defense of his views. But all that has been said in defense of popular taste in connection with the spoken drama may be reiterated and emphasized in the moving-picture field. I can do no better than to quote from the printed word of an expert—one who writes movies as well as of them. He says:

The infancy of motion pictures has been left to the supervision of (take it by and large) the most dangerous element of our population, the element that represents primarily greed. Greed is part ignorance. The two are inextricably interwoven. . . . To them we have intrusted the early years of the motion picture. For this, our children, and our children's children, must pay. With the appearance of the first motion pictures there was a rush to the new field closely comparable to the rush to some new gold district when a strike has been made in most unpromising regions. The first to arrive on new ground are the daring adventurers who take big risks for the possibility of easy profit—the something-for-nothing men. The first writers for the motion-picture industry, taking it as a whole, were those who happened to be on the ground or in touch with the first studio makers, *with nothing better to do*. The office hangers-on, unable to make good in their own field, willing to take a chance at anything—these were the first men to drift into writing for pictures. And, as with the writers, so with the other branches of the industry, so that by the time the moving-picture industry assumed substantial proportions and began to attract a greater number of high-caliber workers, the stamp of inefficiency, ignorance, and an astounding lack of intelligent idealism already marked the new "art." The more competent of the incompetents—keeping always to generalities and avoiding the specific exceptions that mitigate conditions here and there—found themselves in controlling positions, and formed a barrier which the tides of betterment have been able to beat down but slowly. And the pictures turned out represented, in the aggregate, the low mental and moral and spiritual tone of those first drawn to the industry.

In other words, this writer suggests, as I have suggested in the case of the theater, that its worst manifestations—in fact, its general manifestations—do not so much reflect the tastes of the public as the instincts of the group which control it as an industry; that it has not become fully responsive to the wishes of the public, but only to the misguided efforts of unimaginative greed to interpret those wishes.

The other day I sat in a crowded moving-picture house in a small Colorado city. A "comedy" was on the screen. It was a succession of slapstick situations, almost any one of them so grotesquely absurd as to justify laughter, but following one another in such perplexingly rapid succession as to benumb the risibilities of the audience; and it was a patent fact that either an apathetic or a dazed audience, rather than a delighted one, watched the farce. Suddenly into the midst of the plot was introduced an episode of unnecessary and even inconsistent vulgarity. I watched the reaction with interest, and I believe without prejudice. This was a ten-cent matinée audience, crowded with children. It was a "low-caste" audience, if a supercilious critic might be allowed to classify it, and beyond question it was either offended or embarrassed—probably it could not have analyzed its own emotions and told you which. One can easily imagine the process of evolving that scenario. The producer examined it, interpreted the popular demand by means of his own wizened apperceptions, and said: "Give 'em more rough-house," "Put that there young lady into full tights." "Get more suggestion into the third reel. That's what the public wants." Heaven is most unkind to its common people, in that it provides them with such interpreters.

Yet this producer is by no means stupid. If he injects enough of the startling, the shocking, the arousing, his film will advertise itself to curiosity seekers; even the police powers of the city or some crusading clergyman may give it a boost. True, it will die in a day, but in the meantime it "paid" and he has "turned over his capital." As long as unadulterated greed exists unchecked such men will give the public curiosity— not the public taste—what it wants.

The present-day trend in moving pictures is comforting to those who have faith in the popular judgment, for surely the producers have not determined to run contrary to a general demand and force upon the people something better than they want; yet everywhere producers, even the stupidest, are revising their editorial staffs, hunting hurriedly for better sources, and vying with one another to destroy that ugly god which they created in their own image and called Public Opinion; groping for a true god which they have no native means of recognizing.

But let us get along to books. In the field of the theater a brilliant Belasco or an imaginative Hopkins might dispute my assertions and I should be at a loss for retorts. The publishing business is obviously in the hands of more men, more widely distributed. A hundred highly competitive publishing houses are striving to ascertain the popular taste and to cater to it. Moreover, the public may send for the books it wants (from among those it has heard about), while it must take whatever theaters it can get to. What sort of book does it mostly want, and who are the buyers of these books?

My friend Jones is a professional critic. He, too, has gauged the American public. He is fond of saying that it prefers to read "sentimental drivel," or "nasty society stuff." I think he has specifically in mind the highly moral fiction of the Rev. Henry B. Williams. I agree with Jones in his estimate of these writings, but I want to be sure that he is right in saying they determine the popular taste.

Sixty million people in this country never see a book, and only about 4 per cent of our population ever get into a bookstore. The book buyers select from among the books they have heard about. Yet they hear of very few, because, for a popular commodity, books are re-markably underadvertised. This must be so. Mr. Gillette makes one safety razor and his entire advertising appropriation pushes its sales. Mr. Henry Holt publishes one hundred books and whatever advertising appropriation he can afford must be divided among them. Each may get a hundredth part of his budget. Mr. Gillette will make the same razor next year. Mr. Holt will make a hundred new books, with brand-new names demanding entirely different advertising.

Moreover, book-distributing methods are painfully inadequate. It is said that there are fewer retail bookstores in the United States to-day than there were fifty years ago. In a half million homes where reading is desired, what do you find? The Bible, a "home doctor," a history of the world, sold on subscription by some itinerant vender, and then what? *Ben Hur*, perhaps, and a worn volume of Scott or Dickens, and some school books. Please realize that when a new volume of Mr. So-and-So's salacious stuff is tossed from the presses next spring, it is seized upon by the merest fringe of our vast literate population. At the end of six months its sales are dead as a doornail; yet *David Copperfield* is still selling in twenty or thirty different editions, and *A Tale of Two Cities* in forty or more. "Ah," says critic Jones, "that isn't public taste; that's habit. Sets of Dickens aren't books; they are furniture, library wall paper, certificates of culture." Jones would be right if the chief sale of Dickens were by sets, but it is not. One of the many low-priced editions, the year before the war, sold, of *David Copperfield*, 4,700 copies; of *Nicholas Nickleby*, 2,100; *Pickwick Papers*, 2,000; *Tale of Two Cities*, 2,000; *Our Mutual Friend*, 1,100; and other individual volumes of his works in almost negligible quantity. All this was despite the fact that every public library had them. In the year of Dickens's death twenty-one different editions of his works were on sale in America; forty-five years later there were as many as fifty of certain volumes. In that same year before the war a certain best seller went up to one hundred thousand copies in six months and then went down—and out.

It is easy to be misled by flash-in-the-pan successes, when judging popular taste. Mr. So-and-So's society scandals make a very loud noise and then die. Any publisher in the land, if offered a choice between the works of best-seller So-and-So and the works of Joseph Conrad, for instance, would choose the latter, because Conrad's works are a better property in their second year than in their first. Let us substitute the phrase "quick seller" for "best seller" and keep our meanings clear. Two of America's best sellers in the field of copyright fiction are *Ben Hur*, with close on two million sales, and *David Harum*, with more than a million. The publishers of *Tom Sawyer* and *Huckleberry Finn* a few weeks ago manufactured fifty thousand copies each of these two books, to carry them through the coming year, and these stories were first published over forty years ago. It is a safe bet that five out of this year's "six best sellers" will, two years from now, be as the grass that withered; while in the same year *Captain January* and *A Bird's Christmas Carol* and *The Man Without a Country* will approach or enter their second million; and even next year *Lorna Doone* will outsell them all.

What the public wants in the way of literature is a slightly different question from "What does the public like?" I have said that it quite naturally wants to see what it has heard about. And there is always this dominant third question, "What is it able to get?" I am not sure what it likes, but I am optimistic in my guessing.

No, the vast general public, as far as it is buying books at all, is not buying quick sellers, anomalous as that statement may sound. An English publisher announces a new series of cloth-bound books at a low price and of a handy size, and within a few months over a million copies are sold. The editor of the series does not choose his titles from among those books whose sale in their day was due wholly to an aroused public curiosity. He finds the books whose continued sale, however slow, proved that they had *met the approval of popular taste*, and these are republished, and now sell all over again in a fashion to put the six-months-old quick seller to shame.

I have urged that one may not estimate by means of quick sellers the standards of popular literary taste. Yet when one hundred thousand people, out of our small total of book buyers, see fit to buy a new book within six months of its publication, that is a phenomenon that I must not dismiss over lightly. They tell me that those sentimental novels by the Rev. Henry B. Williams, for instance, which to Jones's annoyance have sold so phenomenally, were advertised and distributed with unprecedented lavishness and skill. They were brought to the notice of people who wanted to read, but never had a book thrust upon their attention before, as safety razors had been thrust upon their attention, or made so easy to buy. But perhaps that does not tell the whole story. Jones says, "Those books are without merit; the public buys them; therefore the public has no literary judgment." I admit that I don't like the stories, but, since so many human beings do, there may be certain merits in them that I fail to appreciate. Jones and I proceed from different premises. But it seems to me important to note that certain other books by the same author, although equally sentimental and distasteful to Jones, had the same selling force back of them and yet failed to win public approval. Some simple quality, overlooked by the critic, causes this difference. Perhaps its very simplicity is the reason he overlooks it.

When *David Harum* appeared and gradually secured a sale that was a record-breaker in its day, my friend

Jones and others said it only went to prove the poor quality of popular taste. Now we realize that there was in the book an artistic and spiritually truthful picture of a certain homely American type. That character sold the book and kept on selling it. I have known Jones himself to sit patiently through a great deal of bad vaudeville and feel well repaid when Madame Bernhardt came on. I have heard him extol Drinkwater's "Lincoln" and quite ignore the impossible negro dialect, or the maidservant with English manners out in Illinois in 1859. Perhaps the public, too, does not place the seal of its approval on a whole book when it buys and buys, but only upon some one quality or some one character in the story that it is able to recognize as true in spirit. And it accepts, or ignores as nonessential, certain accompanying characteristics that to Jones may mean the book's damnation.

If so, I am sure it is not any subtle element, for the popular mind is not subtle. Whatever actually suits the public taste must be as simple and as obvious as Millet's "Angelus." Moreover, it may not be cynical or iconoclastic. Virtue must be extolled, sin deplored. The popular taste prefers optimism to pessimism just as the " general public " still believes in God and the ten commandments. It is true that an indecent book if well advertised can can secure a large sale. But publishers will tell you that the limit of sale, though large, is definite and can soon be reached; and no amount of skillful merchandizing could therefore be made to pay. A certain magazine has attained success by appealing to prurient curiosity. It has gradually built up and maintained a definite and profitable circulation. But that circulation is a small fraction of potential magazine readers. On the other hand, those household magazines which have run into circulations of a million and a half or two million, weekly or monthly, find it worldly-wise to be virtuous to the point of vapidity; and they could, if it were not unprofitable to do so, extend their circulations indefinitely.

If I were to create a story that approached literary perfection, and then wrote it in French, no one could assert that popular lack of interest in it proved the public's lack of good taste. The public in this instance would be limited to those with a reading knowledge of French. If my story presupposes a knowledge of applied psychology and makes use of many technical terms in that field of research, then I have again shut out a large portion of the public. My "price of admission" is too high.

A publisher friend of mine calls these superficial qualities of literature "entrance requirements." As you add to their number or to their esotericism, you reduce the number of those who can get into your book. But that limited number has not necessarily a finer sense of what is the good and the true and the beautiful in literature. Many of them may have. But some may be as blind as bats in the sunlight. You have merely a cross section of the public, cut to the lines of your entrance requirements.

I doubt whether it is any disparagement of the public's good taste to say that it prefers the simple and the obvious. Add a frock coat and silk hat to the rudimentary costume of the "Discus Thrower" and, though the fine lines are still underneath, you have made the statue less perfect by reason of these embellishments—and it will become still more grotesque with the passing of the silk hat. It is because of those qualities in the sculptor's achievement which are unhidden by fads and ephemeral embellishments that it still lives. My friend Jones would protest against such a discus thrower, but his faultfinding would be because the frock coat was not a cutaway.

In fact I begin to suspect that Jones enjoys faultfinding. Yet he himself does not face criticism cheerfully. He does not like me to tell him, for instance, that he gains more enjoyment from the contemplation of technique than of accomplishment. Nor does he like me to say that criticism is noncreative and a parasite among the arts, thriving upon literature as mistletoe thrives upon the oak. Far be it from me to wish the mistletoe abolished—it has certain pleasing social functions. But I notice that it only pretends to have roots of its own; and it often injures a delicate oak, while it never builds up a strong one. As for contemplating the beauty of the forest, it may see only the limbs from which it draws its sustenance. Critics can too easily lose touch with the public. They are not sure what it likes, but they know its tastes must be lower than their own.

"But, Mr. Omniscience," say you, "what does the public like?" First, something it can understand; second, something it *recognizes* as spiritually true; third, something that is not destructive of its fundamental faith in the eventual outworking of all things for good; finally, and more specifically, the things it really likes are the things it *keeps on* buying. For this last is not a vague generality. It means that if revivals of "Pinafore" or "Robin Hood" or "Wang" arouse greater enthusiasm forty or thirty or twenty years after their creation than a current light opera six months old, then they are the better criteria of popular taste. It means that any novel which sells successfully ten years after publication is better evidence on which to judge standards of public approval than one which dies in six months.

When Hardy's novels appeared, the public disregarded the judgments of the critics and, having selected certain ones for favor, *kept on buying them.* Critics now say that these certain ones are most worthy of survival. Critics tell us that Dickens must rest his reputation upon a certain three or four books. The public settled upon those books in the beginning, and keeps on buying them.

Let me frankly admit, in conclusion, that whatever arguments I may have presented in the foregoing are largely negative. I would urge that those evidences of the popular taste which you find most depressing are not good evidence. On the stage and in moving pictures the evidence seems to me to indicate that the public likes something much better than it generally gets. In books the greatest percentage of the literate public gets nothing at all. Quick sellers indicate first of all good merchandising methods and some curiosity-arousing quality. What ever else they indicate remains to be proved.

"What do you think of the popular taste in books?" I asked a bookseller of unusually wide experience.

"A most interesting question just now, for this reason," he replied. "Even before the Great War the old classics had begun to give way. Few read George Eliot now. Fewer each year are reading Scott. Before long we shall be unable to measure public taste by old standards. What are the new? Live behind a book counter year in and year out, as I have done, and you may find cause for depression in the stuff that crosses that counter. But it is noting the character of the books that buyers still call for, two and three years after their glory has departed from the advertising spaces, that makes an optimist of me."

A negative argument will not settle anything, it is true. But, as I said in the beginning, I have not sought to settle anything. On the contrary, I want to unsettle something—namely, your mind, in case it is contentedly wearing certain hand-me-down ideas about the "barbarous taste of the public" without first considering whether or not they fit. If they do, by all means wear them.

Why Literature Declines
Robert Lynd

from

Atlantic Monthly, 142, 1928.

WHY LITERATURE DECLINES

BY ROBERT LYND

I

FEW people nowadays believe in the inevitability of progress as confidently as their grandfathers believed in it. The theory of evolution is still accepted, not only by Bishop Barnes, but by the majority of white men who understand it, and even of those who don't; but we no longer apply the theory generally to the affairs of mankind or see any certainty of an orderly progress in civilization itself. There has been steady progress, it is true, in the accumulation of knowledge and in the perfecting of inventions. There is no reason why science should not add story upon story to the tower of human knowledge till it has outgrown the tower of Babel, and there is no reason why, among inventions, wireless should not go on progressing till it has put men in touch with the inhabitants of other planets. But in other spheres of human activity we feel increasing doubts about the future. Prophets who believe that European society will progress slowly toward Utopia are more than balanced by those who believe that it is already in the first stages, or even at an advanced stage, of decay. And when we come to the arts, which are the graces of civilization, not even the professional optimist can see traces of any law of progress at work. Painting, sculpture, music, and literature seem to flourish for a few generations or a few centuries, and then to wither. Golden ages are succeeded by silver ages. Pegasus loses his wings and ambles on his feet. Homer is not followed by greater writers of epics, but, after nearly three thousand years, is still without an equal or a rival. Three great tragic dramatists appear in Athens, and there is no other dramatist fit to be named with them till more than two thousand years later Shakespeare begins to write in England. Phidias is still the greatest sculptor, Plutarch the greatest biographer, as Bach, Mozart, and Beethoven are the greatest composers of music. Nowhere is there any sign of progress. 'If Art was progressive,' said Blake in his 'Annotations to Reynolds,' 'we should have had Michelangelos and Raphaels to succeed each other. But it is not so. Genius dies with its possessor and comes not again till another is born with it.'

Blake, perhaps, went too far in his denial of progress in the arts. Undoubtedly the Greek drama progressed in the hands of Æschylus, and the English drama progressed in the hands of Shakespeare. At the same time, it is true that in literature we do not inevitably pass from peak to higher peak of genius. Literature is just as likely to take a downward direction as an upward. It is supposed to be the mark of a pessimist to say that anything is going to the dogs, and I should not like to say that literature is going to the dogs at present; but so many literatures have gone to the dogs in the past that it is worth inquiring what are the causes and whether these causes are perceptible to-day.

II

My own belief — and there is some evidence for it — is that literature begins to go to the dogs as soon as Earth becomes restive and declares its independence of Heaven. In the great ages of literature, Earth was, if not a suburb of Heaven, a subject kingdom. Heaven and Earth were places on the same cosmic map; civilized men believed in the existence of Heaven centuries before they believed in the existence of America, and believed in it just as firmly as we do in the existence of America to-day. Possibly their ideas of Heaven were even more mistaken than the modern European's ideas of America. But at least the life of mortals was lit up for them by the presence of the immortals, and the gods presided over human destinies. To me it seems impossible to believe that it is a mere accident that all the supremely great epics, from Homer's to Milton's, were written by poets who not only accepted the heavenly background, but wove it into the theme of their narratives. The gods may not be the most interesting of the characters in the *Iliad*, but the mortal characters seem to borrow a radiance from them, and to take part in larger wars than those of which historians write in prose. Take the gods out of the *Iliad*, and you diminish the heroes. The battlefield of Greek and Trojan would, in the absence of the gods, seem as petty as a lamp-lit town over which hung no firmament of stars. We may not be able to explain why this is so, but we know that it is so. We know that in the presence of the stars we feel an exaltation and liberation of the spirit such as we do not feel in the light of the lamps in a street. It is as though the stars enlarged our world and gave us the freedom of the universe. If we could imagine the extinction of the stars, we should think of the world as an infinitely impoverished place. Literature, I believe, would suffer an equal impoverishment as a result of the death of the gods.

There is, I take it, no need to prove by evidence the existence of the religious background in epic poetry. It is too obvious to be overlooked, whether we think of the *Odyssey*, as Poseidon drives Odysseus hither and thither, 'a wanderer from his native land,' and Athene pleads with Zeus to permit his return, or of *Paradise Lost*, in which the poet avows it as his object to 'justify the ways of God to men.' Virgil and Dante see life in the same divine setting. 'Sing, Heavenly Muse' — so Milton invokes inspiration as he writes, and the adjective is not meaningless. There is no other Muse but a Heavenly Muse that has ever produced great epic poetry. According to the Greek legend, the Muses were the daughters of Zeus, and thus song has a heavenly descent. Even in the legendary ages, however, there appear to have been singers who disputed the supremacy of Heaven in poetry. There was at least one mortal who not only attempted to sing without the aid of the daughters of Zeus, but who boasted that he could conquer them in singing, and Homer in the Catalogue of the Ships tells us of his melancholy fate. Thamyris, says Homer, 'averred with boasting that he would conquer, even did the Muses themselves sing against him, the daughters of ægis-bearing Zeus; but they in their anger maimed him, moreover they took from him the high gift of song and made him to forget his harping.' There, I think, we have a fable of the eternal dependence of literature for its highest inspiration on a world larger than a world inhabited by none but mortal men and women. Without this inspiration men lose the high gift of song. I do not mean by this that a man who is intellectually an atheist or an agnostic cannot write great literature. What I do contend is that the literary imagination is akin to the religious imagination, and that literature, while it has its roots in earth, flourishes in its greatest splendor when its branches are stirred by some air from Heaven.

And literature is not unique among the arts in having such close associations with religion. Architecture, sculpture, painting, and music, in at least as great a measure, seem to flower most abundantly when they are in the precincts of the temple or the church. There are no buildings of the Christian era which, either individually or in the mass, reveal imaginative genius in anything like the same degree as the great churches. The age of the most beautiful painting was the age in which men painted the Madonna and the Child, and in which they did not make them lose their divinity in their humanity. Critics differ as to who were the greatest composers, but ordinary men find a pleasure in listening to the music of Handel and Bach, written when music and religion were closely associated, such as they do not find in listening to the music of to-day. I know that, on the other hand, there are critics who explain that the music of Bach is not spiritual, just as there are critics who explain that the poetry of Milton is not Christian. There are critics, again, who deny that there is anything spiritual in the architecture of St. Peter's. Even if we admit this, however, we shall also have to admit that it is a remarkable coincidence that music like Bach's, epic poetry like Milton's, or architecture like that of St. Peter's, has never been produced by artists indifferent to the religious tradition of mankind.

It may be contended that it is a mere accident that the great poets, the great painters, and the great composers belonged to an age more superstitious and less rational than our own, and that, naturally enough, these men of genius reflected in their work the theology of their time, as the younger novelists of our own time reflect the psychology of Freud. There has never yet, it may be urged, been an age of reason, in which men free from the ancient superstitions have had an opportunity of producing work to rival the ancient masterpieces. We constantly hear to-day of literature's breaking new ground and creating new forms, as though we had only to be patient in order to find a better Homer and a better Milton waiting for us round the corner. All talk of this kind, I believe, is based on a profound illusion — the illusion of progress in the arts. We shall never have another Homer until we have a great poet who believes in Olympus. We shall never have another Milton till we have a great poet who believes in the war between Heaven and Hell. It is arguable that these beliefs are superstitions, and that the human race will be both wiser and happier for having abandoned them. But literature, at least, will be the poorer. Literature will always have to return for inspiration to Olympus, though it may be an Olympus transformed. The future of literature is in the past. It is in the recovery and resurrection of the vanished faith of vanished ages.

III

When Thomas Love Peacock wrote mockingly of poetry a century ago, as a kind of literature unsuitable to men in an age of reason, he may have written in jesting fashion, but what he said was fundamentally true. 'A poet,' he declared, 'in our times is a semi-barbarian in a civilized community.

He lives in the days that are past. His ideas, thoughts, feelings, associations, are all with barbarous manners, obsolete customs, and exploded superstitions. The march of his intellect is like that of a crab, backward. The brighter the light diffused around him by the progress of reason, the thicker is the darkness of antiquated barbarism, in which he buries himself like a mole, to throw up the barren hillocks of his Cimmerian labors.' There you have the truth put in a hostile fashion, but it is none the less truth. The march of a great poet's intellect is, like that of a crab, backward — or would be except for the fact that a crab walks sideward. If the belief in Olympus, or in something corresponding to Olympus, is the mark of a semibarbarian, then a modern poet will necessarily be a semibarbarian. He will probably be more at home in the Dark Ages than at a contemporary meeting of shareholders.

This is not to say that either the great poets or the great prose writers of the future will be occupied mainly with religious themes. Religion in itself, in the ordinary sense of the word, is no more likely to produce great literature than party politics. If you look around the shelves of a theological library, you will probably find even less good literature than on the shelves of a purely secular library. Glance through a hymn book, and you will come on very few poems that you feel ought to be included in the *Oxford Book of English Verse*. One of the most astounding facts in literary history is, indeed, that while so many passionately sincere men and women have written religious verse, so few of them have written poems as inspired as the poems that other men have written about nightingales and daffodils. Wordsworth declared that poetry is 'the spontaneous overflow of powerful feelings.' Well, here among the hymn

writers you have surely the spontaneous overflow of powerful feelings, — feelings for which the writers would have been prepared to go to the stake, — yet, as literature, their verses are little better than the sort of verses that could be written in favor of the policy of Mr. Coolidge or Mr. Lloyd George. This does not mean that hymns are not good for their own purposes, which are conceivably as noble as the purposes of literature, or more so. It would be as absurd to complain of the literary quality of hymns as it would be to complain of the literary quality of 'God Save the King.' These hymns move most of us as patriotic songs move us, but they seldom give us the double delight of great poetry — the delight in the thing expressed and the delight in the way in which it is expressed. It may be that the ordinary poet, in writing hymns as in writing patriotic poetry, depersonalizes himself and writes in order to express the emotions of human beings in general rather than his own personal vision of the world. That, I think, is the most reasonable explanation of the mediocrity of most religious verse. When we read Wordsworth's 'Daffodils,' we feel that we have been admitted into the intimate secrets of Wordsworth's soul. When we read Bishop Heber's 'From Greenland's Icy Mountains,' however, we do not feel that we have been admitted into the inner sanctuary of Bishop Heber's imagination. He has not re-created the world for us; he has only exhorted us. We suspect him of writing, not in order to communicate his vision of life to us, but in order to do us good. He writes as the advocate of a cause, and not in the pure delight of the imagination. It may be said that the real failure of the hymn lies in the fact that Bishop Heber was not a man of consummate genius, whereas

Wordsworth was. And that is partly the explanation. But, apart from this, we have to face the fact that a number of men of genius have written both religious and secular verse, and that, while the secular verse is beautiful poetry, the religious verse is scarcely worth reading. Campion wrote both profane and religious verse, and, though his religious verse is not entirely negligible, how uninspired most of it is compared with 'Hark all you ladies that do sleep,' or 'Follow thy fair sun, unhappy shadow'! Donne, again, though Dean of St. Paul's, wrote with nobler inspiration of love than of Paradise. Herrick, another clergyman, was happier when singing 'Gather ye rosebuds' or 'Fair daffadills' than when singing the praises of his Creator. He did, indeed, write a charming thanksgiving to God for his house — in which he recounts his blessings in detail in such simple lines as

> Thou mak'st my teeming hen to lay
> Her egg each day;

but the charm of the poem lies in the picture it gives us of Herrick in his earthly house, rather than in opening up to us a vision of the world transfigured by the light of Paradise. It is as though all these poets wrote of love and earthly things with free imaginations, but of religion under some conventional restraint. You will find a parallel to this if you try to imagine what would happen if all the living poets of genius sat down to write poems about the League of Nations. Probably most of them believe in the ideals of the League of Nations, but, however ardently they believed in them, it is almost certain that they would write about it conventionally and without inspiration. They would write, not from the privacy of their souls, but like public speakers, bent upon influencing an audience. And no great literature comes except from the privacy of the soul. Genius, indeed, demands the same freedom and fullness of expression in religious poetry as in secular poetry.

Whenever a great writer tells us as much of the tumult of his soul in a hymn as Shakespeare tells us of the tumult of his soul in his sonnets, we shall have great religious literature. This is no mere prophecy; the miracle has happened in the past. There has been great religious poetry written in one century after another, in which we wander in new fields of the imagination. When we read Henry Vaughan's 'They are all gone into the world of light' or 'My soul, there is a country, Far beyond the stars,' we become sharers in the deepest experiences of a great writer's soul. Here, we feel, are his profoundest confessions, his autobiography. Here he does not disguise his 'powerful feelings' in the language of convention and restraint. He writes of heavenly things, not as an awkward intruder on his best behavior, but as one who is as familiar with them as Shelley with the song of the skylark. We find the same familiarity and fullness of expression in Francis Thompson's *Hound of Heaven*, and in those verses in which he turns the eyes of men to the vision of

> . . . the traffic of Jacob's ladder
> Pitched between Heaven and Charing Cross.

The religious poets, as a rule, close their eyes to the fact that, even to a religious man, Charing Cross is at least as real as Heaven. They forget that, by making Charing Cross more real, they also make Heaven more real, and that a Heaven that is not related somehow to Charing Cross and the fields of earth is to the imagination merely a vague formula. Literature must be human even when it is divine: otherwise it is not literature, but only divinity.

IV

It is not only in religious poetry, but in religious prose, that you find this deficiency of humanity. The inhumanity of the mass of pious books is, as we say, 'notorious.' Thackeray made fun of the worst kind of them in *Vanity Fair* in his references to Lady Emily Sheepshanks and her 'sweet tracts,' 'The Sailor's True Bivouack,' 'The Applewoman of Finchley Common,' 'Thrump's Legacy,' and 'The Blind Washerwoman of Moorfields.' It is possible, even probable, that works of this kind have helped tens of thousands of people to live happier and better lives, but no one has ever claimed that they possess literary value. They are argumentative in purpose, not imaginative. They are as little literary either in motive or in achievement as a pamphlet in favor of or in opposition to vivisection. On the other hand, let an imaginative man begin to write of religion in terms of his own experiences, and immediately we are in a world as enchanting as the world of the great story-tellers. Bunyan had an edifying, as well as a literary, motive in writing *Grace Abounding to the Chief of Sinners* and *The Pilgrim's Progress*, but he obeyed every rule of imaginative literature as he wrote. He founded his books on human life, and on the passions and experiences that were the most wonderful things that he had known. The ordinary religious story tells us that the salvation of a human soul is wonderful, but it does not make us experience the wonder in our own imaginations. Bunyan does this, and he does it, not only because he is a man of genius, but because he can be true to Heaven without being false to Bedfordshire. Like all great religious writers, he is the inhabitant of two worlds. You see how naturally they interpenetrate one another in that beautiful sentence in *Grace Abounding* describing his conversion: 'But upon a day the good providence of God called me to Bedford to work at my calling, and in one of the streets of that town I came where there were three or four poor women sitting at a door in the sun, telling about the things of God.' How full of light, of grace, of the loveliness of earth, that sentence is, as well as of edification! No one can read it without realizing that the human background is as necessary to religious literature as the religious background is to literature in general.

I have referred to the position of the hymn and the tract in literature chiefly in order to make it clear that, in emphasizing the importance of the religious background in poetry and imaginative prose, I am not contending that men of letters are, or should become, the rivals of preachers, or that they have any kind of propagandist function. I am merely proposing an investigation of one of the chief tributaries that feed the river of great literature, and raising the question of how much literature owes to the acceptance of a larger world than the world we touch with our hands and see with our eyes. So far as epic poetry is concerned, the facts undoubtedly suggest that great epics cannot be written of a world deserted by the gods. The importance of the religious background is not quite so clear, however, when we turn from the epic to drama, lyric poetry, and the novel. Most critics affirm that modern literature flowered into genius largely as a result of breaking free from the authority of religion, and the movement of humanism is praised because it released the human mind from the despotism of theology and enabled it to think and to express itself boldly.

Literature, these critics hold, is

essentially heretical, the opponent of the standards of priest and presbyter, and Walter Pater maintained that one of the strongest characteristics of the literature even of the Middle Ages was a 'spirit of rebellion and revolt against the moral and religious ideas of the time.' As evidence of the heretical and skeptical character of mediæval literature, he quoted the memorable passage in *Aucassin et Nicolette*, in which Aucassin, threatened with the pains of Hell if he does not give up Nicolette, cries scornfully: 'In Paradise what have I to do? I care not to enter, but only to have Nicolette, my very sweet friend, whom I love so dearly well. For into Paradise go none but such people as I will tell you of. There go those aged priests, and those old cripples, and the maimed, who all day long and all night cough before the altars and in the crypts beneath the churches; those who go in worn old mantles and old tattered habits; who are naked, and barefoot, and full of sores; who are dying of hunger and of thirst, of cold, and of wretchedness. Such as these enter in Paradise, and with them I have nought to do. But in Hell will I go. For to Hell go the fair clerks and the fair knights who are slain in the tourney and the great wars, and the stout archer and the loyal man. With them will I go. And there go the fair and courteous ladies, who have friends two or three, together with their wedded lords. And there pass the gold and the silver, the ermine and all rich furs, harpers and minstrels, and the happy of the world. With these will I go, so only that I have Nicolette, my very sweet friend, by my side.'

That is certainly not an orthodox speech, but it is a speech made in a world that believed in Heaven and in Hell. Again and again, even in those early days, we find the priest and the poet in conflict, but they carry on their quarrel against a background that contains other worlds than our own. We see another example of this in mediæval Irish literature, in the famous dialogue that took place between Saint Patrick and Oisin, the long-dead pagan hero, who returns from the Country of the Young to Ireland to find all the heroes dust and Christianity triumphant. To Oisin this Christian Ireland is an Ireland in ruins. He weeps for the vanished pagan world that he had known, and Patrick reproaches him for mourning for heathen companions who are now in Hell. 'Leave off fretting, Oisin,' says Patrick, 'and shed your tears to the God of grace. Finn and the Fianna are black enough now, and they will get no help for ever.' 'It is a pity that would be,' replies Oisin, 'Finn to be in pain for ever; and who was it gained the victory over him, when his own hand had made an end of so many a hard fighter?' 'It is God gained the victory over Finn,' Patrick tells him, 'and not the strong hand of an enemy; and as to the Fianna, they are condemned to Hell along with him, and tormented for ever.' 'O Patrick,' cries Oisin, 'show me the place where Finn and his people are, and there is not a Hell or a Heaven there but I will put it down. And if Osgar, my own son, is there, the hero that was bravest in heavy battles, there is not in Hell or in the Heaven of God a troop so great that he could not destroy it.'

Here, again, we have a passage that seems to suggest that literature has an irreligious rather than a religious temper. But the conflict in this dialogue is not really between religion and irreligion, but between two different kinds of religion. Oisin, like Saint Patrick, has a vision of a world that is on no earthly map. He has the Country of the Young to set against the Saint's Heaven. He cries to Patrick: 'The Country of the Young, the Country of Victory, and, O Patrick, there is no lie in that name. If there are grandeurs in your Heaven the same as there are there, I would give my friendship to God. . . .' Not yet has literature reached that stage of post-humanism where the writer has no eyes except for the earth.

V

With the growth of the drama and the growth of the novel in later times, literature did undoubtedly become more exclusively human. But, even when it was reticent in regard to the religious life of man, it was at its greatest when it was written on the assumption that religion was true. Enthusiastic partisans have attempted to prove that Shakespeare was a Catholic or a Puritan, or that he had no religion at all. I do not know what his convictions were, but it is clear that his plays could never have been written except out of an imagination steeped in Christian conceptions, just as the *Œdipus Rex* could never have been written except out of an imagination steeped in Greek religious conceptions. That profound sense of sin which we find in the tragedies of Shakespeare is essentially a Christian sense. If Shakespeare had brought gods as well as ghosts on to the stage, he could not more clearly have made the life of man seem no mere trivial accident between life and death, but an event in a larger universe.

Take the religious conceptions out of *Hamlet*, and rewrite the play in terms of Freudian complexes, and you will lose almost as great a proportion of beauty as you would lose if you rationalized *Paradise Lost*. Hamlet's cry: —

O all you host of heaven! O earth! what else?
And shall I couple hell?

is no mere figure of speech. Hamlet's actions are again and again governed by his sense of the existence of another world. There is scarcely a great scene in the play in which the divine background of life is not taken for granted. It is all the more interesting to discover that Professor Gilbert Murray, in his latest book, contends that the tragedy of Hamlet has even a quasireligious origin and that it is the perfection of an ancient myth, as is the tragedy of Orestes — that, in fact, both tragedies are sprung from the same mythical seed. 'We finally,' he declares, 'run the Hamlet-saga to earth in the same ground as the Orestes-saga: in that prehistoric and world-wide ritual battle of Summer and Winter, of Life and Death, which has played so vast a part in the mental development of the human race and especially, as Sir E. K. Chambers has shown us, in the history of mediæval drama.'

This is not to say, of course, that Shakespeare consciously wrote *Hamlet* as a fable of the ritual battle of Summer and Winter, of Life and Death, the conception of which is one of the sources of both religion and literature. But it is interesting to discover that the plot he chose can tentatively be traced back to its origin in a myth of the battles of the gods. If this is true, *Hamlet* has a doubly religious lineage, and it would probably not be going too far to say that without the religious imagination it would have been as impossible for *Hamlet* to have been written as it would for the books of the Bible to have been written. And, if we turn to the work of later men of genius who have used the dramatic form, we shall find that the greatest of them, however heretical, have for some reason or other been unable to dispense with, or escape from, the supernatural. If it is possible to write dramatic poetry as great as Goethe's *Faust* and Ibsen's *Brand* and *Peer Gynt* without the assumption of a supernatural background— be it only for dramatic purposes—to men's lives, how is it that no one has ever done so? My own theory is that without this assumption the doom of man loses most of its tragic grandeur, and that for this reason the dramatic, like the epic, poet is inevitably forced to return to a Heavenly Muse for inspiration. The more we consider the matter, indeed, the more we are compelled to the conclusion that literature, while often in revolt against orthodoxy, is inextricably bound up with the religious imagination. Literature might almost be said to be sprung from a seed dropped from the tree of religion. It would be possible, I imagine, to show good cause for believing that the novels of Dickens, no less than the Cathedral of Notre Dame, bear an essential relationship to the religious questionings and affirmations of mankind.

The religious element in literature, of course, is much more obvious in poetry than in the novel. 'It utters somewhat above a mortal mouth,' said Ben Jonson of poetry, and the practice of the great poets has endorsed his saying. They see the world transformed by a 'light that never was, on sea or land.' They release us from the actual, or lead us through it to the universal. 'Poetry,' declared Shelley, 'defeats the curse which binds us to be subjected to the accident of surrounding impressions.' Modern fiction seldom defeats this curse. Many modern novelists devote themselves entirely to the description of surrounding impressions. They are content to observe rather than to imagine, and, as we read their realistic novels about some uninteresting young man or woman in revolt against the uninteresting atmosphere of an uninteresting home, we feel the world growing emptier. Life at its best in such novels is a Canterbury pilgrimage without Canterbury, and with the fun left out.

The aridity of most realistic — or, as it might be called, materialistic — fiction, I believe, is largely due to the fact that the realistic novelists are convinced that the world has outgrown Canterbury. Possibly it has, as it outgrew Olympus, but, just as Homer could not have written the *Iliad* without Olympus in the background, and Chaucer could not have written *The Canterbury Tales* without Canterbury in the background, so, in my opinion, a religious background, either expressed or implied, will always be necessary to the production of great literature. It may be a mere coincidence that the greatest fiction of recent times, the Russian, sprang from what rationalists would describe as the most superstitious soil in Europe; but I do not think so. Some people would deny that there is any religious background in Hardy's work, but it is significant that in *The Dynasts* Hardy found himself compelled to imagine an overworld of spirits and angels as part of the setting of human hopes and fears. As we read the plays of Mr. Bernard Shaw, who invented the life force, again we realize the truth of the old saying that 'if God had not existed, we should have had to invent him.'

Everywhere the imaginative man confronted with the mystery of life and death is forced to adopt a religious attitude to life — the attitude of awe before the eternal mysteries. Without it there can be neither the greatest poetry nor the greatest prose — neither the verse of Milton nor the prose of the Bible and Sir Thomas Browne. Great poetry will cease to be written when poets cease to be men for whom the invisible world exists. And if this is true of poetry, is it not reasonable to believe that it is also true of imaginative prose, which is only poetry in its week-day dress?

Whirligigs of Time and Taste
James Southall Wilson

from

Virginia Quarterly Review, vol. 6, no. 1, 1930.

WHIRLIGIGS OF TIME AND TASTE

By James Southall Wilson

Still am I besy bokes assemblynge,
For to have plenty it is a pleasant thynge
For my conceyt and to have them any in honde;
But what they mene do I not understonde.

THE SHYP OF FOLYS—*Alexander Barclay.*

IF I were trying to arrive at a clear standard of judgment of poetry, a philosophy of taste so to speak, I do not know which I should find more confusing, the books about poetry or the poems of the modern poets. Take half a dozen or more of the recent discussions of poetry, and there arises a Babel of confused voices when taste is matched with taste. Here the voices from a piled half dozen of books speak. Of Byron, Mr. Garrod says that it would not

The Profession of Poetry and Other Lectures. By H. W. Garrod. New York: Oxford University Press. $4.50. *Form and Style in Poetry.* By W. P. Ker. New York: The Macmillan Company. $4.00. *The Cycle of Modern Poetry.* By G. R. Elliott. Princeton: Princeton Press. $2.50. *The Lamp and the Lute.* By Bonamy Dobrée. New York: Oxford University Press. $2.00. *The Craft of Poetry.* By Clement Wood. New York: E. P. Dutton and Company. $3.00. *Practical Criticism.* By I. A. Richards. New York: Harcourt, Brace and Company. $4.00. *Lyrical Poetry of the Nineteenth Century.* By H. J. C. Grierson. New York: Harcourt, Brace and Company. $1.25. *Notes on English Verse Satire.* By Humbert Wolfe. New York: Harcourt, Brace and Company. $1.25. *The Whirligig of Taste.* By E. E. Kellett. New York: Harcourt, Brace and Company. $1.25. *The Fate of the Jury.* By Edgar Lee Masters. New York: D. Appleton and Company. $2.50. *Poems* (complete in one volume). By John Masefield. New York: The Macmillan Company. $5.00. *South and East.* By John Masefield. New York: The Macmillan Company. $2.00. *Collected Poems.* By Edwin Arlington Robinson. New York: The Macmillan Company. $5.00. *Collected Poems.* By D. H. Lawrence. 2 vols. New York: Jonathan Cape and Harrison Smith. $5.00. *Dear Judas.* By Robinson Jeffers. New York: Horace Liveright. $2.50. *New Legends.* By Hervey Allen. New York: Farrar and Rinehart. $2.00. *Black Christ.* By Contee Cullen. New York: Harper and Brothers. $2.00. *Greek Gestures.* By William Griffith. New York: The John Day Company. $2.00. *A Riband on My Reins.* By Nancy Byrd Turner. Hartford: E. V. Mitchell. $2.00. *Golden Falcon.* By R. P. Tristram Coffin. New York: The Macmillan Company. $1.50. *Every Soul Is a Circus.* By Vachel Lindsay. New York: The Macmillan Company. $2.75. *The Litany of Washington Street.* By Vachel Lindsay. New York: The Macmillan Company. $3.00. *Collected Poems.* By Gerald Gould. New York: Payson and Clarke. $3.00. *Blue Juniata.* By Malcolm Cowley. New York: Jonathan Cape and Harrison Smith. $2.00. *Ballyhoo for a Mendicant.* By Colton Talbott. New York: Horace Liveright. $2.00. *The Noise That Time Makes.* By Merrill Moore. New York: Harcourt, Brace and surprise him if posterity "held to 'Don Juan' and let the rest go"; Professor Grierson thinks that Byron's feeling never quite wins through to the magic and music of perfect expression; and Mr. Ker wrote, "It is difficult to defend Byron." Mr. Elliott wonders for his part, "Why is so great a poet so greatly in the shade?" Grierson finds Wordsworth to have achieved "the form as well as the spirit of the great ode as we think of that in connection with Pindar and Milton"; and Elliott, discussing "Milton and the Present State of Poetry," exclaims, "We must appeal from Wordsworth to Milton." In discussing M. Bremond's theory of "pure poetry" which the Frenchman begins with Edgar Allan Poe, Mr. Garrod feels "obliged here to say that I think that French criticism will begin again to be what it should be when it finds out that in the history of aesthetic theory Poe has no place." Grierson, speaking of the poets with whom "colour, imagery, and music are the poet's chief interest," declares, "The poet who first . . . set himself to push this tendency a little further and subordinate statement to suggestion, colour and music, especially the last, was the American poet of the thirties and forties, Edgar Allan Poe . . . 'the artful, subtle, irresistible song of Poe, the new music which none that has heard it can forget,' to quote Henley." Such disagreement among the critics might easily bring one to accept Mr. Kellett's conclusion in "The Whirligig of Taste," wherein he traces with disarming urbanity and charm the varying verdict of the generations to-

Company. $2.00. *Poems by Q.* New York: Oxford University Press. $2.50. *Song and Laughter.* By Arthur Guiterman. New York: E. P. Dutton and Company. $2.00. *Indian Earth.* By Witter Bynner. New York: Alfred A. Knopf. $2.00. *Jade Mountain.* By Witter Bynner and Kiang Kang-Hu. New York: Alfred A. Knopf. $3.50. *Animal Lover's Knapsack.* Edited by Edwin Osgood Grover. New York: Thomas Y. Crowell Company. $2.50. *The Book of Sonnet Sequences.* Edited by Houston Peterson. New York: Longmans, Green and Company. $3.50. *Twentieth Century Poetry.* Edited by John Drinkwater, Henry Seidel Canby, and William Rose Benét. Boston: Houghton Mifflin Company. $4.00. *Chief Modern Poets of England and America.* Edited by Gerald DeWitt Sanders and John Herbert Nelson. New York: The Macmillan Company. $3.00. *Braithwaite's Anthology of Magazine Verse for 1929.* New York: Sully and Company. $4.00.

ward English authors, especially poets, and decides, "There is no sure and tangible criterion of beauty.; nothing to which we can cling and say: 'This at least is good and that at any rate is bad.'" I prefer to believe that there is a variable point on the hither and yon sides of which we may be reasonably satisfied to find the good and the bad. "Taste is still conditioned by the palate; and a safe diet makes a clean palate." That is Mr. Garrod's aphorism and I think it a wise one. The sun is no less the blessed sun though a sand-blind critic or a whimsical Petruchio should bid us call it the moon. Mr. Robert Frost once said that two of the great experiences of his life were the first readings at an interval of years of Francis Thompson's "The Hound of Heaven" and Walter de la Mare's "The Listeners." A man recently said the same to me with regard to "John Brown's Body" and "Tristram." I should know which for me has approved himself of a "clean palate."

Mr. Clement Wood in "The Craft of Poetry" has his word for the critics: "They are not poets, or even adequate versifiers, in the living tradition of poetry.; they are academic parasites, a breed of lingual maggots crawling over the poetry, largely the dead poetry, of the past, seeking dumbly to understand its sealed mysteries and reporting dogmatically their erroneous interpretations of the heart's language, dead to them, yet often living to living poetic hearts." His book is a useful handbook for the young student of the forms of poetry, marred to my reading by the author's effort to make the book a "live" one.

"Practical Criticism," by I. A. Richards, is an amusing effort through a study by laboratory method with thirteen poems "to provide a new technique for those who wish to discover for themselves what they think and feel about poetry . . . and why they should like or dislike it." It provides in a big book material and a method more absorbing than cross word puzzles but this elaborate method used for testing poetic taste leaves me cold.

I have not read for a long time a more delightful book of critical discussions than H. W. Garrod's "The Profession of Poetry and Other Lectures." His topics run from Milton and Massenger to A. E. Housman and Humbert Wolfe, from "Poets and Philosophers" to "How to Know a Good Book from a Bad," and his "clean palate" is as well avouched as his sound learning and sane wisdom. He is an entertaining writer but leaves no consciousness of a nervous effort to be so. His philosophy of poetry is a simple one: "Poetry is a particular manner of expressing life"; and "A man does what he is; and what he does is the man." As professor of poetry in the University of Oxford he has lectured on his contemporaries, but believes that the moderns can be judged only by the critic who knows the literature of the past. "We must be wise as Time is, which always works forwards, never backwards." "Form and Style in Poetry" is a posthumous book by Mr. Garrod's predecessor in the Oxford professorship of poetry, W. P. Ker. The first section treats of the ballad; "the Clark lectures" are devoted the first three to Chaucer and the Scottish Chaucerians and the other four to forms of English poetry, including a discussion of the changes of fashion in literature; the twenty-four London lectures, "Form and Style," constitute a wide-ranging discussion of poetry. It is stimulating and enlightening.

Professor G. R. Elliott in "The Cycle of Modern Poetry" has collected a group of essays on such different themes as Byron, Keats, Hardy, Longfellow, and Frost, but a definite critical philosophy and a pliant prose style give his book unity. It has distinction, for Mr. Elliott thinks his own thoughts and thinks them through. He is courageous enough to defend Byron, and in "Gentle Shades of Longfellow" he makes the best case for that poet that I know. Its philosophy is suggested in this sentence: "Every poet knows that when he succeeds in working well he ceases to be an individual; he loses his life to save it." The subjects of Bonamy Dobrée's "The Lamp and Lute" are Ibsen, Hardy, Kipling, E. M. Forster, D. H. Lawrence, and T. S. Eliot. Dobrée's incisive mind cuts to the heart of things. In his "Restoration Comedy," he cleared up as no critic had done before some of the misconceptions about Wycherley and his contemporaries. Mr. Eliot should thank him now for what appears a lucid journey, through "The Waste Land."

Of three books in the "Hogarth Lectures" series, Professor H. J. C. Grierson's "Lyrical Poetry of the Nineteenth Century" is the wisest, Humbert Wolfe's "Notes on English Verse Satire" is the wittiest, and E. E. Kellett's "The Whirligig of Taste" is the wariest. In a hundred and fifty pages, Grierson comes from Xanadu to the Waste Land; for he is not so cautious as Mr. Kellett who follows his Whirligig of Taste on in the land of "those who are safely dead" because he remembers too well their ferocity to "tempt the moderns." I know no other book on modern poetry where so much of sound judgment and taste is evidenced in so small compass. Humbert Wolfe, himself poet and satirist, has written a delicious book. "Very pretty, Mr. Pope," he says, "but you must not call it poetry." His distinctions are clear as to what is good satire and what is poetry. Mr. Kellett has given me my theme and I am grateful; but the charm of his book was that I so rarely agreed with his ideas. He is surely right, though, when he agrees with Mr. Garrod and Mr. Elliott in rooting the present firmly in the past. Though he blames the critic who deals in "triumphant certainties," he affirms himself that "to attempt a revolution may, at times, be necessary; but the revolutionary doctrine must itself have its roots in the past, or it will assuredly fail." That, however, is history not aesthetics, and Mr. Kellett's consistency remains a firm staff for his whirligig.

II

The year is not a great one in the annals of poetry. The

old voices sometimes say over what they have said better and the new ones often leave me feeling that the fine rolling ground swell of poetry fifteen years ago is spending itself in ripples and foam. Mr. Elliott writes, "A Shelley (or even a Keats) aged fifty and producing a kind of poetry comparable in value with the glamorous verse of his youth is unthinkable." The poets of the earlier years of the century have reached fifty. Those whose work is intellectual rather than "glamorous" continue, perhaps with a ripened wisdom, the work of their earlier years. Edwin Arlington Robinson's "Cavender's House" is a clairvoyant psychograph. Edgar Lee Master's "The Fate of the Jury," if it has none of the sharpness of insight and irony that made the "Spoon River Anthology" approach greatness, is about as successful as earlier long narratives by its author. The women among the lyricists suffer less from the years, but then most of them have fewer years to suffer from; and then again, they are never past fifty. But of some living poets a reviewer breathes—to himself, if he is gentle—the exclamation G. R. Elliott uses of Byron, "This author was not so beloved of the gods that he needed to die young."

It is a period of collected editions and anthologies that gather like autumn baskets the fruit of the passing seasons. Masefield and Robinson have both been "collected" before but their new "Collected Poems" easily take the places of importance in the season's poetry. John Masefield stands here to his full stature. The new volume includes all of his fine work in verse, even the new "Midsummer Night." His "South and East," a lovely fantastic narrative, has been issued separately, illustrated in color by Jacynth Parsons; but it has its place in the collected "Poems." More and more, I believe, Masefield will traditionally come to be the representative English poet of his era. In his hands narrative verse, both realistic and romantic, has glowed with livelier color and awakened a deeper human interest by its Chaucerian vividness. And what has contemporary poetry that surpasses in pure lyric loveliness some of his poems of quiet contemplative beauty, or his sonnets?

The Edwin Arlington Robinson volume includes his full work even to "Tristram" and "Cavender House." I should say that until Robert Frost's work is included in one book there will be no collected volume except Poe or Whitman that can challenge this as the best single American volume by one poet. Here is an author who did not need to die young!

Two handsome volumes contain the "Collected Poems" of D. H. Lawrence. Here may be seen—I quote G. R. Elliott's book again—"Mr. D. H. Lawrence circling around seriously, on the back of a super-sexed life-force." Sons of Whitman, D. H. Lawrence and Robinson Jeffers are surely, but one wonders what portents these sex-tortured men are for the future. The picture I see is not of a dark-bearded man riding a goat; it is a sad-faced poet crucified and writhing on a cross. For Lawrence is a rare and a powerful artist. Shrink as one may from his themes, one feels always his power. There is something splendid about the man's audacity. Dobrée quotes T. S. Eliot as differentiating between the intensity of the emotions and "the intensity of the artistic process, the pressure, so to speak, under which the fusion takes place,"—that is what counts. Lawrence has both and is at his best a great artist; but sometimes the pressure of the artistic process cannot fuse the too intense emotions and there is a running out, of the raw stuff, that is painful. Jeffers, by the way, in his "Dear Judas" carries on his own tradition. To some he will again represent a strange new brilliancy; to others part of his work will have the beauty of an exquisitely phrased poetic prose and some of it the ejaculatory violence of the contortions of a sex-maddened nightmare.

What impresses me as I look over the volumes of new verse is that so few voices lift themselves singing (or even shouting) in the memory when the book is closed. Several of Hervey Allen's poems from "New Legends" are memorable. His character narratives and short poems that embody a mood or catch the spirit of a place are most successful. "Sarah Simon" is fresh and beautiful and significant. "Black Christ" from Contee Cullen's volume of that title is not a poem easily forgotten, and some of the epigrams from William Griffith's "Greek Gestures" bite into one's consciousness like old proverbs. His art packs wisdom and irony, into their small compass, as when he makes "A Pupil of Plato" say:

> I seem never to go anywhere,
> In my mind,
> But that I meet Plato coming back.

Poems like "Return" and "Going up to London" from Nancy Byrd Turner's "A Riband on My Reins" chime differently even in an untenacious memory. It is altogether a delightful little book and if it becomes widely known is likely to please more people than many a more "important" volume. These poems have sentiment and are sometimes sentimental; which is to say they are not in the modern vein. They are charming verses by an adequate technician who is very human. There are poems in Robert P. Tristram Coffin's "Golden Falcon" that are memorable for color and the firm beauty, of modeling.

"A Litany of Washington Street" is a sort of dithyramb in prose on the American spirit, and especially Virginia, by Vachel Lindsay. In his new volume, "Every Soul is a Circus," the poem that most reminds me of the power of Lindsay's earlier work is "The Virginians Are Coming Again," of which the author says it is a poetic summary of the "Litany." Mr. Lindsay remains one of the most vigorous and interesting personalities of American poetry, but I do not feel in the new poems the fire and color, the creative force by which his earlier work lives.

They are so different, these poets of the twentieth century, that I am sure the taste of no one reviewer is a match for them all. Here are the cool, beautiful verses of the "Collected Poems" of Gerald Gould proving to me again what competent craftsmen the better English verse-writers are— yet leaving no clear impress of a distinct flavor of his own. "Blue Juniata" of Malcolm Cowley, "Ballyhoo for a Mendicant" of Colton Talbott, and "The Noise That Time Makes" by Merrill Moore are individual but the first two impress me as "too clever by much"; and the crisp intellectual phrases of Merrill Moore pique me into an admiration for qualities that I do not find chiefly poetical. "Poems by Q" is easier to describe. It is a collection of the verse written throughout a fairly long life by Sir Arthur Quiller-Couch. There is no poor work in it: the verse has grace and beauty. It is rarely memorable. Arthur Guiterman's "Song and Laughter" and Witter Bynner's "Indian Earth" are in the manner familiar to their readers. Guiterman's volume has some of his best work. He is skilful and clean-cut in his more serious work and certainly one of the deftest in his lighter moods. Bynner writes on Mexican themes in "Indian Earth," but in "Jade Mountain" he has in collaboration with Kiang Kang-Hu made a translation of Chinese poems that is more satisfying to me than any other I have read. They give me a haunting sense of beauty and human emotion.

New volumes that I have not seen, by poets the quality of whose work is well known, include Grace Hazard Conkling's "Witch and Other Poems," Joseph Auslander's "Letters to Women," Anna Hempstead Branch's "Sonnets from a Lock Box," Eunice Tietjens' "Leaves in Windy Weather," Conrad Aiken's "Selected Poems," and J. C. Squire's "Poems in One Volume." Percy McKaye's "Weather-goose Woo!" and Lizette Woodworth Reese's beautiful autobiographic essays, "A Victorian Village," ought for their poetic qualities—though not verse collections—to be mentioned in this survey.

The anthologies suggest again the multi-colored variety of contemporary verse when for example in the "Animal

Lover's Knapsack," Edwin Osgood Grover with cosmopolitan taste includes animal poems by Edgar A. Guest, Osbert Sitwell, and Robert Bridges. Houston Peterson's wisely chosen gathering of the best sonnet sequences, "The Book of Sonnet Sequences," runs from Sidney to Leonard. It gives emphasis to the contemporaries, including at least ten out of twenty-one sequences that belong to our own day.

Two books worthy of a place on the shelves of every lover of poetry are "Twentieth Century Poetry" edited by John Drinkwater, Henry Seidel Canby, and William Rose Benèt, and "Chief Modern Poets of England and America," by G. D. Sanders and J. H. Nelson. The first is the most wisely chosen anthology of English and American poetry of our day that I know. It leaves out some of the finest individual poems (perhaps because they are so familiar) and gives too few poems from some of the truest poets, but those chosen are not the hackneyed ones, so that it will constitute for most readers a new collection. The "Chief Modern Poets" is the sort of anthology that has long been needed. It includes a large enough group of poems to be representative of each of fifteen of the most distinguished English and eleven American poets. Were I making such an anthology I should make few changes in the list of poets included; my choice of the individual poems, naturally, would be quite different. It is an admirable book for courses studying contemporary poetry and it is a good book to restore the faith of the general reader who from too much reading of strange forms has come to distrust all modern poets; for this is a conservative book.

For a full view of the scope of American contemporary verse Braithwaite's "Anthology for 1929" must be read. William Stanley Braithwaite has been heroic in his task for American poetry. He is broadly inclusive, it must be admitted; but he never selects work below a recognizable standard. His new volume contains a surprizingly large quantity of distinctive and genuine poetry.

Fame Versus Fashion in Literature
Laurence Housman

from

Essays in Divers Hands, n.s., 21, 1945.

Reprinted by permission of the Executors of the
Laurence Housman Estate.

FAME *VERSUS* FASHION IN LITERATURE.

By Laurence Housman, F.R.S.L.

[Read June 7th, 1943.]

The two words " Fame " and " Fashion " begin with the same two letters. After that, they have not a letter in common. And what is true of their spelling is true also of what they stand for : fame and fashion have very little in common. What makes a writer fashionable is not what makes him famous ; in a good many cases a writer would probably have achieved fame, had all—or most of the elements—which made him fashionable been left out. It would be going too far to say that a writer owed his fashion—his popularity—to all his bad qualities, and to none of his good ; but it is very generally true that some at least of the qualities which helped him to fashion are not the qualities which add lustre to his fame in after years. They had been better away.

Let us take some instances from the day before yesterday : the Victorian Age, which, during the last generation, has stepped into history. Two of the most famous writers of that day (famous and fashionable) were Dickens and Tennyson. Now there can be very little doubt that the popularity of Dickens was enormously enhanced by the way he played down to the intellect of his readers—he was sedulously " low-brow." Dickens is never difficult to understand—he is always terribly easy. He dots the I's and crosses the T's of his characters not once but a dozen times. And where his rich humour wears thin (as it sometimes does) he carries on with an arch facetiousness, and a heavy-handed exaggeration of statement, which not merely require no effort of the intellect for their appreciation, but require that the intellect shall be temporarily non-existent, or dormant, to make them at all credible, or tolerable.

Take for instance the letter written by Fanny Squeers to Mr. Ralph Nickleby after Nicholas had thrashed her father. Blind admirers of Dickens regard that letter as a masterpiece of humour. It is humorous in patches ; but parts of it are heart-rending. I will read it to you. I am afraid I shall not read it well, for it hurts my feelings to read it at all. But I will do my best not to put into my tones the malignity towards Dickens that it causes me to feel:

"Sir : My Pa requests me to write to you. The doctors considering it doubtful whether he will ever recover the use of his legs, which prevents his holding a pen. We are in a state of mind beyond everything, and my Pa is one mask of bruises, likewise two forms are steepled in his goar. We are Kimpelled to have him carried down into the kitchen, where he now lays. You will judge from this that he has been brought very low. When your nephew, that you recommended for a teacher, had done this to my Pa, and jumped upon his body with his feet, and also langwedge which I will not pollute my pen with describing, he assaulted my Ma with dreadful violence, dashed her to the earth, and drove her back-comb several inches into her head. A very little more and it must have entered her skull. We have a medical certificate that if it had, the tortershell would have affected the brain. Me and my brother were then the victims of his fury, since which we have suffered very much, which leads us to the arrowing belief that we have received some injury in our insides, especially as no marks of violence are visible externally. I am screaming out loud all the time I write, and so is my brother, which takes off my attention rather, and I hope will excuse mistakes. The monster, having satisfied his thirst for blood, ran away, taking with him a boy of desperate character that he had excited to rebellion, and a garnet ring belong to my Ma, and not having been apprehended by the constables is supposed to have been took up by some stage-coach. My Pa begs that, if he comes to you, the ring may be returned, and that you will let the thief and assassin go ; as, if we prosecuted him, he would only be transported, and if he is let go he is sure to be hung before long, which will save us trouble, and be much more satisfactory. Hoping to hear from you when convenient—I remain Yours and cetrer.
"FANNY SQUEERS.

"*P.S.*—I pity his ignorance and despise him."

Now, as I say, blind admirers of Dickens do not in their pious blindness regard that performance as a crime to be condoned or hidden away ; they regard it as a gem ; and its postscript (which by itself is not so bad) has passed into the currency of our language. Why is it, then, that I find it so painful an exhibition of unscrupulous pandering to the cheapest sense of humour ?

In ultra-burlesque, incredible statements *are* permissible— they are part of the game ; but in comedy, and in novels, some relation to real life is demanded. And when Fanny says that she is " screaming all the time that she writes," and that her

" mother's back-comb was driven several inches into her head, and a little more and it would have entered her skull "—well, as a bit of isolated extravaganza you may be able to laugh at it (I notice that some of you do). But as part of a letter possible to be written by an angry young woman, whose father has been assaulted—it simply won't wash : it is so absolutely unreal, and so abysmally silly. It is supposed to represent a character prone to exaggerate ; and Dickens is not artist enough in restraint to make the exaggeration funny without making it incredible.

Dickens discovered that he could get the cheap laugh from scores of thousands of his fellow-countrymen, and he yielded to the temptation. It helped his popularity, but it has not helped his fame.

Another of his popular qualities was his sentiment, as expressed in the deaths of Paul Dombey, Little Nell, Dora, and other small fry, whose dyings were a delight to the Victorian Age— but delight us less now.

Dickens is famous because he created a collection of characters of extraordinary vividness and variety, which (in spite of, and not because of his absurd exaggerations about them) remain alive. And because his rich sense of life was infectious, he made his readers feel that—filled though it was with the bad and the indifferent as well as the good—life was aboundingly worth while. Not a sense of beauty, but a sense of vivacity, of exuberant spirits, is what we get from Dickens, in full measure pressed down, and bubbling up again. Had Dickens been less extravagant as a caricaturist, and less of a sentimentalist, he would have been just as famous in the present day, but less fashionable in his own.

Then take Tennyson. When Tennyson came into literary being, he was the adored of a small group of sensitively cultured minds ; but the older critics disliked him. A highly educated Don of Cambridge said, "Tennyson is poetry gone mad." Curiously—after his death—the charge against Tennyson was that he was " poetry gone tame." And it is quite true that, in the interval, much of his poetry—in spite of (perhaps because of) its technical delicacy and polish—had gone tame. Tennyson achieved his popularity—his fashion—by a taming process, which luckily did not infect all his poems. It infected ' The May Queen,' ' The Princess,' ' Enoch Arden,' ' The Idylls of the King.' It did not seriously infect ' In Memoriam ' (which was a far bolder poem for its time than we now realize it to be) ;

it did not infect at all his best short lyrics, or ' Maud,' or certain other pieces that one could name. But ' Maud ' with Tennyson's contemporaries was never popular—it was deprecated as morbid, hysterical, and unwholesome. And it is only within the last few years that a Neo-Georgian poet, Mr. Humbert Wolfe, has come along to assert boldly that ' Maud ' is Tennyson's finest poem, and his surest claim (outside his lyrics, and a few other pieces) to permanent fame. What made Tennyson fashionable was not what has re-established his fame. It was not on the ' Idylls of the King ' that his reputation recovered from the slump that followed a few decades after his death. The only one of the Idylls which keeps its hold is ' The Passing of Arthur,' which he cribbed largely from Mallory, and made a very beautiful poem.

One of Tennyson's faults was that he was so self-consciously polished in his diction that sometimes he could not call a spade even remotely a spade. When he wanted to talk of King Arthur's " moustache," he called it " the manly growth which fringed his lip." (And his Victorian readers thought that was poetic.) And it is a curious fact that in poetry poets have allowed themselves to talk freely of a man's beard, but not of his moustache, or of his whiskers. I don't know why; it simply is not done.

Similarly a lover will invite his " Nita," his " Juanita," to lean upon his breast, but not upon his chest. So (with the weight of tradition against it) perhaps one ought not to be too hard upon Tennyson for being so wordily evasive in mentioning King Arthur's moustache, though " bearded lip " would have been more straightforward, and sensible.

Some writers are, of course, in a way " fashionable " (the vogue of a certain set) without achieving popularity in the larger sense. Swinburne was never popular; but he was once very much the vogue. He is less so to-day. That is not to say that Swinburne has no claim to rank among famous poets, only that the degree of his fame is by no means yet settled. But it was with some amazement that I heard, not many years ago, a man of brilliant critical discrimination (himself a poet) say that he would not be surprised if, eventually, Christina Rossetti took higher place than Swinburne. And it amazed me not because I do not think highly of Christina Rossetti myself—she attracts me more deeply than Swinburne; but because it seemed so unlikely that a general estimate of cultured minds could be so drastically reversed; yet there was a critic of penetration, sensitive to the higher values of poetry, saying that it might be so. He may be wrong ; but he may be right. We can't tell. And in the inability of even highly cultured minds to be independent of vogue and fashion, there is something of a mystery. It seems as if fame is necessarily a product of the ages ; that it cannot be conferred with certainty by one generation alone ; and that —as the Church Militant draws for its sustenance on a Communion of Saints reaching all down the ages, as a necessary link with the Church Triumphant (to which its own contemporary virtues cannot so effectively give it access)—so similarly, in the realm of Literature, we require a communicative gift from age to age, to make us more sure of ourselves in giving right judgments concerning Fame. For fashionable judgments we can rely entirely on ourselves.

If you look through the history of Literature, with its contemporary judgments, you will be able to pick out great names which would have died and been buried, had their final disposal been in the hands of their contemporaries. And many names (little considered to-day) would have been foisted upon us as great had the voice of contemporary approval been able to decide the matter. But it was not. It never will be. Therefore, in delivering our dictums of blessing or cursing on the upstarts whom we fashionably adore, let us remember that those judgments are not likely to be final ; and with caution (avoiding arrogance) be courteous towards experiments which are not popular.

For what becomes easily popular seldom lasts. In my own day I have seen reputations go up like a rocket and come down like the stick. It would, perhaps, be unkind to mention names— some are still with us, or have near relations still living. But what is worth notice is that, when those reputations were on the up-grade, they were vouched for by most of our leading critics in poetry and literature. The 1890's were terribly anxious to discover a poet of the first rank (and I still think that some really fine work was then produced). But somehow, most of it had not staying-power. Possibly hereafter some of it may be retrieved, and single pieces may have fame accorded them. For we have, in poetry, instances of single poems to which the rank of fame has been rightly given, where almost everything else by the same writer is forgotten except by students. And, of those single poems, one can say confidently that they are first-rate—that, of their kind, nothing has been better done.

Take, for instance, Drayton, whose 'Agincourt' is a well-known poem, of good but not tremendous quality. But Drayton wrote one sonnet which ranks with the sonnets of Shakespeare, and higher than all Milton's sonnets except his very best. I mean the sonnet which begins—" Since there's no help, come let us kiss and part ! " And in case there may be one or two here who do not know it (though that is unlikely) I will read it to you :

> Since there's no help, come let us kiss and part !
> Nay, I have done, you get no more of me ;
> And I am glad, yea, glad with all my heart,
> That thus so cleanly I myself can free.
> Shake hands for ever, cancel all our vows,
> And when we meet at any time again,
> Be it not seen in either of our brows
> That we one jot of former love retain.
>
> Now at the last gasp of Love's latest breath,
> When, his pulse failing, Passion speechless lies,
> When Faith is kneeling by his bed of death,
> And Innocence is closing up his eyes,—
>   Now, if thou wouldst, when all have given him over,
>   From death to life thou might'st him yet recover.

Take another—John Donne—John Donne never was, and never will be popular ; but he has written passages of love-poetry, and of religious poetry, which are unbeaten in their intensity of bitter and sweet emotion combined. Yet it is only in the last generation that Donne's intellectual stature among the poets has been fully recognized. And there is more likelihood of that belated appreciation being well founded, than had it been accorded in his own day. Between then and now, so great an authority as Pope belittled him ; and Dr. Johnson had not much to say for him of good.

And having mentioned Pope, I have mentioned a writer who was once tremendously the fashion ; but whose fame is not now (and never will be, I think) so great as fashion once made it. Nevertheless he remains (quite worthily within his limitations) a very considerable figure in English literature.

There are signs to-day of an attempt to " boost " him back into a higher rank among the immortals than his qualities warrant ; and I don't wonder that the untidiness of our present school of poetry should have given the expert tidiness of Pope an attraction (by force of contrast) for those whom untidiness repels. Yes, polish—expert tidiness—was one of Pope's pre-eminent qualities.

Now, as parody is a good short-cut for getting in with one's criticism (the 'Two Voices' parody of Wordsworth by J. K. Stephens is one of the best criticisms of him that I know), perhaps a little parody may help to indicate one of the defects of Pope's qualities. And so I have tried to write a small poem in that manner of delicate balance and perfect sobriety, which formed so large a part of the recipe for writing poetry which Pope imposed on the Augustan Age.

In thinking of Pope in terms of parody—a see-saw (you who are his admirers will be horrified to hear) came at once to my mind. And my thought was: "If Pope had set himself to rewrite 'See-saw, Margery Daw,' how would he have done it ?" I suggest that he would have done it (far better no doubt), something like this:

> " Now up, now down, supported, Margery swings ;
> The swaying plank supplies her mind with wings :
> Not uninspired, but with a balanced brain,
> She hurls herself to Heaven—then down again.
> To-morrow Johnny goes—dejected boy—
> To a new master, and to new employ :
> Himself a clod, his fellow-clod he turns,
> Slow as a slug ; and small the wage he earns :
> Copper, not gold, the goal to which he strains,
> A penny-piece the price for all his pains.
> To narrow mind what matters the amount ?
> His goose is cooked—and this the cooked account."

Now the construction of these lines will have told you, I imagine, why, when one comes to parody Pope, one thinks of a see-saw. I think his mother must have swung daily on a see-saw while she was expecting him.

Can a see-saw become the vehicle of genius ? It can ; and Pope is the exponent of that extraordinary fact. You may despise the see-saw as an instrument of locomotion ; but you cannot despise Pope. Nevertheless you can place him (where he has placed himself, with a gusto which shows how thoroughly the instrument satisfied him), you can place him on the see-saw, and can watch him exercising himself upon it by the hour. Of course, parody exaggerates ; but in saying this, do I exaggerate ? Am I not merely stating a patent fact ?

Listen to this : it is from the poem selected in 'The Oxford Book of English Verse' as representing Pope at his best :

> " O ever-beauteous, ever friendly ! tell
> Is it, in Heaven, a crime to love too well ?
> To bear too tender, or too firm a heart,
> To act a lover's or a Roman's part ?

> Is there no bright reversion in the sky
> For those who greatly think, or bravely die ?
> Who can atone (O ever-injured shade !)
> Thy fate unpitied, and thy rites unpaid ?
> No friend's complaint, no kind domestic tear
> Pleased thy pale ghost, or graced thy mournful bier.
> By foreign hands thy dying eyes were closed,
> By foreign hands thy decent limbs composed,
> By foreign hands thy humble grave adorned,
> By strangers honoured, and by strangers mourned."

In that poem of 82 lines, dedicated to the death of an unfortunate lady, I can only find 14 of genuinely inspired and moving poetry. And that does not seem to me the proportion due from a great poet, when he composes a dirge upon a beautiful and blameless character hounded into suicide. Moreover, not only is the mechanism, though skilful, too obvious for spontaneity of feeling to survive, but the sentiment itself does not bear examination; for, in spite of the statement, "Thy fate unpitied and thy rites unpaid," we find, in the concluding lines, that the rites were abundantly paid by foreign hands, and her fate abundantly pitied by strangers. If Pope had really meant us to be heartwrung, he would have accentuated the indifference with which strangers buried her. But, having given grief a graceful turn, Pope is satisfied.

Now if (on referring to that poem) you can convince yourselves that above a quarter of it is more than polished artifice, you will think me unfair, and will be the readier to agree with those who rate him more highly. But I should run some risk of unfairness in any case if I based my criticism on one poem alone. I turn for further illustration, not to less considered examples, but to another of his most famous poems. And there still I find the see-saw at work.

I take the following from the impassioned address of Eloisa to her absent lover, Abelard—giving (in Pope's words) " so lively a picture of the struggles of grace and nature, virtue and passion " :

> " I ought to grieve, but cannot what I ought.
> I mourn the lover, not lament the fault ;
> I view the crime, but kindle at the view,
> Repent old pleasures, and solicit new :
> Now, turned to Heaven, I weep my past offence ;
> Now think of thee, and curse my innocence.
> Of all affliction taught a lover yet,
> 'Tis sure the hardest science to forget !
> How shall I lose the sin, yet keep the sense ;
> And love the offender, yet detest the offence ?

> How happy is the blameless Vestal's lot,
> The world forgetting, by the world forgot :
> Eternal sunshine of the spotless mind !
> Each prayer accepted, and each wish resigned ;
> Desires composed, affections ever even :
> Tears that delight, and prayers that waft to Heaven ;
> Grace shines around her with serenest beams ;
> And whispering Angels prompt her golden dreams."

That is " the lively picture " ; a sparkling performance, tersely phrased, brilliant in diction. But does it really touch your emotions ?.

And now, for my last example—the brilliance of which, I think, nobody can dispute : here is Pope doing the thing he was meant to do, and using his recipe—touching it with sharp, delicate flavours—like the chef of genius that he was :

> " Peace to all such. But were there none whose fires
> True genius kindles, and fair fame inspires ;
> Blest with each talent, and each art to please,
> And born to write, converse, and live with ease ;
> Should such a man, too fond to rule alone—
> Bear, like a Turk, no brother near the throne,
> View him with scornful, yet with jealous eyes,
> And hate for arts which caused himself to rise :
> Damn with faint praise, assent with civil leer,
> And, without sneering, teach the rest to sneer ;
> Willing to wound and yet afraid to strike,
> Just hint a fault, and hesitate dislike,
> Alike reserved to blame, or to commend,
> A timorous foe, and a suspicious friend,
> Dreaded by fools, by flatterers besieged,
> And so obleeging that he ne'er obleeged,
> Like Cato give his little senate laws,
> And sit attentive to his own applause—
> Who but must laugh, if such a man there be :
> Who must not weep, if Atticus were he ? "

Now that is top-notch ; and it is, of its kind, perfect form. Why ? Because it is a satirical attack. Because it is incisive ; because it is giving a series of short sharp stabs ; and because, for dexterity, a stab must be short, sharp, and quick : if it's long, it's blundering ; it must keep its pace even in the final *coup de grâce* which closes the account. And that is why, for this sort of thing, Pope's device of couplets (each couplet containing two antitheses) is a perfect device of its kind. And that is why it is a less suitable device—a device which descends into mechanism— when he tries to apply it to the softer emotions, or to continue, for page after page, what should be kept to give climax and clinch to the venomous sentiments which God sent him into the world to express—better than any other poet I know.

And in order to show you just how, to my mind, this system of antithesis becomes a second-rate thing when removed from satire to sentiment, I take the most antithetical passage from Shakespeare that I can remember, and translate from the manner of Shakespeare into the manner of Pope:

> " Mercy, with mind serene, pursues her path,
> Free from constraint, and far removed from wrath ;
> As the fermenting cloud, distilled in rain,
> Bedews with general moisture hill and plain,
> Twice blest it goes : sheds blessing as it leaves
> The donor's hand, and blesses who receives.
> Where man's most mighty it but adds renown,
> And upon Kings confers a statelier crown.
> Of temporal power the sceptre is the sign—
> Awful in weight, majestic in design ;
> There sits the dread of Kings, and there the fear—
> Guilt cowers or flees, while trembling hope draws near.
> But Mercy plies no lash, and wields no rods,
> She prompts the hearts of Kings to be like God's ;
> And earthly power then shows the more divine,
> If Justice melts when Mercy makes the sign."

For that sort of thing Pope's method imposes shackles which even the genius of Pope (so ready of wit, so quick in turn of phrase) is unable to escape.

From Pope (too highly esteemed in his day) let us turn to one whose fortune was just the opposite : one of the most remarkable examples in English literature of contemporary neglect, followed, after a considerable interval, by fame.

Sixteen years ago the centenary of William Blake's death was commemorated by the unveiling of a tablet to his memory in St. Paul's Cathedral. To the critics of his own day, Blake—long-lived, frugal, industrious, but poverty-stricken—was not merely " poetry gone mad "—he *was* mad, and nothing else. The charge of madness was allowed to wipe out from the comprehension of his contemporaries (except a very few : Charles Lamb and Wordsworth were two of them) any critical sense of the extraordinary beauty and value of his poems and paintings. And even 50 years ago (when I edited a selection of his writings and poems) a leading critic, Mr. Andrew Lang, began his review of it with the words : " It is the mark of a clique to admire Blake." It was true enough then—if the word " clique " means a small minority.   But it would be difficult to-day to find anyone of serious literary standing who (whatever he thought of Blake's sanity) failed to recognize the rare and high qualities of his genius.

Now the case of Blake, and the life-long neglect and dislike of him by his contemporaries, brings up the question of the effect of environment and of contemporary modes of thought and fashion on a man's work—the work of a man of genius.

I once heard a lecturer make the acute remark that, had Shakespeare lived in the reign of George II, he could not have been anything like the Shakespeare we know ; he could not have produced so well, or so spontaneously.   For a man of his temperament the Age would have been out of joint ; and his genius could **only have** revealed itself with difficulty.   That unpropitious atmosphere would either have damped down, or exacerbated, the workings of his brain.   Undoubtedly that did happen to Blake. He suffered from his environment.   His Age would not have him ; and, as a consequence, he rebelled against it, kicked violently, forced his note, and said things extravagantly, to annoy and puzzle a generation which (from his point of view) was extraordinarily stupid.

The unimaginative assault and battery which was paid out to Blake by that unreceptive Age (and paid back by him more imaginatively in explosive fireworks, which still do his fame some harm) was also, in a certain sense, directed by that same Age against Shakespeare.   But Shakespeare was dead, so it did not affect him ; it only affected his work in the way it was published and presented during the 18th century.

The mangling (and "improvement" to suit contemporary taste) of Shakespeare's Plays had begun under the Restoration ; and during the 18th century it went on.   Why ?   For the simple reason that Shakespeare and the 18th century had not the same sense of beauty, or the same sense of truth, or the same sense of life's values.

"Exuberance is beauty," said Blake.   "Exuberance is bad taste" said the 18th century.   And Shakespeare, in his large grasp, and love, and interpretation of human nature was exuberant.

The 18th century had the defects of its qualities ; it could not help it.   Shakespeare had also the defects of *his* qualities ; but they were better qualities.   And so, to an Age which did not specially value those qualities—they were not merely a falling short of the perfection aimed at ; they were in bad taste.   What else did the 18th century dislike, or wish to make different ?   Its undervaluation of Shakespeare was not likely to stand alone. And it didn't.

Not only was the 18th the century which least understood Shakespeare (being least in sympathy with all that Shakespeare stood for), it was also lacking in sympathy or understanding for two other great influences of the past—Christianity, and Gothic Architecture. (It is, of course, of the cultured 18th century that I am now speaking.)

John Wesley had nothing in common with the cold culture of the Age in which he lived ; his living Christianity seemed shockingly out of taste. Similarly Gothic Architecture had become a curiosity : like Christianity, people preferred to see it in ruins ; it was more suitable to look at than to live with. And Horace Walpole's reconstruction of Gothic in a toy version for his own domestic amusement was no more than a pet fancy—on a par with the contemporary ' Tapestries ' which Miss Lindley worked in imitation of oil-paintings, and framed into pictures. And that being the taste of the Age, we find that at the theatre King Lear was made tolerable by being given a happy ending. And Garrick's acting versions of other plays are an accurate measure (in their departure from the text) of the separation between Shakespeare and the 18th century.

Two of its most prominent characters passed judgments on him which are representative enough to be worth quoting. " Was there ever such stuff as Shakespeare wrote ? " exclaimed George III irritably ; while Dr. Johnson declared that you could not find anywhere in Shakespeare six consecutive lines of good poetry.

And yet Dr. Johnson had a great mind—was, indeed, a most sensible person ; and if he sometimes said foolish things, those foolish things nevertheless had sense to back them ; he said them with a reason.

There was, therefore, something the matter, either with Shakespeare or with the 18th century to cause this critical coldness in a great mind so representative of its Age to the form of Shakespeare's poetry (Johnson did not have to question his greatness).

That matter was (as I have already said) that their defects ran in opposite directions. The 18th century was over-correct in its literary conventions—too much ruled by rule, and too limited in vision, to be able to think or write freely.

Shakespeare, on the other hand, had no use for correctness—followed no rule, obeyed an almost limitless vision, was careless of scholarship, and had an exuberant love of human nature, which he expressed on an heroic scale.

A critic for whom I have a natural respect (A. E. Housman), comparing the perfections of Milton with the imperfections of Shakespeare, said that Milton was a great artist, and that Shakespeare was not : that Shakespeare lacked Milton's great gift of " sobriety."

That is the opinion of a fine scholarly mind. I am not scholarly ; and perhaps it is for that reason that I am inclined to retort, " Who but a pedant wants sobriety from Shakespeare ? " Had Shakespeare expressed himself with sobriety, how much of Shakespeare would have remained ?

But from the Restoration period onward, producers of Shakespeare for the stage were constantly trying to reduce him to sobriety, by pruning down the too exuberant language of his characters. And so, when Macbeth (his overwrought speech expressive of an overwrought mind) cries out to the messenger of Doom :

> " The Devil damn thee black, thou cream-faced loon !
> Where got'st thou that goose-look ? "

Davenant comes along, and reduces the phrase to " sobriety " by making Macbeth say : " Now, Friend, what means thy change of countenance ? " And the character of Macbeth, and the state of Macbeth's mind—sacrificed to sobriety of statement—become, for the moment, non-existent. Macbeth is wiped off the stage.

But though Shakespeare often indulged in overwrought phrases with less excellent dramatic excuse than in the instance I have just given, Shakespeare was always consciously using a form which helped to produce a cumulative effect.

You hear a passage of Shakespeare at his worst, it is still in the Shakespeare style of big utterance ; it remains consistent—of a piece—with Shakespeare at his best : with the scale, that is to say, on which Shakespeare moulded his characters, and gave them accompanying speech. But (and here is the clue to the dramatic value of Shakespeare's range of style) you might hear a short, specially selected passage of Shakespeare at his dramatic best, and not know that it was Shakespeare, unless you came on it in its dramatic setting ; and then—if you were intelligent— you would say (not because of its form, which might be extraordinarily stark and simple ; but because of the greatness of its invention for the place in which you found it) that nobody but Shakespeare could have thought of it—just there.

Take, for instance, this :

> " Thou'lt come no more for ever   .   .   .
> Never, never, never, never, never.
> Pray you, undo this button. Thank you, Sir."

Disjointed from its setting, it is nothing : there is no style, no form about it.   One line of it is even bad verse—bald, uneventful, monotonous.   But in its place, in that last scene when Lear is dying, with Cordelia dead in his arms, it becomes a tremendous invention, a thing of absolute genius.

Out of that general background of large utterance to which he scales his characters, comes now and then this utter poignancy of the vox humana, stark, and stripped of ornament, terse, direct, simple.

That is what Shakespeare's form leads up to : to moments when mere form disappears : and the very simplest thing that can be said has a tremendous significance—pure human nature emerges pinnacled in tragedy—brought to an ultimate simplicity that is more revealing of the springs of being than any ornament of imagery or rhetoric, however grand.

The actual range of Shakespeare's form is, therefore, very wide —from the most elaborate language to the most simple ; and it has that range for dramatic reasons—not for mere literary. That is a point which critics sometimes miss.   There are occasions in the play when dramatic value is far more important than literary value, and, Shakespeare being a dramatic artist, is the greater artist because his form varies.   In some of his great scenes " sobriety " would be out of place.   It is nonsense to demand it.

To go back, then, to this question of the separation which had arisen between the mind of Shakespeare and the mind of the 18th century—How did it arise ?   How should one define it ?

One might account for a great deal of it in a single word— " Enthusiasm." Shakespeare, in his exuberance, was of an enthusiastic temperament ; the 18th century was not.   The very word had (for the 18th century) a reprobate meaning. I turn to an 18th century dictionary, and there I find—" Enthusiasm— a vain belief of private revelation ; a vain confidence of Divine favour ; heat of imagination."   " Enthusiast—one who vainly imagines a private revelation ; one who has a vain confidence in his intercourse with God ; one of a hot imagination."   And it is only reluctantly, as a last alternative, that the more favourable definition is conceded, "One of elevated fancy, or exalted ideas."

The earlier definition has etymology behind it ; but the word "vain" is opprobriously thrown in without any etymological justification whatever. And so, maybe, to many cultured minds of the 18th century, Shakespeare was " a vain fellow," a man who, by his enthusiastic language, showed that he had a vain confidence of his intercourse with God, in terms of beauty.

Now if Shakespeare needs any excuse for the exuberance of his language (the high key in which he pitched most of his dramatic dialogue), it should be remembered that he was doing, on the plastic stage of his own day, what (in the pictorial stage of our day) is not so much required. Shakespeare's dramatic figures stood out on a platform-stage, without scenery, and practically without background ; with the audience on three sides of it. And the whole of his atmosphere and environment had to come from the gestures and language of the actors. When they spoke, they provided their own scenery, which we now provide for them. They had to do a good deal more (when they spoke) than actors have to do nowadays in order to give the setting. They carried the scenery on their backs, as it were, and spoke it in words. That condition alone made it impossible for Shakespearean drama to be naturalistic in form. But it did, nevertheless, aim at giving you human nature. The large utterance of Shakespeare's characters tends to give them a larger scale, enabling the actors to hold the stage in the difficult circumstances of having so much more than themselves to express. And this particular condition of the Elizabethan stage suited the exuberant temperament of Shakespeare ; he adapted himself to it *con amore*.

But if you were to ask me if there was not also a fashion in Shakespeare's day, which made merely for popularity, and which has done some harm, if not to Shakespeare's fame, to the form in which his Plays have come down to us, I should be bound to say " yes."

Shakespeare's Plays would have been better than they are (more acceptable, more completely appealing to the mind of posterity) had they not been affected—adversely affected—by certain fashions of his own day. Certain things which then made for popularity give them a certain unreality now. They are less convincing, less satisfying to us, because they accepted certain rather cheap conventions, devices, and make-shifts, which the public of his day liked and were always ready to swallow whole.

The public of his day liked ghosts—they demanded them ; if you had a murder, you almost always had to have a ghost also. Without the ghost (if it was murder of an important person) the murder was not complete.

You have a curious instance of that in Webster's 'Vittoria Corombona' or 'The White Devil.' The wife of one of the characters has been murdered. The husband, who does not know it, begins thinking of her. Immediately her ghost enters. The husband does not know that it is her ghost; he does not know that the ghost is there at all. But the author wants the audience to know; and so, there the ghost stands, while in soliloquy he talks about his wife. And when he has done talking of her, the ghost goes again. It is quite silly; but the fashion of that day required that sort of thing, and got it—got it from Shakespeare along with the rest. And sometimes (not always) Shakespeare's ghosts would be better away. We could do better without them.

Another of the contemporary stage-fashions of Shakespeare's day, which has become unreal to us, was the comedy—or the tragedy—carried to fantastic lengths—of mistaken identity— two people exactly alike; sometimes a boy and a girl: twins. (Of course on the Shakespearean stage both actors were boys, which made it just a shade more possible.) But though we accept that stage convention to-day, for the sake of laughter, it is not in the least convincing. And if it had not been the fashion of his day, acceptable, and readily swallowed by all playgoers, Shakespeare would hardly have condescended to it, although in comedy the fairy-tale element in which the play is cast may give it a sort of rightness. But when you have similar devices of mistaken identity in tragedy the result is sometimes lamentable in its mock make-believe.

Take, for instance, the play 'Cymbeline,' which contains one of the loveliest of Shakespeare's female characters—Imogen. But that play is almost ruled out for modern audiences by the crude and clumsy device of Cloten's headless body, left a nasty mess for Imogen to weep over. And because the body wears the clothes of her husband, she proceeds to identify him, with a particularity which leaves one gasping at the nonsensicalness of an age which could swallow such stuffing devoid of all reason:

> " ' I know,' she cries—
> I know the shape of his leg; this is his hand!
> His foot Mercurial, his martial thigh,
> The brawns of Hercules; but his Jovial face—
> Murder in Heaven! 'Tis gone!'"

Murder in Heaven! 'Tis nonsense! Here you have a devoted wife examining the anatomy of another man, piece by piece, and swearing it to be her husband's, with a particularity which I can only call "luridly domestic." With an Elizabethan audience that sort of thing (in spite of its wild improbability) went down. They liked it.   We don't.

As for 'Titus Andronicus,' that orgy of bloodshed and mutilation—I don't know what the latest scholars say about it : for myself, I devoutly hope that Shakespeare did not write it.

There you get two instances of the bad effects of fashion on the great literature of its day. We meet with them, it is true, in plays—one negligible ; the other—one which (in spite of its many beauties) does not take decisive rank.

But I will give you instances, from two of Shakespeare's finest plays, where it seems to me that fashion has imposed on him a stage-device which had been better away.   In 'Julius Caesar,' in the tent-scene (after the quarrel with Cassius, and the military discussion, and the Boy's song that follow), Caesar's ghost appears to Brutus.   And if the Ghost must appear at all, it is done exceedingly well.   But I cannot help feeling that Brutus was not the sort of character to see ghosts visibly.   Indeed, his way of dealing with the Ghost when it appears shows a philosophic acceptance of the pass in which fate has landed him, which the apparition does not trouble.   Brutus needs no ghost for the stirring of his conscience, or the rousing of his fears ; for it does neither.   But the audience of Shakespeare's day did need it ; so—enter ghost !

Ghosts have another drawback for modern audiences, in addition to their frequent superfluousness.   When the Ghost appears and all see it alike (as they do see it in the opening scene of 'Hamlet'), then the apparition is consistent, and the scene remains all of a piece.   But in the scene between Hamlet and his mother (when Hamlet sees it and she does not) credibility is strained. If Horatio and the rest saw the Ghost on the ramparts, why does not Hamlet's mother see it also ?—especially as she is a rather guilty party to the business ?   Still, I admit, there is no possible getting rid of the Ghost in Hamlet.

But the other instance, to which I wish specially to call attention, is in that ghost-ridden tragedy 'Macbeth.'   That play is, of course, so steeped in the supernatural (in the scenes with the witches and in the whole machinery of Doom foretold) that ghostliness has its right setting.   But in that play there is one very effective scene, where an apparition is described but remains invisible.   I mean in Macbeth's dagger-soliloquy, beginning :

" Is this a dagger that I see before me—
The handle toward my hand ? "

It is reported in the annals of the stage, that at some time or another, upon the opening of that speech, it was customary for a material dagger to be let down from the flies, like bait to a fish, for Macbeth to bite on. Nobody would do anything so foolish to-day. The haunted state of Macbeth's mind is better depicted if no dagger is there.

But apply that—I ask you to apply that same consideration to the banquet scene, where the Ghost of the murdered Banquo comes and occupies the seat which is waiting for Macbeth. As the scene is written, nobody sees the Ghost except Macbeth. Even Lady Macbeth, his partner in guilt, sees nothing.

Now I am convinced that that scene would be very much more effective, and terrible, and haunting, if no Ghost appeared ; if the chair were to remain vacant while Macbeth (to the bewilderment of all present) speaks to a Ghost which only he sees. That, I believe, has been done at the " Old Vic." in London ; and it is a thoroughly sensible thing to do. And I believe that Shakespeare would have done it, had he not been tied down by the stage-fashion of his day, which—after a murder—demanded on all possible occasions a visible ghost.

Well, Fame *versus* Fashion has been my subject to-day ; I have tried to show by example how little fashion is helpful to fame ; how sometimes it imposes (even on great writers) the acceptance of puny devices to which they would not have descended had they been more free from the tricks and entanglement of contemporary taste.

*   *   *   *   *

A good deal of what I have been saying to-day has probably been said by others. I do not suppose that I am the only lover of Shakespeare who finds his mistaken identities and his long-armed coincidences too good to be true, and therefore a little unreal in their dramatic effect ; and his Ghosts sometimes a little superfluous, a little trying. These are heresies—if heresies they be—which I share with others.

But I would like, before I close, to give you one suggestion— one bold bad piece of innovation, which, I believe, is entirely my own. . . . It flies in the face of all tradition ; and yet, I believe, it is right, and (for stage purposes) an improvement.

I believe that Lady Macbeth's last appearance is not when she makes her exit in the sleep-walking scene. It is true that she never speaks again ; but I believe that she appears again, and that in ' Macbeth ' (which shows signs of having been hastily completed, or left incomplete) there is a lost stage-direction, which (had it been given) would have accounted for her death.

I believe that Lady Macbeth committed suicide. It is a much-debated point ; but I will give you my reasons.

I would begin by saying that William Shakespeare was a dramatist who knew what he was about. He was no bungler; and if he puts into the mouth of one of his characters a significant remark, he does so for a reason.

In 'Macbeth' two of the characters make significant remarks, for which there is no reason, unless Lady Macbeth committed suicide. And if she did commit suicide, why (when you hear the cry of the women) are you not told that it was suicide ? Why did Shakespeare prepare you for suicide, and then not tell you of it ?

It is, I suggest, because something has been left out which would have told you.

The first significant remark that I refer to is that made by the Doctor, in the sleep-walking scene, when (after the exit of Lady Macbeth) he tells the Waiting-woman what to do . . . " Look after her," he says.

> " Remove from her the means of all annoyance,
> And still keep eyes on her."

Now there. clearly, the Doctor indicates that she may attempt her own life ; all such " means of annoyance " are, therefore, to be kept out of her reach, and she is to be watched.

Shakespeare, I repeat, was no bungler. Unless so significant a warning was to be followed by the event, why give it ? . . .
The second significant remark is made by Malcolm, in the closing speech of the play. We have not seen Lady Macbeth die ; we have only heard the wail of the women and the brief statement of the fact :

> " The Queen, my Lord, is dead."

Malcolm, in his final speech (having referred to Macbeth as " This dead butcher), then goes on :

> " and his fiend-like queen,
> Who, as 'tis thought, by self and violent hands,
> Took off her life."

Again I say—Shakespeare was no bungler. Had it not been true, he would not have made Malcolm say so. Therefore it seems quite certain that she did " by self and violent hands " (" hands " mind you) take off her life.

And now the question that I raise is this : Is there not an opportunity—a point in the action of the play—where the audience can see the Doctor's caution against leaving means of annoyance within her reach, break down ?

I believe there is. The stage-directions of most of Shakespeare's plays are few and incomplete. Often, for lack of them, producers are badly puzzled. It is not, therefore, unlikely that the stage-direction for the last silent entry and exit of Lady Macbeth has been left out of a play which seems to have been finished but roughly.

Remember what the stage of Shakespeare's day was like : a platform, with a small inner stage at the back, used sometimes for interiors, and above it a gallery, with an upper entrance of its own.

In the last Act there is a scene where Macbeth (accompanied by the Doctor) receives news of the English invasion, and calls for his armour. The Attendant says that the armour is not yet wanted : 'tis too soon. But Macbeth will have it. Shakespeare wants it for this scene. Why?

The Doctor is there, waiting for consultation. Why is the armour brought on before it is really needed ? Shakespeare had a reason for bringing the armour on. And so, armour is brought out, and presumably arms also. And if these are brought down or handed down from the gallery to those below, then it is quite possible that, on the wooden balustrade, a sword or dagger is left lying. Then, while Macbeth's armour is being put on him by an attendant), he talks with the Doctor. The subject of their talk is the Queen's illness. . . . And as I see that scene, Macbeth, impatiently putting on his armour, and impatiently listening to the Doctor—listening with a growing impatience to that hopeless account of a sickness that cannot be cured—I see the Queen enter the gallery above, and stand listening. All hope has gone out of her life ; and now the omens of doom are gathering thick and fast. Her hand falls on the dagger that has been left lying. She takes it, turns, and goes in.

A minute later you hear the cry of the women. Macbeth—in the middle of a speech defiant of coming fate—stops to inquire, " What is that noise ? "

" It is the cry of women, my good Lord."

And Macbeth (with a premonition of what has happened) makes the speech which begins :

" I had almost forgot the taste of fears,"

and ends :

> " I have supped full with horrors ;
> Direness (familiar to my slaughtered thoughts)
> Cannot once start me . . .   Wherefor was that cry ? "

(Word has come)

> " The Queen, my Lord, is dead."

And how she has died, the audience knows, and needs no more words to tell it.

There, then, is my proposed innovation : a new scene for Lady Macbeth, to explain the manner of her death—a silent soliloquy, spoken by action without words—

> " Is this a dagger that I see before me ? "

I offer it to any producer who may be here, free, gratis, for nothing ; for I should really like to see it done. And it may interest you to know that Sybil Thorndike has promised me that if she ever plays Lady Macbeth again, she will try out my innovation on an English (or a Scottish) audience—if the producer will allow her to do it. So I still live in hopes of being able to give Shakespeare a " leg up " in one of his scenes. If that ever happens I shall be a proud man.

Poetry and Society
Marshall McLuhan

from

Poetry, 84, 1954.

POETRY AND SOCIETY

Dream and Responsibility, by Peter Viereck. University Press (Washington, D.C.). $1.50.

THE CONCERN HERE is with "four test cases of the tensions between poetry and society": "1. Ezra Pound. 2. Stefan George. 3. Art vs. Propaganda. 4. The Poet in the Machine Age." Why does Mr. Viereck seem to be out of his depth in handling these familiar and even banal topics? Is it that he is a real David rattling about in the armor of Saul? If so, the sooner he resorts to the humble sling the better. At mid-century there are too many readers who still have some slight recollection of the prose performances of Yeats, Wyndham Lewis, and Valéry to act as a standard for the great themes of dream and responsibility. That this standard still obtains where these themes are concerned may be unfortunate for Mr. Viereck, but it may well be for the good of letters.

No new light is thrown by the first essay on the problems of the Pound case or the com-Pound ghosts evoked by the art of the *Cantos*. No critic or poet could be the worse for some mastery of the *Cantos*, and without such mastery no critic should venture to guide the perplexed into the fields of light. Mr. Viereck leaves the inquiring reader with the uneasy sense that an assured rhetorical manner is being substituted for actual perception and rejection of poetry.

A great deal could be done to reveal the theology underlying the *Cantos*. Presumably this theology has something to do with both the politics and the poetics of the *Cantos*. Why have all the critics of Pound avoided mention of his theology? Why have they failed to state their own? What are the divergent theologies behind the "vertical" and "horizontal" symbolisms and poetics of Blake and Mallarmé (and of Yeats and Eliot) as cited by Mansell Jones in *Modern French Poetry?* John Lindberg's recent *Foundations of Social Survival* does go into the theology behind vertical and horizontal, but in the sphere of politics only.

In discussing Stefan George and the Nazis, Mr. Viereck has to hint, at least, at the theological issues. One aspect of the issue is the war between cognitive and magical views of art and its social functions. Is the artist a substitute for the witch-doctor or is he the witch-doctor in disguise? George proclaims his adherence to the magical position in commenting on Napoleon's remark: "I love power as an artist." George retorted: "I love art as power." Everybody is familiar with Eliot's magical theories of art and communication, which he shares with Coleridge and many others. If the health of letters in the Western world depends on the conceptual, rationalist tradition in opposition to the magical poetics, then why not say so? Why impugn the products of "magical" poets when it is their theory that is repugnant?

Perhaps such a view as this last is natural to Catholics, for whom both vertical and horizontal theories, and the dichotomies of both time and space, rational and irrational, are, ontologically, nonsense.

Mr. Viereck concludes his remarks about art *vs.* propaganda with a statement about the Soviet condemnation of poets who express "emotions of private love and loneliness" and concludes that: "Whatever expresses ethics, beauty, and love with genuine individuality, is thereby a blow against tyrants (whether communists, fascists, or domestic American thought-controllers)."

This provides his transition to *The Poet in the Machine Age*. Here the dilemma of the vertical or individualist theory becomes acute. The machine was made in the Western world. It is a product of individualist genius and tenacity. But its effects are entirely collectivist and horizontal. As gimmick, the machine is useful. As object, as companion, as environment-shaper, it is magical. Marx was right to that extent. He saw that the machine would necesarily transform human feeling and sensibility. It would change habits of association and work. It would re-structure one's idea of the world and of oneself. It was the revolution. For the vertical partisans it was the Trojan Horse. The vertical poet and critic approaches the machine as a theme. He wonders what to say *about* it, quite unaware that the machine has already had a great deal to say about him, having altered the sense of rhythm and changed the shape of his life, as well as having modified his attitude toward himself and others. The machine could only have been made in the West—but its spiritual home, as Bergson saw, is the East, where the entire cosmos is a giant assembly line for the psychic bits and parts of time's masquerade. It is for that reason that horizontal poetics can cope with some of the features of mechanized culture and that vertical poetics cannot. But vertical and horizontal alike are poor substitutes for reason and reality.

MARSHALL MC LUHAN

Myth and Mass Media
Marshall McLuhan

from

Myth and Myth-making, H.A. Murray (ed.). George Braziller,
New York, 1960.

Myth and Mass Media

MARSHALL McLUHAN

WHEN AN ATTEMPT is made to bring the relatively articulated concept of "myth" into the area of "media"—a concept to which surprisingly little attention has been given in the past—it is necessary to reconsider both "myth" and "media" in order to get at relevant data. For example, English is itself a mass medium, as is any language employed by any society. But the general use of the phrase "mass media" would seem to record an unfavorable valuation of new media, especially since the advent of the telegraph, the telephone, moving pictures, radio, and television. These media have had the same kind of drastic effect on language and culture that print had in Europe in the sixteenth century, or that it is now having in other parts of the world.

It might even be well to avoid so highly charged a phrase as "mass media" until a little more thought can be given to the problem. Languages as human artifacts, collective products of human skill and need, can easily be regarded as "mass media," but many find it difficult to consider the newer media deriving from these languages as new "languages." Writing, in its several modes, can be regarded technologically as the development of new languages. For to translate the audible into the visible by phonetic means is to institute a dynamic process that reshapes every aspect of thought, language, and society. To record the extended operation of such a process in a Gorgon or Cadmus myth is to reduce a complex historical affair to an inclusive time-less image. Can we, perhaps, say that in the case of a single word, myth is present as a single snapshot of a complex process, and that in the case of a narrative myth with its peripety, a complex process is recorded in a single inclusive image? The multilayered montage or "transparency," with its abridgement of logical relationships, is as familiar in the cave painting as in cubism.

Oral cultures are simultaneous in their modes of awareness. Today we come to the oral condition again via the electronic media, which abridge space and time and single-plane relationships, returning us to the confrontation of multiple relationships at the same moment.

If a language contrived and used by many people is a mass medium, any one of our new media is in a sense a new language, a new codification of experience collectively achieved by new work habits and inclusive collective awareness. But when such a new codification has reached the technological stage of communicability and repeatability, has it not, like a spoken tongue, also become a macromyth? How much compression of the elements of a process must occur before one can say that they are certainly in mythic form? Are we inclined to insist that myth be a reduction of collective experience to a visual and classifiable form?

Languages old and new, as macromyths, have that relation to words and word-making that characterizes the fullest scope of myth. The collective skills and experience that constitute both spoken languages and such new languages as movies or radio can also be considered with preliterate myths as static models of the universe. But do they not tend, like languages in general, to be dynamic models of the universe in action? As such, languages old and new would seem to be for participation rather than for contemplation or for reference and classification.

Another way of getting at this aspect of languages as macromyths is to say that the medium is the message. Only incidentally, as it were, is such a medium a specialized means of signifying or of reference. And in the long run, for such media or macromyths as the phonetic alphabet, printing, photography, the movie, the telegraph, the telephone, radio, and television, the social action of these forms is also, in the fullest sense, their message or meaning. A language is, on the one hand, little affected by the use individuals make of it; but, on the other hand, it almost entirely patterns the character of what is thought, felt, or said by those using it. And it can be utterly changed by the intrusion of another language, as speech was changed by writing, and radio by television.

Is, then, what concerns us as "myth" today a photograph or "still" shot of a macromyth in action? As a word uttered is an auditory arrest of mental motion, and the phonetic translation of that sound into visual equivalence is a frozen image of the same, is not myth a means of static abstraction from live process? A kind of mythmaking process is often associated with Hollywood and with Madison Avenue advertising agencies. So far as advertisements are concerned, they do, in intention at least, strive to comprise in a single image the total social action or process that is imagined as desirable. That is, an advertisement tries both to inform us about, and also to produce in us by anticipation, all the stages of a metamorphosis, private and social. So that whereas a myth might appear as the record of such extended metamorphosis, an advertisement proceeds by anticipation of change, simultaneously anticipating causes with effects and effects with causes. In myth this fusion and telescoping of phases of process becomes a kind of explanation or mode of intelligibility.

What are the myths by which men have recorded the action of new media on their lives? Is there significance in the fact that the Oedipus myth has so far not been found among the preliterate? Is the action of literacy in the shaping of individualism and nationalism also severe on kinship structures? Is the Gorgon myth an account of the effects of literacy in arresting the modes of knowledge? Certainly the Cadmus myth about letters as the dragon's teeth that sprang up armed men is an image of the dynamics of literacy in creating empires. H. A. Innis in his *Empire and Communications* has given us a full exegesis of the

Cadmus myth. But the Gorgon myth is in much greater need of exegesis, since it concerns the role of media in learning and knowing. Today, when by means of a computer it is easy to translate a mere blueprint of an unbuilt plane into a wind-tunnel test flight, we find it natural to take all flat data into the domain of depth interpretation. Electronic culture accepts the simultaneous as a reconquest of auditory space. Since the ear picks up sound from all directions at once, thus creating a spherical field of experience, it is natural that electronically moved information should also assume this spherelike pattern. Since the telegraph, then, the forms of Western culture have been strongly shaped by the spherelike pattern that belongs to a field of awareness in which all the elements are practically simultaneous.

It is this instantaneous character of the information field today, inseparable from electronic media, that confers the formal auditory character on the new culture. That is to say, for example, that the newspaper page, since the introduction of the telegraph, has had a formally auditory character and only incidentally a lineal, literary form. Each item makes its own world, unrelated to any other item save by date line. And the assembly of items constitutes a kind of global image in which there is much overlay and montage but little pictorial space or perspective. For electronically moved information, in being simultaneous, assumes the total-field pattern, as in auditory space. And preliterate societies likewise live largely in the auditory or simultaneous mode with an inclusiveness of awareness that increasingly characterizes our electronic age. The traumatic shock of moving from the segmental, lineal space of literacy into the auditory, unified field of electronic information is quite unlike the reverse process. But today, while we are resuming so many of the preliterate modes of awareness, we can at the same time watch many preliterate cultures beginning their tour through the cultural phases of literacy.

The phonetic alphabet, which permits the translation of the audible into the visible, does so by suppression of meaning in the sounds of the letters. This very abstract technology has made possible a continuous one-way conquest of cultures by the Western world that is far from finished. But it would seem that with the commercial use of the telegraph during more than a century we have become accessible to Eastern art and technology as well as to preliterate and auditory cultures in general. At least, let us be prepared to consider carefully the formally auditory character in the telegraph and in subsequent electronic forms of codifying information. For the formal causes inherent in such media operate on the matter of our senses. The effect of media, like their "message," is really in their form and not in their content. And their formal effect is always subliminal so far as our ideas and concepts are concerned.

It is easy to trace some of the effects of phonetic writing since they are coextensive with the most familiar features of the Western world.

The phonetically written word, itself an abstract image of a spoken word, permits the prolonged analysis of process but does not greatly encourage the application of knowledge to action beyond the verbal sphere. It is not strange, therefore, that the ancient world should have considered applied knowledge under the mode of rhetoric. For writing made it possible to card-catalogue all the individual postures of mind called the "figures" of rhetoric. And these became available to all students as direct means of control over other minds. The oligarthic reign of these figures was swiftly liquidated by printing, a technique that shifted attention from the audience to the mental state of the individual reader.

Writing has given the means of segmenting many phases of knowing and doing. Applied knowledge by the lineal segmentation of outward motion comes with print, which is itself the first mechanization of an ancient handicraft. And whereas writing had fostered the classification of the arts and sciences in depth, print gave access to the arts and sciences at high speed and on one plane at a time. While manuscript culture required gloss and commentary to extract the various levels of meaning it held for the awareness, because of the very slow reading necessary, print is itself commentary or explanation. The form of print is single-leveled. And the print-reader is greatly disposed to feel that he is sharing the movements of another mind. Print drove people like Montaigne to explore the medium as a new art form providing an elaborate means of self-investigation in the act of learning as well as self-portraiture and self-expression.

By contrast, today we live in a postliterate and electronic world, in which we seek images of collective postures of mind, even when studying the individual. In some respects, myth was the means of access to such collective postures in the past. But our new technology gives us many new means of access to group-dynamic patterns. Behind us are five centuries during which we have had unexampled access to aspects of private consciousness by means of the printed page. But now anthropology and archæology give us equal ease of access to group postures and patterns of many cultures, including our own.

Electronic tape permits access to the structure and group dynamics of entire languages. My suggestion that we might regard languages on one hand as mass media and on the other hand as macromyths seems obvious to the point of triteness to the structural linguists to whom I have mentioned these approaches. But it may be useful to point to some of the many nonverbal postures, both individual and public, that accompany changes in the media. That is to say, a new form is usually a cluster of items. For example, in the very first decades of printing at the end of the fifteenth century, people became vividly aware of the camera obscura. The relation of this interest to the new printing process was not noted at the time. Yet printing is itself just such a camera obscura, yielding a private vision of the movements of others. While sitting in the dark, one has in the camera obscura a cinematic presentation of the outside world. And in reading print, the reader acts as a kind of projector of the still shots or printed words, which he can read fast enough to have the feeling of re-creating the movements of another mind. Manuscripts could not be read at a speed sufficient to create the sense of a mind actively engaged in learning and in self-expression. But here, centuries before the movie, is the ultimate magic and myth of the movie in the camera obscura. Perhaps as the camera obscura was the first, the movie is the last phase of print technology.

The movie, which has so little in common with television, may be the last image of the Gutenberg era before it fuses via the telegraph, the telephone, radio, and television, and fades into the new world of auditory space. And as the habits of reading print create intense forms of individualism and nationalism, do not our instantaneous electronic media return us to group dynamics, both in theory and in practice? Is not this shift in media the key to our natural concern with the concept and relevance of myth today?

Printing evoked both individualism and nationalism in the sixteenth century, just as it will do again in India, Africa, China, and Russia. For it demands habits of solitary initiative and attention to exactly repeatable commodities, which are the habits inseparable from industry, and enterprise, production and marketing. Where production precedes literacy, there is no uniform market and no price structure. Industrial production without well-established markets and literacy makes "communism" necessary. Such is the state of our own ignorance of our media that we are surprised to find that radio has very different effects in an oral society than it had in our highly literate culture. In the same way the "nationalism" of an oral world is structured quite differently from the nationalism of a newly literate society. It would appear that to see one's mother tongue dignified with the precise technology of print releases a new vision of unity and power, which remains a subliminal devisive force in the West even today. Unawareness of the effects of our media these past two thousand years and more would seem to be itself an effect of literacy that James Joyce designated as "ab-ced" or absent-mindedness.

The sentiment of spatial and territorial nationalism that accompanies literacy is also reinforced by the printing press, which provides not only the sentiment but also the centralized bureaucratic instruments of uniform control over wide territories.

Perhaps we tend to define myth in too literary a way, as something that can be verbalized, narrated, and written down. If we can regard all media as myths and as the prolific source of many subordinate myths, why cannot we spot the mythic aspect of the current hulahoop activity? Here is a myth we are living. Many people have puzzled over the fact that children refuse to roll these hoops on roads or walks. A mere thirty years ago a hoop was for rolling. Today children reject the lineal use of the hoop in an external space. They use it in a nuclear mode as a means of generating their own space. Here, then, is a live model or drama of the mythic power of the new media to alter sensibility. For this change in child behavior has nothing to do with ideas or programs.

Such a changed attitude to spatial form and presence is as definitive as the change from the photographic to the television image. In his *Prints and Visual Communication* (London: Routledge and Kegan Paul, 1953), William M. Ivins explains how the long process of capturing the external world in the "network of rationality," by the engraver's line and by ever more subtle syntax, finally reached conclusion in the photograph. The photograph is a total statement of the external object without syntax. This kind of peripety will strike the student of media as characteristic of all media development. But in television the striking fact is that the image is defined by light *through*, not by light *on*. It is this fact that separates television from photography and movie, relating it profoundly to stained glass. The spatial sense generated by television experience is utterly unlike that of the movie. And, of course, the difference has nothing to do with the "content" or the programming. Here, as ever, the medium itself is the ultimate message. The child gets such messages, when they are new, much sooner than the adult. For the adult instinctively retards awareness that will disturb a cherished order of perception or of past experience; the child would seem to have no such stake in the past, at least when he is facing new experience.

It is my point that new spatial orientation such as occurs in the format of the press after the advent of the telegraph, the swift disappearance of perspective, is also discernible in the new landscapes of Rimbaud in poetry and Cézanne in painting. And in our time Rouault anticipated the mode of the television image by decades. His use of stained glass as a means of defining the image is what I have in mind.

The mythmaking power of a medium that is itself a myth form appears now in the postliterate age as the rejection of the consumer in favor of the producer. The movie now can be seen as the peak of the consumer-oriented society, being in its form the natural means both of providing and of glorifying consumer goods and attitudes. But in the arts of the past century the swing has been away from packaging for the consumer to providing do-it-yourself kits. The spectator or reader must now be cocreator. Our educational establishment naturally lags behind the popular media in this radical change. The young, when exposed to the television image, receive at once a total orientation in spatial matters that makes the lineality of the printed word a remote and alien language. Reading for them will have to be taught as if it were heraldry or some quaint codification of reality. The assumptions about reading and writing that accompanied the monarchy of print and the related rise of industrial forms are no longer valid for, or acceptable to, those being re-formed in their sensibilities in the electronic age. To ask whether this is a good or a bad thing is to express the bias of efficient causality, which is naturally that of the man of the printed word. But it is also a futile gesture of inadequacy to the real situation. The values of the Gutenberg era cannot be salvaged by those who are as unaware of how they came into existence as they are of why they are now in the process of liquidation.

Philosophic agreement is not necessary among those who are agreed that the insistent operation of media-forms on human sensibility and awareness is an observable, intelligible, and controllable situation. Today, when ordinary consciousness is exposed to the patternmaking of several media at once, we are becoming more attentive to the unique properties of each of the media. We can see both that media are mythic "images" and that they have the power of imposing subliminally, as it were, their own assumptions. They can be viewed at the same time as intelligible explanations of great tracts of time and of the experience of many processes, and they can be used as a means of perpetuating such bias and preference as they codify in their structure.

It is not strange that we should long have been obsessed with the literary and "content" aspect of myth and media. The "form" and "content" dichotomy is as native to the abstract, written, and printed forms of codification as is the "producer" and "consumer" dichotomy.

Unfortunately for the direction and control of education, such a literary bias is quite unable to cope with the new "images" of the postliterate age. As a result of our using literary lenses, the relevant new data have escaped our scrutiny. My book, *The Mechanical Bride: Folklore of Industrial Man,* is a case in point. Turning literary guns on the new iconology of the Madison Avenue world is easy. It is easy to reveal mechanism in a postmechanical era. But I failed at that time to see that we had already passed out of the mechanistic age into the electronic, and that it was this fact that made mechanism both obtrusive and repugnant.

One of the great novelties effected by printing was the creation of a new sense of inner and outer space. We refer to it as the discovery of perspective and the rise of representation in the arts. The space of "perspective" conditioned by an artificially fixed stance for the viewer leads to the enclosing of objects in a pictorial space. Yet so revolutionary and abstract was this new space that poets avoided it in their language for two centuries after painters had accepted it. It is a kind of space very uncongenial to the media of speech and of words. One can gain some idea of the psychic pressures exerted by print in the work of William Blake, who sought new strategies of culture to reintegrate the segmented and fractured human spirit. In fact, the explicit mythmaking of Blake is the greatest monument and antidote to the mythic pressures of the printing press, to "single vision and Newton's sleep." For the matrix of movable type contains the totality of industrialism as well as the means of global conquest, which, by peripety, brought the preliterate world once more into the heart of the industrial metropolis.

The prevalent concept that the mass media exert a baneful influence on the human spirit has strange roots. As Marjorie Nicolson has shown in *Newton Demands the Muse*, it was Newton's *Opticks* that taught poets the correspondence between the inner and outer worlds, between the structure of seeing and the structure of the scene. This notion planted in poets the ambition to gain control over the inner life by a calculus of landscape composition. The idea of verbally constituted landscape, as a lever upon the psychic eye of man, was a dichotomy quite congenial to the culture of the printed word. And whereas external landscape has been abandoned for inner landscape since Rimbaud, Madison Avenue clings to the earlier Romantic concept of consumer control by means of externally arranged scenes. The recent flutter about "subliminal" advertising indicates the delayed shift of attention from outer to inner landscape that occurred in many of the arts in the later nineteenth century. And it is this same shift that today focuses attention on myth in all its modes. For myth is always a montage or transparency comprising several external spaces and times in a single image or situation. Such compression or multilayering is an inescapable mode of the electronic and simultaneous movement of information, whether in popular media or esoteric speculation. It is, therefore, an everyday occurrence for academic entertainment to stress "content," while displaying complete illiteracy with regard to media old and new. For we have now to possess many cultural languages for even the most ordinary daily purposes.

The newspaper will serve as an example of the Babel of myths or languages. When information from every quarter arrived at the same time, the paper became a daily snapshot of the globe, and "perspective" in news became meaningless. Editorials could still try to tie some items together into a chain or sequence with a special point of view or vanishing point. But such views were really capsules for passive readers, while, paradoxically, the unprocessed, uninterpreted, raw news offered far more challenge to the reader to find his own meanings. Today it is easy to see how Edgar Allen Poe, both in his symbolist poems and in his detective stories, had anticipated this new mythic dimension of producer orientation by taking the audience into the creative process itself. Likewise, it is easy to see how the spot news of the telegraph press really acts like the yes-no, black-white dots of the wire-photo in creating an inclusive world image. Yet even now the sponsors of pre-electronic media continue to overlay the new myth by injections of earlier myth, creating hybrids of the "horseless carriage" variety in the interests of superior culture.

The same type of confusion exists in education in the concept of "audio-visual aids." It would seem that we must do in education what the poets, painters, and composers have done, namely, to purge our media and test and define their unique powers before attempting Wagnerian concerts. The Gutenberg myth was not a means of modifying the Cadmus myth, any more than the Henry Ford myth modified the horse and buggy. Obliteration occurred, as it will with the movie under the impact of television, unless we choose to restrain the operation of form on form by due study and strategy. We now stand at that point with regard to all myth and media. We can, perhaps we *must*, become the masters of cultural and historical alchemy. And to this end, we can, I suggest, find means in the study of media as languages and languages as myths. For our experience with the grammar and syntax of languages can be made available for the direction and control of media old and new.

Popular Religion of the 1930s as Reflected in the Best Sellers of Harry
Emerson Fosdick
Richard H. Potter

from

The Journal of Popular Culture, vol. 3, 1970.

Richard H. Potter
Department of American Studies
University of Maryland
College Park

POPULAR RELIGION OF THE 1930'S
AS REFLECTED IN THE BEST SELLERS OF
HARRY EMERSON FOSDICK

Popular religion might be defined as religion which reflects the beliefs of a broad spectrum of the populace. In some cases popular religion may be no more than a set of ideas upon which a large number of persons tend to agree. In other cases it may become formalized into specific doctrines and practices exhibited by organized groups. But formalized religion can be classified as popular only if there is acceptance of its basic beliefs by many persons beyond the boundaries of the group.

The study of popular religion is particularly difficult since an attempt is made to determine what people basically believe. Examinations of cults or sects, if they can be shown to embody similar beliefs, might be one approach to such a study. Ideological movements that find expression in new groups and/or adoption by established groups might offer another means of study. A third approach might be to study a particularly popular figure whose religious ideas appeal to a wide audience. In any of these cases the assumption must be made that if a set of beliefs appeals to people these ideas become a part of the individual's religious thinking. The study of a popular religious figure seems to offer the best means of interpreting popular religion simply because it involves only one subject.   Yet the method to be used in such a study presents a new problem.   Schneider and Dornbusch in their book Popular Religion contend that an examination of inspirational religious best sellers offers an acceptable means of studying popular religion.   Such books would have to deal with ordinary, daily problems and offer techniques to assure salvation.   In addition, these books would have to satisfy the best seller requirement. [1]   Thus it would seem that a popular religious figure who was also an author of inspirational best sellers would be an excellent means of studying popular religion.

No other man has as many inspirational best sellers on the Schneider and Dornbusch list as Harry Emerson Fosdick.   In the decade of the thirties alone, five of Fosdick's six published books are classified as best sellers in Popular Religion.   Fosdick was also popular as a religious leader apart from his books.   During the decade, he was pastor of the non-denominational Riverside Church in New York City where he consistently preached to overflowing crowds.   His message also reached the public each Sunday evening via his national radio broadcast "National Vespers." Numerous religious articles were written by him for national, mass magazines.   Books, magazines, pulpit, and radio all paid tribute to the national popularity and religious prominence of Harry Emerson Fosdick in the 1930's.   Thus we have chosen to analyze popular religion through a study of Harry Emerson Fosdick's best sellers in the 1930's.

Fosdick's first major publication of the decade was As I See Religion.   This book, published in 1932, is probably the best single statement of his religious ideology.   As such it lays the theoretical foundation for his remaining best sellers.   These other works, published in 1933, 1934, 1935, and 1937, are collections of sermons preached at the Riverside Church and for "National Vespers." Reaching the public in two forms, these sermons seem particularly relevant for our study.   Fosdick's only other major publication in the decade was A Guide to Understanding the Bible.   Although not a best seller, this book is considered by many to be his best and most influential work.

Fosdick's major theoretical concern of the thirties seems
to have been an attempt to clarify and somewhat systematize his
basic ideas on religion and Christianity. He expounded not only
the basic tenets of Christianity as he saw them, but he also defended
these concepts against anti-religious elements. In addition, he re-
defined his theological position.

Theologically, Fosdick belonged to the liberal movement
with its appeals to social gospel and critical common sense. The
liberals had reached their height in the twenties in their conflict
with fundamentalism. In the thirties a reaction against the liberal
theology appeared called neo-orthodoxy. According to this movement, "liberalism failed to keep pace with the religious needs and
experiences of a world in crisis."[2] Too much emphasis on the
resources of human nature and the logic of historical progress had
caused the liberals to deny basic aspects of religion that were
essential, such as grace and pious trust in God. The recognition
of this humanistic, complacent aspect of the liberal movement was
Fosdick's basic theological concern in the thirties.

He never rejected the important contribution liberalism
had made, however. For liberals had "insisted that the deep and
vital experiences of the Christian soul with itself, with its fellows,
with its God, could be carried over into this new world and understood in the light of new knowledge."[3] Yet he saw that liberalism
had become too occupied with intellectualism at the expense of the
spiritual needs of the individual. They had pictured God simply as
a kind and affectionate father, evil as practically non-existent, and
progress as automatic and inevitable. "Whatever was harsh, grim,
forbidding in the old religion was crowded to the periphery or thrust
out altogether and whatever was lovely, comforting, and hopeful
was made central."[4] Fosdick recognized that "this world is a much
wilder, fiercer, profounder place than such superficial liberalism
ever took account of."[5]

Fosdick felt that the solution to the liberal failing lay in
making Christianity more practical and useful to daily living. Basically, Christianity needed to be less concerned with theological
arguments and more concerned with making religion meaningful to
the individual. As he noted, "religion is the relationship of a man
as a whole to the meaning of his life in this universe as a whole."[6]
Christian thinking should be concerned with that individual man.

But how should religion be related to this modern individual?

For Fosdick, William James seemed to have begun the correct analysis of individual religion by showing its psychological basis. For "religion is increasingly dealt with today not in ecclesiastical or theological but in psychological terms. Increasing numbers of people mean by religion, not first of all a true church or orthodox system.of theology, but a psychological experience."[7] To Fosdick this was natural. Numerous psychologists since James had recognized that mental health requires a religion or some substitute which gives life meaning and purpose. So it could be seen that "our real task is to achieve a religion which saves people and such religion must be primarily an individual psychological experience."[8]

Fosdick, however, does not leave religion simply as psychological fulfillment. He sees true religion as requiring an individual spiritual experience. Of such experiences he says,

> Whatever elevates life, beautifies it with significance, makes its appreciation of nature keener, its happiness in art richer, its moral practices more wholesome, its social relationships more humane is spiritual. Whatever gives men creative joy in their work, redeems life from drudgery, and baptizes it with purposeful meaning is spiritual.[9]

In essence, then, true religion is a psychological, spiritual experience. What is such an experience like? Fosdick defines it thus: "Whenever anybody thus finds any goodness, truth, or beauty concerning which he feels not that it should give itself to him but that he should give himself to it and be its loyal servant, that man has entered into an authentic religious experience."[10]

A religious experience and a meaningful religion are not necessarily the same. Where various types of experiences may be described as religious, "all profound religion ministers to three basic needs: the need of a great metaphysics, a philosophy of life to put meaning into living; the need of a great morality, principles of conduct, personal and social to ennoble living; the need of a great mysticism, profound resources of interior power by which to live."[11] Thus an individual spiritual experience which fulfills basic religious needs becomes the goal of any authentic religion.

Such a religion is Christianity. Since man did not create the spiritual world of goodness and beauty and truth, Christianity is based on the concept of God. Such a God provides us with "a moral universe, a superhuman allegiance, the external reality of spiritual values, and the endless possibilities of personality."[12] But accepting God does not mean that man can believe in an optimistic, progressive universe. To Fosdick the Christian God is not paternal nor capricious but just. "What God guarantees is that this is a law-abiding universe, where whatsoever a man or nation soweth, that shall he reap. What God guarantees is that there is no salvation, personal or social, without sacrifice."[13] This is not to imply, however, that God is transcendent. "To believe in the Christian God is to believe that in spiritual life at its best we have touched the hither side of God."[14]

The most perfect spiritual revelation of this God was Christ. From Christ comes our best knowledge of God and the unique ingredient that makes Christianity a religion. Fosdick believes that Christ "thought of personality as the central fact in the universe and used it as the medium of interpretation for all other facts."[15] It is this respect for the worth and value of the individual human being that sets Christianity apart as a religion. At its best, Christianity is primarily concerned with the advancement of personality, "its divine origin, spiritual nature, infinite worth, and endless possibilities,"[16] and its immortality.

Harry Emerson Fosdick sees the Christian religion providing for the psychological and spiritual needs of men. But this will not happen unless men take upon themselves the task of living the Christian life in the world. "A religious experience that is not deceitful will be one in which a man does not endeavor to escape the actual world but to transform it."[17] It is not the Christian purpose to make life easy; rather it demands sacrificial labor on the part of men since goodness in the world will only be realized when it is made attractive enough for men to accept. Thus Christians should be persons whose lives become examples for others to follow. As Fosdick summarizes Christianity, "it is a way of thinking about life and living life to be wrought out personally and socially on earth."[18]

One of the basic religious problems of the thirties to Fosdick was the prevalence of various substitutes for Christianity. Thus he devotes much in his works to an analysis and evaluation of these movements. Non-theistic humanism espouses a universe in which personality has evolved simply because of propitious circumstances.[19] Materialism offers a universe in which spiritual

experiences have no explanation.[20] Atheism denies man has worth
and thus subjects him to despair.[21] Progressivism sees everything
evolving toward some inevitable good.[22] Nationalism teaches
obedience and devotion to the state is the highest end of man.[23]
Polytheism worships any aspect of life which offers reward.[24]
Secularism offers a world in which Christ is systematically
crowded out of daily living.[25] Each of these seems capable of only
partially fulfilling man's religious need.

If these substitutes do not match Christianity, Fosdick
does recognize that they succeed largely because they have offered
men something which Christianity has seemed to lack. Christianity
must, therefore, face the task of showing men the practical applicability of its doctrines to daily living. "This," Fosdick says,
"is the outstanding challenge to us in the churches--our attitude
not on theological questions but on practical, ethical, social
questions.[26]

In approaching this task of making Christianity more
practical, Fosdick naturally found himself involved with the society
of his day. In the first part of the decade, this society was in the
throes of an economic depression. The later years of the decade
saw the growing threat of war as society's gravest enemy. To
such practical social realities Fosdick directed much of his
message in the 1930's.

Fosdick saw all human tragedy or pain resulting from
four basic factors: (1) the law-abiding nature of the universe by
which a man receives the fruits of his actions; (2) the progressive
nature of life which causes man to constantly fight to overcome
ignorance, disease, poverty, and war; (3) the individual characteristics of initiative and self-determination; (4) the interlocking
relationships of life so that what happens to one happens to others.[27]

If, then, tragedy is a logical, common sense result of
preceding factors, the   depression and war could be explained
and perhaps corrected by recognizing their basic causes. To
Fosdick the depression had been caused by our inability to provide
for mass consumption--our refusal to adequately share the
prosperity of the twenties. "Our Western civilization," he said,
"has broken all laws of social health, transgressed the principles
of a civilized society, and the fact that in consequence we are
now in trouble does not indicate that the world is crazy but rather,
that the foundations of the world are laid in moral law so that
whatsoever a civilization soweth, that shall it also reap."[28]

Fosdick sees the guilt for the depression lying largely with the privileged, those who had used the power of wealth and position only for their personal advancement. Yet Fosdick also recognizes that "the trouble in this country has been not alone the people who have succeeded but the way the rest of us have thought about success and tried to get it."[29] The measurement of success by size and wealth: the attempt to maintain the status quo; devotion to class interest; an adherence to a comfortable adjustable, undemanding religion: such attitudes found in the majority of Americans had, in reality, brought on the depression. The avoidance of further economic distress naturally lay in correcting such attitudes.

As for war, Fosdick views it as the greatest enemy of mankind. It is a waste, a process by which nations sacrifice their finest youth on an altar of hate and violence; it is a process by which family and home are torn by destruction and sorrow; it is a process by which our finest talents are usurped to produce new, more total means of destruction; it is the denier of individual freedom and individual worth. Civilization, democracy, government, Christianity are all doomed unless man is willing to effectively thwart the cause of war.

Belief in national sovereignty and the morality of defensive engagements are the excuses offered for maintaining the war philosophy. Yet any nation can maintain that any war is defensive necessity for its national independence. The fact is that nationalism is too often promoted not by patriotism but by munitions makers and others who have a vested interest in maintaining a belief in the efficacy of violence. And it is here that Fosdick sees the basic cause of war.

In no one thing is Fosdick so adamant as in his attitude toward war. A supporter of World War I, throughout his works in the thirties he ardently pleads for world peace. In one of his best known sermons, he sums up his attitude on war:

> I renounce war. I renounce war because of what it does
> to our men....I renounce war because of what it compels
> us to do to our enemies, bombing their mothers in
> villages, starving their children by blockades.... I
> renounce war for its consequences, for the lies it lives on
> and propagates, for the undying hatred it arouses, for
> the dictatorships it puts in place of democracy, for the
> starvation that stalks after it. I renounce war and never

again, directly or indirectly, will I sanction or support another.[30]

Society was faced with two basic problems--economic inequalities and international relations. Although somewhat nebulous in his ideas concerning the rectification of international tensions and the achievement of world peace, Fosdick does offer guidelines in the realm of economics. He believes that "the sole defense of any economic order is to make it work for the welfare of all the people."[31] A "social structure which best opens the doors of possibility to all the people"[32] must become our goal. To do this, collectivism or socialism may be necessary. For "a man's welfare or a man's disaster depends on world-wide conditions, which he cannot handle for himself, so that only social-mindedness, cooperatively handling them together for good of all can meet the issue.[33] So it is that the basic key to the improvement of the social order and, presumably world conditions, lies with the individual. This is natural to Fosdick for most social evils originate in men. "There is no social sin whose central respon-sibility is not inside individuals,"[34] he asserts. Thus it follows that "there is no problem on earth so large that its cause and cure do not root back in individual responsibilities."[35]

Because of their belief in the sacredness of personality, Christians ought to be particularly sensitive to the individual role in social reform. Fosdick sees the basis of Christian service lying in love--the constructive, creative force that discovers and ad-vances personal and social possibilities. Each man achieves his greatest worth insofar as he loves and is loved. For "being a Christian involves essentially...caring enough for persons and causes to sink our lives in them."[36] Each Christian can make a social contribution for it is the family which is the center of our culture and upon the youth of our families rests society's future.

The ideal of Christian service may bring social reform, but it is not possible without first achieving individual reform. The fact is that despite the problems of the decade, the popular attitude is one of indifference, confusion, disillusionment, hope-lessness, uncertainty, and prejudice. So it is that world change and improvement cannot rest in theory or society but with the altering of the personal life.

However, Fosdick recognizes that "a man is impotent to face the onslaught of the objective world until he has restored harmony within the borders of his soul."[37] For "whatever else life may give or may deny, one thing is absolutely indispensable-- that a man should not break faith with himself, that he should keep his honor bright in his own eyes, that whatever else may fail he should not inwardly be a failure,"[38] So it is that man lives in a world where his major struggle is no longer with himself.

Fosdick saw a world in which the moral, emotional, and mental pressures of modern life forced men to seek means of escape. "The most difficult task in the world for most people," he noted, "is courageously to deal with reality."[39] One of the most common means of escape was to sink into despair, giving up our lives to cynicism, disillusionment, and fear. The other common means of escape was to become enamored with one's own worth. The result of this latter technique was seen in the prevalence of egocentric pursuits of power, prestige, possession, and popularity in the world. In essence, then, man seeks to be saved from the realities of life-- disease, ignorance, poverty, and fear-- and to such pursuits he devotes himself. The obvious conclusion is that "salvation is the chief preoccupation of all intelligent and earnest minds."[40]

Although popular salvation frequently takes the forms of desperation or egocentricity, true salvation does not necessitate as much of an escape from reality as an acceptance of the basic reality. For, in essence, the basic realities of life are not the visible, tangible things, but the invisible and spiritual. Only when man sees life in spiritual terms and identifies himself with it can he really be saved from the tragedies of life.

One of man's basic psychological needs is to give himself to some cause, idea, or being beyond himself--something to which he can give his devotion and allegiance. Man seeks something to "worship and serve, belong to and care about, the unifying loyalty which draws his life together and gives it centrality and singleness of aim,"[41] As Fosdick sees it, "we must give ourselves to something, make a god of it and serve it, or there is no meaning or direction in our lives."[42] For inevitably "we are being used by ideas. All we can do is to choose which ones should use us."[43] In essence, our attempts to escape or be saved from the world are manifested in those ideas which use us. "The ultimate meaning of our lives, therefore, lies in the ideas which we allow to use us."[44]

In accepting the concept of reality as spiritual, Fosdick
sees our main task becomes that of enslaving our will not to the
trivial or worldly but to persons, causes, or ideas which will
inspire us to spiritual goals and which we will serve for spiritual
ends. For "happiness is not primarily a matter of the means by
which we live; it is a matter of the spiritual ends for which we live."[45]
Christianity with its spiritual God and its concept of personal worth
is an eternal cause to which each individual can devote his highest
essence. In this matter man is able to achieve the true and ultimate
salvation which he seeks.

Yet Christianity is more to individual life than a means of
spiritual salvation. It is also a source of inner strength, providing
man truly worships and is sensitive to its message. With inner
sustenance to face life realistically, and inner harmony restored
by the spiritual loyalty, one is able to fully appreciate the worth
of personality so vital to Christian thinking. The Christian is
then enabled to "pioneer for the application of Christ's ideals to
personal and social life."[46] For it is in this realm of Christian
service that the individual is able to practice and fulfill the
spiritual life.

Such service must be achieved in a real world of trouble
and tragedy, a world where happiness becomes victory, not
pleasure. But the Christian must remember that "all our calamities
come from the same factors that provide our opportunities and
joys."[47] Trouble and adversity are really tests and moulders of
character, challenges to be met and conquered. It is inevitable
that Christian living in a hostile and adverse world will require self-
denial, self-restraint, and sacrificial labor. Yet, in the end, the
Christian will triumph if his faith in and devotion to the spiritual
and personality aspects of Christian living remain firm. For, as
Fosdick concludes, "a spiritual victory won in the face of hostile
environment--that is what a Christian is all about."[48]

Thus far in examining Fosdick we have endeavored to
isolate and discuss his basic themes in the thirties. However, the
characteristics of any given period can best be recognized only
as one sees their uniqueness in that period. We are not able to
fully understand which of these themes, considered singly, is
actually unique to the thirties. In order to better determine what
of Fosdick can be considered truly reflective of popular religion

in the thirties, it seems of value to compare his ideas of this period with his ideas in the preceding decade.

In reality, Fosdick's ideas in the 1930's were simply an outgrowth of his work in the earlier decade. The practical, social, and personalized religion he espoused in the thirties was anticipated throughout much of his work in the twenties. Thus in 1924 he observed

> So long as profits rather than service is the motive of our industrial life, so long as money rather than personality is its ultimate concern, so long as autocracy rather than democracy is its method of organization, and imperialism rather than international cooperation is its consequence, our economic system cannot be thought Christian. [49]

Yet despite the fact that no concept of the latter decade is entirely without precedent in his works of the 1920's, we can note a changing emphasis between the periods. A dual theme permeated his major writings in this early decade: Christianity needs to be constantly reinterpreted and rephrased in the light of a progressive, modern world; this is needed because Christianity must form the basis for a vigorous, total way of life.

Fosdick viewed the inequalities of the twenties as largely a result of an inadequate Christianity. "We are committed," he said, "to the hope of making progress and the central problem which Christianity faces in adjusting her thoughts and practice to the modern age is the problem of coming to intelligent terms with this dominant idea."[50] It was evident to him that "one of mankind's most insistent needs is the interpretation of religion in terms of service and the attachment of religion's enormous driving power to the tasks of service."[51]

As Fosdick viewed the twenties, he saw that the primary religious necessity was to bring Christianity out of the clouds of irrationality and blind tradition. Modern Christianity did not have to be in conflict with scientific principles or common sense. It should adjust itself in the light of new knowledge and new circumstances rather than clinging to concepts originated in and designed for pre-scientific eras.

Fosdick recognized that this was not merely a clerical or theological problem of his time, but also one which led to personal dilemma and uncertainty among many. As he said, "There is a

widespread, deep-seated, positive desire on the part of many
Christians in all churches to recover for our modern life, for its
personal character and its social relationships, the religion of
Jesus as distinguished from the accumulated, conventionalized,
largely inadequate and sometimes grossly false religion about
Jesus. "[52] What was needed was not a new creed or a new sect
but rather a unified "kind of Christianity that will send men out
courageously to apply their Christian principles to our social,
industrial, and international order. "[53]

As the nominal leader of the liberal, modernist movement
of the twenties, he struck out against the complacent, stagnant,
Fundamentalist religion of his day. He defined this Liberal movement as seeking "to subordinate the details of ritual, creed, and
church to the major objects of Christianity--the creation of personal
character and social righteousness. "[54] It was "a spirit of free
inquiry which wishes to face the new facts, accept whatever is
true, and state the abiding principles of Christian faith in cogent
and contemporary terms. "[55]

Fosdick not only tried to show the need for a reexamina-
tion of Christian beliefs and traditions, but he also sought to present
these basic truths. "What is permanent in Christianity," he said,
"is not mental frameworks but abiding experiences that phrase
and rephrase themselves in successive generations' ways of
thinking and that grow in assured certainty and in richness of
content. "[56] In "human personality, its divine origin, its spiritual
nature, its supreme value, its boundless possibilities"[57] he found
the Christian base. In "the social life from which personality springs
and by which it is tremendously affected, "[58] he found the Christian
goal. In the twenties he rethought, reviewed, reinterpreted, and
restated Christianity so that its personal and social value could
be better understood and utilized.

From Fosdick's works of the twenties we see Christianity
in a state of flux. People were faced with a static, traditional
religion which often seemed in conflict with their progressive,
changing world. There was a need for a rational, common sense
basis for religion within the framework of modern knowledge. There
was a need for spiritual strength and security as a result of the
lost confidence in traditional religion. There was a need for realistic, workable, ethical guidelines by which man could live in

harmony with his fellows. So men searched in the twenties for a meaningful religion, and Fosdick reflected this uncertainty as he sought to provide solutions.

In spite of our cursory examination of the twenties, we can still observe specific areas of variations in emphasis between the two decades. In general, the thirties can be viewed as a reaction to the uncertainties of the earlier decade. These latter themes were a responsive outgrowth of the concepts which Fosdick had expounded in the twenties. We can see this reaction in our three general areas of discussion.

Theoretically, this reaction is seen in a de-emphasis on questioning and reexamining standard or traditional religion. A more authoritative and demanding religion was advocated as opposed to the easy, optimistic, progressive theology of the twenties. The thirties saw Fosdick less concerned with reconciling scientific findings and religious thought. Fosdick saw the people of the thirties as confused, uncertain, and often unbelieving because of the lack of religious authority in the twenties. Virtually no new attacks were launched against the Church, its creeds, or the fundamentalist interpretation, a direct contrast to the earlier decade. Actually, sermons were frequently preached on the theme of the importance of traditional religion in the Church. Overall, theoretical discussion in the thirties was concerned largely with trying to establish and clarify systems of beliefs and practice which had been disputed in the twenties. Although theoretical discussions were less numerous in the thirties, it was in this realm of theory that Fosdick differed most from the twenties.

Fosdick's social themes also reflected a reaction to the 1920's. This is most evident in his concern with the economic order which he believed was a result of the economic inequalities of the 1920's. The thesis of inevitable social progress had been one to which Fosdick was linked in the 1920's: but during the thirties he rejected this idea. In the 1920's, the privileged had been generally above criticism while in the 1930's they were frequently lambasted for their contribution to the depression. Laissez-faire economics and government had been advocated in the 1920's while the following decade saw Fosdick advancing limited socialism. Theories of optimistic social evolution gave way to needs for practical, current means of correcting social evils. The Social Gospel had been popular in the twenties, but it had been primarily a form of private service; the 1930's saw the idea of Christian social responsibility become a collective enterprise. Evolution had been behind social evil in the 1920's; in the thirties the basis of social evil was usually individual wrongs. Where war had been rarely mentioned in the 1920's, it became a major theme in Fosdick's works of the 1930's. Somewhat related to this was the increased concern with all types of international problems. In general, Fosdick's social themes of the 1930's became less theoretical and more applicable to current situations.

In Fosdick's personal themes we can again see a reaction to the twenties. Basically there had been a de-emphasis of personal themes in the 1920's. A counter reaction appeared in the 1930's in the form of a greater concern with personal religion. In the 1930's there was a greater attempt to make religion adaptable for individual consumption: there were more religious appeals made with psychological overtones; there was an increased attempt to systematize religion to overcome individual confusion and uncertainty; there was greater emphasis on the practical role of religion in daily life; there was less concern with theological problems and more concern with individual problems.

Throughout Fosdick's works in the thirties runs a constant emphasis on individual improvement and individual worth. This individualized religion was perhaps the most profound change between the two decades, seemingly a direct reaction to a decade of prosperity and theoretical questioning.

We have attempted to analyze the best sellers of Harry Emerson Fosdick by content, theme and comparison. From this we can now attempt to draw certain conclusions concerning popular religion in the 1930's.

Fosdick reflected a religion that might be termed a way of living. His basic concern seemed to have been trying to bring religion to a level where people could understand it and could practice it. His was an attempt to simplify and systematize, to personalize and individualize religion. Starting with a simple, basic Christian theory he sought to form guidelines for Christian living, simple guidelines that would appeal to logical, common sense but still would require responsibilities.

The religion expounded by Fosdick in the 1930's might be summarized in five points. (1) Religion or its equivalent is a psychological necessity for man because man must have something to which to give himself. (2) Man is more than matter: he has a spiritual essence expressed in truth, beauty, and goodness. To find life's true significance man must give himself to spiritual ideas. (3) God is the creative, unifying aspect of life which gives the spiritual essence of man significance and support. (4) Christianity is a religion which accepts the reality of the spiritual man and advances the concept of reverance for all personality. (5) Christian living demands cultivation of one's inner resources and service to one's fellows. This, then, is the basis of popular religion of the 1930's as reflected by Harry Emerson Fosdick.

FOOTNOTES

[1]Louis Schneider and Sanford M. Dornbusch, Popular Religion: Inspirational Books in America (Chicago: The University of Chicago Press, 1958), passim.

[2]Herbert Wallace Schneider, Religion in Twentieth Century America, rev. ed. (New York: Altheneum, 1963), 143.

[3]Harry Emerson Fosdick, Successful Christian Living: Sermons on Christianity Today (New York: Harper and Brothers, 1937), 154.

[4]Harry Emerson Fosdick, As I See Religion (New York: Harper and Brothers, 1932), 104.

[5]Harry Emerson Fosdick, The Power to See It Through: Sermons on Christianity Today (New York: Harper and Brothers, 1935), 74.

[6]Ibid., 35. [7]Fosdick, As I See Religion, 4. [8]Ibid., 9.

[10]Ibid., 11. [11]Fosdick, The Power to See It Through ..., 132.

[12]Harry Emerson Fosdick, The Secret of Victorious Living: Sermons on Christianity Today (New York: Harper and Brothers, 1934), 178.

[13]Harry Emerson Fosdick, The Hope of the World: Twenty-five Sermons on Christianity Today (New York: Harper and Brothers, 1933), 139.

[14] Fosdick, The Secret of Victorious Living..., 167.

[15] Fosdick, As I see Religion, 42.

[16] Ibid., 44.   [17] Ibid., 124.

[18] Fosdick, The Secret of Victorious Living..., 50.

[19] Fosdick, As I See Religion, 70.

[20] Fosdick, Successful Christian Living..., 46-47.

[21] Fosdick, Secret of Victorious Living..., 140.

[22] Fosdick, Successful Christian Living..., 79.

[23] Fosdick, The Hope of the World..., 159.

[24] Fosdick, Successful Christian Living..., 55.

[25] Fosdick, The Power to See It Through..., 241.

[26] Ibid., 8.   [27] Fosdick, As I See Religion, 54.

[28] Fosdick, The Secret of Victorious Living..., 25.

[29] Ibid., 47.   [30] Ibid., 97-98.   [31] Ibid., 61.

[32] Fosdick, The Power To See It Through..., 103.

[33] Ibid., 93.   [34] Fosdick, Successful Christian Living..., 135.

[35] Fosdick, The PowerTo See It Through..., 239.

[36] Fosdick, The Secret of Victorious Living..., 33.

[37] Fosdick, Successful Christian Living..., 26.

[38] Fosdick, The Power To See It Through..., 4.

[39] Fosdick, As I See Religion, 101.

[40] Fosdick, Successful Christian Living..., 80.

[41] Ibid., 55.   [42] Ibid., 36.   [43] Fosdick, The Power to See It Through..., 175.   [44] Ibid., 174.

[45] Fosdick, The Hope of the World..., 42.

[46] Fosdick, The Secret of Victorious Living..., 78.

[47] Fosdick, As I See Religion, 55.

[48] Fosdick, The Power to See It Through..., 13.

[49] Harry Emerson Fosdick, The Modern Use of the Bible (New York: The Macmillan Co., 1924), 203.

[50] Harry Emerson Fosdick, Christianity and Progress (New York: Fleming H. Revell Company, 1922), 41-42.

[51] Harry Emerson Fosdick, The Meaning of Service (New York: Association Press, 1920), 1.

[52] Harry Emerson Fosdick, Adventurous Religion and Other Essays (New York: Harper and Brothers, 1932), 309.

[53] Ibid., 204. [54] Ibid., 247. [55] Ibid., 245-246.

[56] Fosdick, The Modern Use of the Bible, 103.

[57] Fosdick, Adventurous Religion..., 36-37.

[58] Fosdick, The Meaning of Service, 33.

Thrill as a Standard
Howard D. Roelofs

from

Southern Review, vol. 6, no. 4, 1941.

THRILL AS A STANDARD

Howard D. Roelofs

T<small>HE</small> Symposium on American Culture conducted by the American Philosophical Society is more perplexing than enlightening. That each contributor to the symposium was a specialist, one an editor, another an anthropologist, another a physicist, and so on, is not to be wondered at. It is our accepted modern procedure. If we have a particular problem falling entirely within a recognized field, we go to the appropriate expert; if we have a general problem which no one specialty can encompass, we ask the aid of the experts from the adjacent fields. We wish reliable information, and the expert is the man to supply it. Unfortunately, by fulfilling this requirement the result sometimes fails in its purpose. The experts speak as experts, that is, they speak about their specialties, and the totality of what they contribute remains a mere aggregate. The general problem is approached but not reached.

This is too much the case with this symposium. The contributions are very uneven in quality, but good and bad, they remain almost wholly each within its own special field. Mr. Allen speaks like a promoter regarding the popularization of culture in the fields of literature, music, and the drama. Mr. Kidder sounds a solemn warning based upon anthropology, that if we do not achieve the control of culture which earlier cultures did not achieve, we too, like them, shall pass away. Mr. Compton extolls the benefits of science so much that he arouses our suspicions. When he quotes with approval this boast: "In the last fifty years physics has exerted a more powerful beneficial influence on the intellectual, economic, and social life of the world than has been exerted in a comparable time by any other agency in history," one is tempted to remind him that the hand that rocks the cradle rules the world, and that the influence for good of mothers' love in any fifty years has always been greater than that of physics—not to mention the influence of cooks. Mr. Taylor certainly gives excellent grounds for being hopeful about the future of American painting. If the Federal Art Project really enabled the American artist to become "a simple workman who could take his dinner pail to work in the morning and be accepted by the plasterers, the masons, and the carpenters, as an ordinary, regular member of society . . . [to enter] once again into the life of the people from whom he came and with whom he has been happiest from time immemorial"—if the Federal Art Project accomplished that, its expenditures are abundantly justified. But none of this reaches the central theme.

Reflecting on this perplexing result, there came to mind another statement made by Mr. Taylor: "In the last three generations intellectual disproportion and inequality of judgment have probably done more to weaken the vitality of democratic thinking than any other single factor. We have became the victims in many instances rather than the beneficiaries of some one else's specialized thought." These two sentences provide both a sound judgment and a fair warning when applied to the very symposium in which they appear. The several contributions from the different experts fail to reach a common focus. Nonetheless they are useful. Viewed in another way, they themselves become data for a study of American culture.

Approached in this way, two characteristics of American culture not usually brought together are found to be deserving of a common consideration. In this symposium one is present in almost every article, the other comes to mind because it is left out. The first is best indicated by a series of brief quotations, each, with one exception, from a different speaker. ". . . there is an exciting thought . . ." ". . . cultural progress in a new and exciting way . . ." ". . . the American public which is actually excited about art . . ." ". . . that it [an important assertion] could be seriously made is something excitingly new." ". . . Montana . . . the most thrilling spot in the world." "One of the most thrilling experiences I have ever had was directing for a few months the Federal Art Projects in the New England States."

This persistent reliance on "thrilling" and "exciting" to indicate high importance and notable achievement might be only a stylistic deficiency, evidence that these men possess only a limited command of the English language. But this interpretation is not supported by the rest of their writings, and it would be odd if a meager vocabulary should manifest itself with constant regularity in the use of just those terms. Further, it is not these men alone who rely on just those terms to name whatever is finest and best. A new dentifrice is recommended because it offers "America's latest taste thrill." Cocktails have long been said to be "exciting" and in New York City one can obtain a "Double Thrill" cocktail, "Master-Mixed with bonded liquor, fresh fruit juices and fresh ice and served in a sterilized glass." (*Fresh* ice!) A new cooked cereal is now urged upon us to give a "breakfast thrill." And an editor of one of our intellectual quarterlies, to describe new music he has just heard, uses the one sentence, "It's exciting!"

This is not a symptom of a mere vocabulary deficiency. Learning a number of synonyms for "thrilling" and "exciting" might relieve the verbal monotony, but it would not correct the basic error. Persons, foods, music and pictures, the fulfillment of duties, achievements in virtue and in crime, drinks, and toiletries are all reduced to a common measure. Do they excite? Do they give us a thrill? Their reality and their worth are tested and verified by their effectiveness as devices for giving our emotions a kick.

One thing has escaped. One thing is not yet openly urged upon us for its thrill. It is religion. And religion also is not to be found among the characteristics of American culture considered in the American Philosophical Society's symposium. Both the escape and the omission are, to say the least, very odd. Few things can equal the range and intensity of the emotional effects of religion. This aspect of religion has been both abused and studied. It certainly is well known. The outer fringes of religious experience are, to some extent, cultivated simply for the emotional result—unbelievers go to church because, as they say, it makes them feel better. But the worship of God is not yet measured by degrees of emotional excitement. Not yet are men urged to repentance and obedience for the sake of a thrill.

On the other hand, the relation of religion to culture would seem to be too obvious to be overlooked. If culture is understood to mean the pattern and structure of the life of a people, religion is a distinctive element in that pattern. If culture is taken in the more usual sense of meaning the refined and sensitive appreciation of all things lovely and good, religion provides both a source and an object of such appreciation. If in the future culture of America, science is to perform the functions of religion, as Mr. Compton seems to suggest, a change of such magnitude merits explicit consideration. But religion simply does not appear among the subjects of this symposium. One wonders why. No reading of the printed proceedings can supply assured knowledge of the motives and reasons of the organizers and contributors, but this much can be said. There is certainly no evidence of any hostility to religion. The appearances suggest rather that religion was left out because no one thought to include it. And the record shows its absence provoked no vigorous comment.

Religion in one way or another is at least mentioned three times, and the occasions and what is said are worth noting. Mr. Mumford in speaking of the importance of balance, expresses the hope that "in the long run, agriculture and industry, education and religion, the means and the ends of living, will work in harmony toward a common good." Mr. Edward V. Huntington, from the audience, says he was struck by the modernism of all the speakers: not one mentioned a certain book by Carl Snyder— "Also, nobody mentioned any form of theology." That, judging by the "also," is now only supplementary evidence of modernism. But if theology is not mentioned, there is one direct appeal to God. Mr. Kidder confronts the possibility that we have become so dependent on culture "that we have left it to do our evolving for us." He then exclaims: "If so, God help us, for our culture, like Frankenstein's monster, is a soulless thing." It is not an impertinence to suggest to Mr. Kidder that if we ourselves have no souls, our culture's similar lack is not of much moment. But if we have souls, our attention to God had better be something more than a rhetorical appeal for His aid. Yet these three references constitute, unless

I missed something, the whole of this symposium's consideration of religion. That is the revealing, the significant fact. In more ways than one it is "later than we think."

I am not going to argue that in the persons who contributed to this symposium there was a specific connection between emphasis on excitement and neglect of religion. But in American life today there is extensive preoccupation with getting the thrills out of life, and religion is ignored by many people. The conjunction of this concern for emotion and indifference to religion is an aspect of contemporary culture worth examining.

The intimate relation of the emotions and art, morality, and religion has always been recognized. We speak normally of a feeling for beauty. The last word on both religion and morality is that we are to love God and we are to love our neighbor. But while feeling is the dominant mode of our relationship to the beautiful, the good, and the divine, the emphasis is not on the feelings, not on experiencing this or that emotion, but on objects—on things which are beautiful, on fine actions, on noble ideals, on God. As early as Aristotle it is stated explicitly that our feelings are to be trained, disciplined, directed. What is required is not that we have feelings, anyone can have them, but that we have the right feelings for the right things. Culture manifests itself in the union of correct judgment and appropriate emotional response to what is genuinely beautiful and splendid. To go into ecstasy over something tawdry or ugly is almost as bad as to be insensitive to beauty. So also the good man not only knows and does what is right, he delights in it; and to take pleasure in mean or evil actions is the certain mark of a depraved moral character.

From this comes the importance of determining what things are beautiful, what actions are good. The long history of man's efforts to accomplish this is not a record of constant success. *Tot homines, tot sententiae, de gustibus non disputandum est* is an ancient expression of the opinion that we might as well admit we cannot discover universally valid standards of beauty and of goodness. Yet the conviction that there are such standards on the whole has persisted. And I think it is a serious misreading of history not to recognize that the evidence given by human experience has slowly but steadily mounted in support of that conviction. But with the swift, spectacular advances of the natural sciences in modern times, the contrast between science and the arts upset the judgment of many able men. On the one hand there seemed to be a steady, rapid increase in demonstrated knowledge, accepted by all; on the other, a mere welter of opinion. The interpretation of nature as a vast expanse of matter or energy without color and without form, a theory claiming the support of science, still further undermined the older confidence in the objectivity of beauty and goodness. Variations in manners and customs among men were treated as equivalent to fundamental oppositions in moral standards. Beauty was said to exist only in the eye of the beholder; and virtue was made out to be the name for types of behavior which in the long run brought the most satisfaction to the most interests.

This is not a proper occasion for even a summary of the controversy over the true nature of value, aesthetic, moral, religious; of the rivalry of theories, subjective, functional, behavioristic. From the confusion one fact emerged with notable distinctness. In most situations the *feeling* each of us experiences can be readily determined: when I feel tickled I feel tickled; on that I am infallible. These results are initially restricted by reference in each case to single individuals, but the results are certain. Once obtained they can be counted, classified, studied. Consider the different character of the results obtained by asking a number of people for their considered judgment on the beauty of a picture, and asking another group merely how they feel about the picture. In the first case, some will reply they do not know; and for the definite replies, the picture is beautiful, it is ugly, there remains the problem of determining what is meant in each case, whether the answer is unbiased, whether it expresses an estimation of the picture or a response to the picture's reputation, etc. But in the second case, although some may say they experience mixed feelings, all reports are definitive, final. If three people say they are thrilled, then the picture does thrill three people. What thrill means we all know or can learn from direct experience. What difference does it make whether it was just the picture or the picture's reputation which did the business; they were thrilled, weren't they?

On this is based a new method for both research and practice in the field of the arts. For this method important claims are made. It is claimed to be experimental: a picture is presented to each observer and he reports his feeling. It is scientific: the results can be counted, a kind of measurement, and then subjected to mathematical analysis. It is democratic: each person's feelings count for one, no more than one, and we all can *feel*. It is useful: the types of pictures found to be most effective in producing specific feelings in the most people can be determined and then used; feelings of a given sort can be produced almost at will. The old moralists recognized that feelings can be trained, but they aimed at our having the right feelings for things which are good, and their methods were unreliable. Now the aim is only to give people the feelings they want and the methods are tested.

A fundamental shift in emphasis has been made. Whereas formerly sound judgment and right feeling were united in a common reference to objects, now feelings just as feelings are decisively important. Feeling becomes the *terminus ad quem* of all artistic activity; objects once called beautiful are now mere instruments for producing, if they can, a thrill. Once people debated the importance of art and found they were not even agreed on the meaning of importance. Now that question is settled by discovering which people are "excited about art." When this position is adopted, there is no longer any problem of the cultivation of good taste or the refinement of the emotions. There is only the problem of the production of feeling. Whatever will do that is serviceable; what fails, is useless. Culture gives place to sensationalism.

I have no desire to exaggerate the extent of this degeneration in art or in morals. The giving of a good deal of attention to our feelings is not a new phenomenon in the history of man. In many situations our feelings are quite properly the final arbiters. Why shouldn't we choose a dentifrice for its taste thrill? The law protects us fairly well from dangerous cleansing agents; consumers' research organizations pronounce upon differences in therapeutic values; in a field so narrowly restricted and with brushing the teeth an intrinsically objectionable necessity, let taste decide choice. Who would cavil at that?

It is ordinary people, common people, who rely largely on feeling to guide them. It is also ordinary people who give least attention to theories. In this case, that is their protection. They have, if I may put it in this way, a sound feeling about the importance of their own feelings. They frequently laugh at the expert in art, as well they may, but they will attend to his judgments with respect; they do not think their own feelings are the ultimate criterion of beauty.

Errors in theory produce their first evil effects among those who deal with theories at first hand, who consciously accept or reject them. In the field of culture these are also the people in whose charge is the maintenance of standards. To give standards effectiveness, to protect them from being debased, is a struggle in which the welfare of the many depends upon the tenacity and integrity of a few. All sorts of drivel is written and said about an aristocracy of taste. It is often forgotten that aristocrats need not be, in fact, cannot be snobs, and they do not have to be given special privileges. What is required of them in the field of taste is that they work harder than the rest of us and for our benefit. If the word aristocrat is objectionable, let it be dropped. But culture for all of us depends upon the special gifts and integrity and hard work of some of us.

When people whom we expect to perform this function, talk the language of thrill and ignore religion, the situation is serious. It means they have abandoned the theory upon which the health of culture depends and do not even look at the one field in which that theory is still dominant. Religion, as has already been noted, has thus far escaped or has successfully resisted the alternative theory that excitement is the supreme goal of life. The mystic, if God grants it, may experience the ecstasy of union with God. The most ordinary penitent receives the peace of sins forgiven. But the mystic strives not for the ecstasy, but for union with God. Bastard mysticism regularly betrays itself by making ecstasy its end and trying all sorts of easy means to get it. Fraudulent penitence seeks to use confession as a means to a thrill. St. Augustine did not say his soul found rest in a religious experience. His words were: "My soul is restless till it rests in Thee." Despite its many errors and shortcomings, religion maintains these distinctions clearly and firmly. In religion one can still learn at first hand that the quality of our emotions is inextricably bound up with the quality of our actions, and with the character of the objects to which our feelings are a response.

This holds not only in religion, but in morality and in art. To bastard mysticism there corresponds a bastard aestheticism, a bastard moralism. They all carry the same distinguishing mark, preoccupation with feeling for its own sake. Feeling may be more precious than cognition or will; at least it is their equal. But feeling, or as we commonly say, love, is blind. Religion knows that. We are to love God; yes, with all our mind. Those who concern themselves with culture need to know that also. They need to know that feeling is the accompaniment, not the fulfillment of culture. If they have not learned that elsewhere, let them study religion.

Proletarian Literature
William Empson

from

Scrutiny, 3, 1935.

Reprinted by permission of the author and Cambridge
University Press.

PROLETARIAN LITERATURE

I T is hard for an Englishman to talk definitely about proletarian art, because in England it has never been a genre with settled principles, and such as there is of it, that I have seen, is bad. But it is important to try to decide what the term ought to mean ; my suspicion, as I shall try to make clear, is that it is liable to a false limitation.

As for propaganda, some very good work has been that ; most authors want their point of view to be convincing. Pope said that even the *Aeneid* was a ' political puff ' ; its dreamy, impersonal, universal melancholy was a calculated support for Augustus. And on the other hand proletarian literature need not be propaganda ; *Carl and Anna* is simply a very good love-story ; it counts as proletarian because no other social world (ideology) is brought in but that of the characters who are factory-workers. Of course to decide on an author's purpose, conscious or unconscious, is very difficult. Good writing is not done unless there are serious forces at work ; and it is not permanent unless it works for readers with opinions different from the author's. (On the other hand the reason an English audience can enjoy Russian propagandist films is that the propaganda is too remote to be annoying ; a Tory audience subjected to the same degree of Tory propaganda would be extremely bored.) Anyway it is agreed that there is some good work which a Marxist would call proletarian ; the more pressing questions for him are whether some good work may be bourgeois and whether some may not be class-conscious at all.

Gray's elegy is an odd case of poetry with latent political ideas.

> Full many a gem of purest ray serene
> The dark, unfathomed caves of ocean bear ;
> Full many a flower is born to blush unseen
> And waste its sweetness on the desert air.

What this means, as the context makes clear, is that eighteenth century England had no scholarship system or *carrière ouverte aux talents*. This is stated as pathetic, but the reader is put into a mood in which one would not try to alter it. (It is true that Gray's society, unlike a possible machine society, was necessarily based on manual labour, but it might have used a man of special ability wherever he was born). By comparing the social arrangement to Nature he makes it seem inevitable, which it was not, and gives it a dignity which was undeserved. Furthermore a gem does not mind being in a cave and a flower prefers not to be picked ; we feel that the man is like the flower as short-lived, natural, and valuable, and this tricks us into feeling that he is better off without opportunities. The sexual suggestion of *blush* brings in the Christian idea that virginity is good in itself, and so that any renunciation is good ; this may trick us into feeling it is lucky for the poor man that society keeps him unspotted from the world. The tone of melancholy claims that the poet understands the considerations opposed to aristocracy, though he judges against them ; the truism of the reflections in the churchyard, the universality and impersonality this gives to the style, claim as if by comparison that we ought to accept the injustice of society as we do the inevitability of death.

Many people, without being communists, have been irritated by the complacence in the massive clam of the poem, and this seems partly because they feel there is a cheat in the politics implied ; the 'bourgeois' themselves do not like literature to have too much 'bourgeois ideology.'

And yet what is said is one of the permanent truths ; it is only in degree that any improvement of society could prevent wastage of human powers ; the waste even in a fortunate life, the isolation even of a life rich in intimacy, cannot but be felt deeply, and is the central feeling of tragedy. And anything of value must accept this because it must not prostitute itself ; its strength is to be prepared to waste itself if it does not get its opportunity. A statement of this is certainly non-political because it is true in any society ; and yet nearly all the great poetic statements of it are in a sense 'bourgeois,' like this one ; they suggest to many readers, though they do not say, that for the poor man things cannot be improved even in degree. This at least shows that the distinction the communists try to draw is a puzzling one ; two people may get very different experiences from the same work of art without either being definitely wrong. One is told that the Russians now disapprove of tragedy, and that there was a performance of ' Hamlet ' in the *Turk-Sib* region which the audience decided spontaneously was a farce. They may well hold out against the melancholy of old Russia, and for them there might be dangerous implications in any tragedy which other people do not see. I am sure at any rate that one could not estimate the amount of bourgeois ideology ' really in ' the verse from Gray.

The same difficulty arises in the other direction. Proletarian literature usually has a suggestion of pastoral, a puzzling form which looks proletarian but isn't. I must worry the meaning of the term for a moment. One might define proletarian art as the propaganda of a factory-working class which feels its interests opposed to the factory owners ; this narrow sense is perhaps what is usually meant but not very interesting. You couldn't have proletarian literature in this sense in a successful socialist state. The wider sense of the term includes such folk-literature as is by the people, for the people, and about the people. But most fairy-stories and ballads, though ' by ' and ' for,' are not ' about,' whereas pastoral though ' about ' is not ' by ' or ' for.' The Border ballads assume a society of fighting clans who are protected by their leaders since leaders can afford expensive weapons ; the aristocrat has an obvious function for the people, and they are pleased to describe his grandeur and fine clothes (this pleasure in him as an object of fantasy is the normal thing, but usually there are forces the other way). They were class-conscious all right but not conscious of class war. Pastoral is a queerer business but I think permanent and not dependent on a system of class exploitation. Any socialist state with an intelligentsia at the capital that felt itself more cultivated than the farmers (which it would do ; the arts are produced by over-crowding) could produce it ; in a subdued form it is common in Russian films and a great part of their beauty (for instance the one called *The General Line* when it came to England). My reason for dragging this old-fashioned form into the discussion is that I think good proletarian literature is generally Covert Pastoral.

Before theorizing about this it is best to look at some recent

English artists. A book like Lionel Britton's *Hunger and Love,*
one of the few ostensibly proletarian works of any energy that
England has to show (I disliked it too much to finish it) is not at
all pastoral ; it is a passionate and feverish account of a man
trying to break his way out of the proletariat into the intelligentsia,
or rather the lower middle classes into the upper. As such it may
be good literature by sheer force, and useful propaganda if it is not
out of date by the time it is written, but what the author wanted
was the opportunity not to be proletarian ; this is fine enough, but
it doesn't make proletarian literature. D. H. Lawrence's refusal
to write it was an important choice, but he was a complicated
person ; to see the general reasons one had best take a simpler
example. George Bissill the painter, who worked from childhood
in the mines and did some excellent woodcuts of them, refused
to work for the *New Leader* (which wanted political cartoons)
because he had rather be a Pavement Artist than a proletarian
one. As a person he is obviously not ' bourgeois,' unless being
determined not to go back to the mines makes you that. Such
a man dislikes proletarian art because he feels that it is like pastoral,
and that that is either patronizing or ' romantic.' The Englishman
who seems to me nearest to a proletarian artist (of those I know
anything about) is John Grierson the film producer ; *Drifters* gave
very vividly the feeling of actually living on a herring trawler and
(by the beauty of shapes of water and net and fish, and subtleties
of timing and so forth) what I should call a pastoral feeling about
the dignity of that form of labour. It is very much under Russian
influence. But herring fishermen are unlikely to see *Drifters* ; for
all its government-commercial claim to solid usefulness it is a
' high-brow ' picture (that blasting word shows an involuntary
falsity in the thing) ; Grierson's influence, strong and healthy as
it is, has something skimpy about it. Of course there are plenty
of skilled workers in England who are proud of their skill, and
you can find men of middle age working on farms who say they
prefer the country to the town, but anything like what I am calling
pastoral is a shock to the Englishman who meets it on the Continent. My only personal memory of this sort is of watching
Spaniards tread out sherry grapes and squeeze out the skins afterwards, which involves dance steps with a complicated rhythm.
I said what was obvious, that this was like the Russian Ballet,

and to my alarm the remark was translated ; an English worker would take it as an insult, probably a sexual one. They were faintly pleased at so obvious a point being recognized, and showed us the other dance step used in a neighbouring district ; both ways were pleasant in themselves and the efficient way to get the maximum juice. The point is not that they were living simple pretty lives by themselves ; quite the contrary ; some quality in their own very harsh lives made them feel at home with the rest of civilization, not suspicious of it. This may well show the backwardness of the country ; for that matter there were the same feelings in Russia for the Soviets to use if they could get at them. They seem able to bring off something like a pastoral feeling in Spain and Russia, but in an English artist, whatever his personal sincerity, it seems dogged by humbug, and has done for a long time (Johnson was I think the first to say so). This may well be a grave fault in the English social system, but it is not one that an English artist can avoid by becoming a proletarian artist.

The essential trick of the old pastoral, which was felt to imply a beautiful relation between rich and poor, was to make simple people express strong feelings (felt as the most universal subject, something fundamentally true about everybody) in learned and fashionable language (so that you wrote about the best subject in the best way). From seeing the two sorts of people combined like this you thought better of both ; the best parts of both were used. The effect was in some degree to combine in the reader or author the merits of the two sorts ; he was made to mirror in himself more completely the effective elements of the society he lived in. This was often absurdly artificial ; the praise of simplicity usually went with extreme flattery of a patron (dignified as a symbol of the society), done so that the author could get some of the patron's luxuries ; it allowed the flattery to be more extreme because it helped both author and patron to keep their self-respect. So it was soon parodied, especially to make the poor man worthy but ridiculous, as often in Shakespeare ; nor is this merely snobbish when in its full form. The simple man becomes a clumsy fool who yet has better ' sense ' than his betters and can say things more fundamentally true ; he is ' in contact with nature,' which the complex man needs to be, so that Bottom is not afraid of the fairies ; he is in contact with the mysterious forces of our own nature, so that the clown has the wit of the unconscious ; he can speak the truth because he has nothing to lose. Both versions, straight and comic, are based on a double attitude of the artist to the worker, of the complex man to the simple one (' I am in one way better, in another not so good '), and I think that this recognizes a permanent truth about the aesthetic situation. To produce pure proletarian art the artist must be at one with the worker ; this is impossible not for political reasons but because the artist is never at one with any public. It may be that to produce any good art he must be somehow in contact with the workers, it may be that Russia is now going to produce very good art, with all the vigour of a society which is a healthy and unified organism, but I am sure that it will not be pure proletarian art and I think it will spoil itself if it tries to be.

The realist sort of pastoral also gives a natural expression for a sense of social injustice. So far as the person described is outside society because too poor for its benefits he is independent, as the artist claims to be, and can be a critic of society ; so far as he is forced by this into crime he is the judge of the society that judges him. This is a source of irony both against him and against the society, and if he is a sympathetic figure he can be made to suggest both Christ as the scapegoat (so invoking Christian charity) and the sacrificial tragic hero, who was above society rather than below it, which is a further source of irony. Dostoevsky is always using these ideas ; perhaps unhealthily, but as very strong propaganda. But I doubt whether they are allowed in proletarian literature ; the Communists do not approve of them, either as tragic or Christian, both because they glorify the independent man and because they could be used against any society, including a Communist one.

The great poetic statements of human waste and limitation, whose function is to give strength to see life clearly and so to adopt a fuller attitude to it, usually bring in, or leave room for the reader to bring in, this whole set of ideas. For such crucial literary achievements usually involve an attempt to reconcile some conflict between the parts of a society ; literature is a social process, and also an attempt to reconcile the conflicts of the individual, in whom those of society will be mirrored. (The belief that a man's ideas are wholly the product of his economic position is of course as fatuous as the belief that they are wholly independent of it). So ' fundamentally true ' goes to ' true about people in all parts of society, even those you wouldn't expect,' and this implies the tone of humility normal to pastoral. ' I now abandon my specialized feelings because I am trying to find better ones, so I must balance myself for the moment by imagining the feelings of the simple person. He may be in a better state than I by luck, freshness, or divine grace ; value is outside any scheme for the measurement of value, because that too must be valued.' Various paradoxes may be thrown in here. ' I must imagine his way of feeling because the refined thing must be judged by the fundamental thing, because strength must be learned in weakness and sociability in isolation, because the best manners are learned in the simple life ' (this last is the point of Spenser's paradox about courtly ' ; the Book of Courtesy takes the reader among Noble Savages). Now all these ideas are very well suited to a socialist society, and have been made to fit in with the dogma of the equality of man, but I do not see that they fit in with a rigid proletarian aesthetic. They assume that it is sometimes a good thing to stand apart from your society as far as you can. They assume that some people are more delicate and complex than others, and that if such people can keep this distinction from doing harm it is a good thing, though a small thing in comparison with our common humanity. Once you allow the arts to admit this you will get works of art which imply that the special man ought to be more specially treated, and that is not pure proletarian literature.

It is for reasons like this that the most valuable works of art so often have a political implication which can be pounced upon and called bourgeois. They carry an implication about the society they were written for ; the question is whether the same must not be true of any human society, even if it is much better than theirs. My own difficulty about proletarian literature is that when it comes off I find I am taking it as pastoral literature ; I read into it, or find that the author has secretly put into it, these more subtle, more far-reaching, and I think more permanent ideas.

W. EMPSON.

Introduction to 'Clubland Heroes'
Richard Usborne

from

Clubland Heroes: a Nostalgic Study of Some Recurrent Characters in the Romantic Fiction of Dornford Yates, John Buchan and Sapper by Richard Usborne. Constable, London, 1953.

Reprinted by permission of Barrie and Jenkins Limited.

INTRODUCTION

I AM forty-three now. I was eight when the First World War ended. I read my first Buchan (*Greenmantle*) when recovering from measles, my first Sapper (*Bulldog Drummond*) when recovering from mumps, my first Dornford Yates (*Berry and Co.*) when recovering from chicken-pox. After that I grabbed everything of each of them that I could lay my hands on in sickness and in health. If, in General Papers or scholarship *viva voce*, I was asked who my favourite authors were, I said Homer, Virgil, Shakespeare, Bunyan, Dickens and Thackeray. I lied. The authors I preferred, and whose books got about my schoolboy wits more than any others, were Dornford Yates, John Buchan and Sapper.

They might have been Conan Doyle, Edgar Wallace and A. E. W. Mason. They might have been P. G. Wodehouse, Michael Arlen and Gilbert Frankau. But they were not. I am not saying that my three were the best or only. But they were my three.

Some years ago I found, in an essay of George Orwell's, a derogatory remark about the type of middle-aged man who still lived a fantasy life in the works of Sapper. Well, even now I can never walk past, let alone into, the Ritz, Hatchett's or Half Moon Street without vaguely imagining myself to be Bulldog Drummond. I spent a large portion of the recent war working for a strange department referred to, even in Teheran, as 'Baker Street'. Practically every officer I met in that concern, at home and abroad, was, like me, imagining himself as Hannay or Sandy Arbuthnot. Three years ago, going to France for a holiday, I headed for the Pau–Biarritz area deliberately, imagining myself (albeit in a Ford 8, with family and sleeping-bags) to be a charter member of Berry and Co.

I decided to get all the books and read them through again, and to renew my acquaintance with three sets of characters whom I have, for thirty years, happily regarded as real people.* In the following chapters I often stray into examining them, rather unfairly, *as* real people. This could be called The Lower Criticism. Charles Morgan writes, in an essay,

> 'A critic's duty is (among much else) to discover a novelist's merit or demerit within the territory of the novelist's own purpose; not to praise or condemn him, as clique-critics and party-hacks invariably do, for having interpreted, or failed to interpret, life in terms of the critic's temperament or fashion.'

I do not think I am a clique-critic or a party-hack; but I break Mr. Morgan's rules.

And it is even more unfair, since I am often criticising between-wars books, characters and authors from the standpoint of 1953. 'Age is apt to react against what ravishes youth,' wrote Buchan in his book on Scott. My boyhood heroes lived lives I wanted to live myself. They were rich, and had Rolls Royces and many servants in the 1920's. I was envious, perhaps hopeful, then. One day I might help a wealthy woman across the street and be made her heir. Then I, too, could have a Rolls

---

* I was introduced in 1942 to a Syrian notable, who asked me if I was a descendant of an officer of my name who was killed at Waterloo. With a spin of the mind as remarkable as any of Richard Hannay's, I guessed he was thinking of George Osborne in Thackeray's *Vanity Fair*. And so indeed he was. He had forgotten the name of the book, and of its author; but George Osborne remained in his mind forty years after his last reading of the novel. He had forgotten that it was a novel. George Osborne was now a historical character to him.

and servants, and a dangerous job offered to me by the British Secret Service. But I feel that forty-three is too old for such fortuitous inheritance. Today I am probably soured by disappointment (that's what made some of the villains villains in Sapper and Yates). With time telescoped, fiction tested as fact and a purely personal approach, my judgments are the judgments of The Lower Criticism, and highly subjective.

History itself has been a little unkind to my authors and their heroes. The world has shrunk since the days when Jim Maitland and Sandy Arbuthnot went wandering in the far places. In what style could Berry and Co. travel in France and Carinthia on today's allowance of foreign currency? They could hardly buy priority for the clearance of the Rolls at the Dieppe Customs for a year's francs. England is no longer the governess of half the globe. *Ius Brittanicum* does not apply over so many lands of palm or pine. There are fewer Government Houses flying the Union Jack. The Embassies and Consulates that have replaced them cannot summon the gunboats to revenge a British traveller thrown to the sacred crocodiles.

By extension, the Englishman's traditional mistrust and dislike of the foreigner, the Dago and the lesser breeds cannot be so frankly expressed today. Their expression by the heroes and decent fellows in the books of Buchan, Yates and Sapper is noticeable now. I didn't notice it when I read them between the wars. On the Jewish Question particularly the decent fellows now seem to be badly at fault. Reading their views today one tends to forget that they were expressing them before the rise and fall of Hitler. But, in artistic compensation, the Russian wheel has come full circle. Ideologically Russian

Communism was the face at the window of Clubland in the 1920's; it is there again today. A good deal of the Sapper background, and a little of Yates' and Buchan's, is, in that respect, in focus once more. When I first read Sapper's *The Black Gang*, at the age of fourteen, I was duly thrilled. I happened to read it again in 1943, and was appalled by its cheerful, muscle-bound 'fascism'. Today it reads like the book it was, a venial political rant in the guise of a beefcake thriller.

I imagine that many of my age-group used to read my three authors with a good deal of youthful enthusiasm too. I have thought the books worth re-examining because, even in middle age, I often find that they have conditioned my mental reflexes. I like to think that this is only so on subjects on which I have had little cause or opportunity to form my own judgments from experience: subjects such as the Ritz Hotel, Darkest Africa, bar-room brawls in Tampico, sacred man-eating crocodiles in the Nile, Rolls Royces, crashed Balliol men, the erecting of woodland gallows and the digging of woodland graves in the South of France, buried treasure, rare Borgia poisons, disguises, men-servants, deer-stalking, the protocol at great country-house week-end parties, resigning from Clubs, and the British Secret Service.

Buchan, Sapper and Dornford Yates have given me a Code which might serve me well if I ever *did* find myself stalking deer, fighting in a bar-room in Tampico or hanging a villain in a dingle in France. But can I be sure that they haven't conditioned some of my thinking, and the thinking of my class and age group, about Jews, money, foreigners, leisure, killing, dogs, games, girls and how to make love to girls, beer, champagne, Success, England, America, the lower classes, the upper classes, servants, and West-End Clubs?

I have called this book 'Clubland Heroes' because the heroes of the books I am examining were essentially West-End Clubmen, and their clubland status is a factor in their behaviour as individuals and groups. It is not so usual for the heroes of today's thrillers to be gentlemen of leisure. In the 1920's I suppose that the man of sufficient private income and absolute leisure did not excite comment. Naturally he had a West-End club. He probably had several. The beefy type of hero was a man's man. So his club life meant a lot to him. Today's heroes are mostly professionals of one sort or another, special agents, Insurance investigators or straightforward cops, like P.C.49. But in Buchan, Sapper and Yates the men of action were recruited from the leisured class. When Scotland Yard was baffled, Inspectors MacGillivray, MacIver and Falcon put through 'phone calls to Clubland numbers.

A man's London club offers him a fortress, with many of the amenities of home, but without the distractions of, or the obligations to, his womenfolk. He can hole up at his club, and sulk there if he wants to. He can have his letters addressed there (which wives know, and some wives regret). The Hall Porter of a man's club is a reasonable picket against women, creditors and hunchbacked foreigners. A London club is a convenient place for authors to put their heroes.

Sometimes the smoother villains get in too. Where but in a London club can a villain, his face green in the light reflected from the baize cloths, peer in at the small circular window in the door of the billiard-room to see the hero and his friends playing snooker? Ronald Standish says, in one of Sapper's books, 'You won't believe it, but the police know of four men at large in London today . . . two of them members of first class clubs . . . who have all committed murder.' Sapper's Carl Peterson, in one of his disguises, was a member of the R.A.C. Friar, Oxford don, legal luminary and crook, was a member of (wasn't it?) the Athenæum until Jonah Mansel cancelled his membership with sudden death. Dominick Medina, M.P., Hannay's and Arbuthnot's opponent, was, by implication, a member of Boodle's. The German spy that Berry and Co. helped to apprehend in the summer of 1914 had been a member of the Travellers.

St. James's Square and its purlieus have, in derring-do romances, some of the advantages that the Western Desert had as a battle-ground. There are no women or children, and you have plenty of room to manœuvre your vehicle.

I am not saying that the Clubland-hero type was typical of the members of his club. Many a member of Brooks's hadn't the time or the inclination to go hunting villains Jonah-fashion. The Junior Sports Club must have had many more serious members than Drummond and his gang. And in Sandy's and Hannay's St. James's Street club Sandy and Hannay were probably looked upon as rowdy young trouble-makers. The romance-hero of my period is a Clubman; but he is not, in fact, typical of his club. Much more is he typical of the English Public School Prefects' Room.

He has advanced a number of years in time from the Prefects' Room. But his ethic is much the same still. He spends most of his time now administering free-lance justice, often rough. Come to man's estate, he no longer has fags to show off to, or rotters to punish for letting down the tone of the school. Now there are crooks, rotters and foreigners to punish for the good of England. If the hero likes punishing them (Jonah definitely had a sense of mission, and Drummond liked

dicing with death for its own sake), it is partly a psychological hangover from school days.

The public-school system sets boy over boy, prefect
over fag, with powers of command, reproof and corporal
punishment. It is a little world of junior law, vacuum-
sealed from the State Law. It may have justified itself
over the years by the production of the leader-of-men
type. The Prefect System trains men to assume responsibility. It also trains men to take the law into their own
hands.* A very reasonable and justifiable training for
your (then) Indian Civil Servant and your Sanders of the
River. But such public servants were ultimately responsible to Government for their actions. Was Jim Maitland? Was Drummond? Was Jonah Mansel? It is
worth noticing that Buchan himself, and his major hero,
Hannay, were not English public school products. The
Buchan adventurers chased and, if absolutely necessary,
killed their men on behalf of Government or governmental authority. They did not kill in private quarrel.†

Maitland, Drummond and Jonah Mansel fearlessly
attacked their cads, crooks and rotters without authority,
and without thinking very deeply about the legal implications. Admittedly, since they were on a usefully 'old-boy'

---

* There was a story in my House at school that a boy had been beaten
by the Head Prefect for leaving his (bottled) appendix in the dining-
room. This was an action against which there was no written or unwritten
law. The Head Prefect had decided it was wrong, and, by summary
corporal punishment, had aimed to stamp out the possibility of it becoming
a trend in the house.

† The adventure of *The Island of Sheep* was purely private enterprise.
Hannay, Arbuthnot and Roylance went out to help Haraldsen the Dane
rid himself of his inherited enemies. Haraldsen did a good deal of killing
in a berserk mood at the end of the book; the British heroes came back
without blood on their hands. But you cannot say that Buchan or his
heroes always regarded private killing with horror. Lewis Haystoun of
The Half-Hearted, written when Buchan was in his mid-twenties, argued
that on a purely private expedition of exploration it might be right for the
Englishman to execute a bad native porter to encourage the others.

level with the high-ups at Scotland Yard and in Embassies, they stood to lose little if their killings were interpreted as over-enthusiastic at the post-mortems. But in spirit they behaved as they were encouraged to do at their public schools. They didn't stop to wonder whether they really had the right to torture a dago bar-tender in Valparaiso (because he was a white-slaver) or hang a Hebrew jewel-robber (because he tried to paw an English girl). Drummond, though gone fairly berserk at the time, had no qualms or regrets afterwards about transfixing a Russian revolutionary, in peace-time, to the wall of an Essex mansion with the Russian's own bayonet. The Russian had tried to murder Drummond's wife. That was enough.

Was there any legalistic thinking at all behind these immediate responses in the brains of these admirable English heroes? If so, it had been done for them at school. They had, they thought, as much right, and indeed as much of a duty, to kill their crooks as they had had, as school prefects, to cane Jones Minor for missing a catch in the house match or for burning their toast at tea.

The spirit of *Stalky and Co.* hangs heavy over the books of Sapper and the thrillers of Dornford Yates. But the public-school/Clubland attitude of rough justice goes back farther than Kipling. There is a letter of Horace Walpole's in which he describes an alarm about a burglar:

> 'The next step was to share my glory with my friends. I despatched a courier to White's for George Selwyn, who, you know, loves nothing on earth so well as a criminal, except the execution of him. . . . (The drawer) stalked into the club-room . . . and said "Mr. Selwyn! Mr. Walpole's compliments to you, and he has got a house-breaker for you!" A squadron

immediately came to reinforce me. . . . Col. Seabright with his sword drawn . . . and then I, a carbine upon my shoulder.'

Crook-hunting was sport for the Clubland hero of the eighteenth century too.

Of course the art-form requires that, wherever possible, the villain should meet his death hand to hand with the hero. It is the expected ending. It is far less exciting if the police, or forces of authority, do the killing. And frankly, in Buchan's books, one feels rather cheated by the recurrent soft-heartedness of the heroes when they have their enemies (and the enemies of England) at bay. Heroes must be brave. It is presumably part of their bravery that they can take a lethal decision quickly. Perhaps, in a good book, the reader is panting along so fast that he does not stop to consider whether a decision to kill without trial in peace-time is ever justified; nor does he flinch because the killing is not even pondered, by the heroes, with any sense of awe. A public-school prefect learns not to waste time being awe-struck. Bull-fighting would not be a commercial proposition if the 'moment of truth' were omitted and the beaten bull reprieved from death. Readers look for the death-grapple, and authors, if they know their stuff, give it to them. The readers require—and it is part of Drummond's, Maitland's and Jonah Mansel's code—that the heroes administer the ultimate penalties of free-lance justice themselves, wiping the blood (if it has been messy) off their hands with never a qualm that it will bring them sleepless nights.

It is too much to ask that heroes of thriller-fiction should let the pale cast of thought sickly their every action. The George Orwell, product of Eton, who, as a police officer in Burma, had to shoot and witness the death of a rogue elephant—and hated every minute of it —would not have lasted long in Sanders' job in Africa. Not of such is the hero of thrillers. But a little less relish for their lethal work might not have harmed Jonah Mansel, Jim Maitland and Bulldog Drummond. They were endangering their own lives, yes. But does your own voluntary—indeed, sought-out—endangering of your own life give you the right, even if he shoots first, to shoot a peace-time opponent dead? Drummond is such a lovable old cloth-head that one scarcely expects him to weigh the rights and wrongs. But Jonah is a thoughtful chap. He never goes berserk (a 'well, he was beside himself' excuse for killing once used palliatively by Buchan, and often by Sapper). Jonah kills quietly, without losing his temper, for revenge and with a sense of mission, relieving the hangman of his job. And often enough he kills in revenge for something that in Law would not be a job for the hangman at all. Here we are, back in the Prefects' Room.

In *Perishable Goods* Jonah threatens the evil Jute, 'Rose' Noble's henchman, with death. But only to get information out of him about the captured Adèle (whom Jonah loves). Jonah does not murder his prisoners of (peace-time) war. And if Jute refuses to squeal, Jonah won't, in fact, carry out his threats. But then Jute produces from a pocket, and with a sneer, an envelope containing the white silk blouse that Adèle was wearing when 'Rose' Noble captured her. Someone, perhaps Jute, has stripped it off her back, just as, previously, someone, perhaps Jute, had cut off her glorious hair and sent it to Jonah in a box labelled 'Cut Flowers'. So Jute dies. The servants, Carson and Bell, rig the gallows and dig the grave. Jute has committed an offence which no legal system punishes with death. But the Clubland hero, with a code perhaps somewhat strengthened by reading such fiction as this, carries out his own sentence. It is partly revenge, partly social justice. It is legal only in Lynch-Law. It is whole-heartedly acceptable to the reader.

'The art of Life', says Jonah, 'is to make valuable friends.' He had made a valuable friend (was it at Harrow?) of Chief Inspector Falcon of Scotland Yard. Hannay knew he could find Sir Walter Bullivant (Foreign Office and Secret Service) and MacGillivray (Scotland Yard) at the Rota Club. Many's the Sapper book at the end of which Drummond emerges from a relished blood-bath and drifts round to see Old Tum-tum (whose fag he had been at school) at the Home Office. He has slain the Demon King and many of the Demon King's dirty-collared, Communist-inclined, revolutionary henchmen with names ending in -*sky*. 'There'll be questions about this in Parliament,' says Tum-tum. Or words to that effect. 'What are we going to say?' 'Oh, come, come,' says Drummond, 'haven't I done the Home Office and Parliament a good turn?' 'Oh, all right, you old rough-houser!' says Tum-tum. And Drummond toddles out, wondering how he's going to kill time until the next opportunity offers to kill cads.

Buchan called the self-protective cell the 'totem'. For all these pecunious gentlemen adventurers there is a background of powerful friendships. It is the 'totem', the system of the Club. The hero is a decent chap, and, as far as possible, he kills only bad chaps. If something goes wrong, and an innocent man gets killed, well, his powerful friends know that the hero meant no harm. Drummond once opted a safe-breaker to help him with a little job of pilfering. Some cad threw a bomb at the boys, and the safe-breaker (who was silly enough not to obey Drummond's order to lie down) was killed. Drummond felt badly about this. But it was nothing that £2,000 could not wipe from his conscience. He paid, in large-hearted semi-anonymity, £2,000 to the safe-breaker's widow. And how Tum-tum and Drummond and Co. laughed when she was arrested for drunkenness four nights in a week! By some mysterious working of the thriller-reader's mind, and cunning presentation by the author, Drummond positively seemed to come out of that little accident with credit. But then, if you have a spare £2,000 for such widows lying idle at your banker's, your credit is sure to be good.

It is no blame to their authors that Drummond, Maitland, Mansel & Co. get away with it every time, and with our sympathy. The authors know what we want, and they give it to us. They give us our blood-letting, and we enjoy it vicariously. We like to identify ourselves with such brave power and such straight shooting; we who could not fight our way out of a paper bag. But let us acknowledge, even while we envy, the cell-system which protects the hero. Not for us, perhaps, a life of gallantry on a private income from inherited wealth (though Hannay made his own pile). But, vicariously, through these cunning books, we can all be 'wonderful fellahs'; we can all know Old Tum-tum at the Home Office, and be sure he'll turn a blind eye to our few paltry murders; we can all belong to good West-End Clubs and leave our revolvers in the cloak-room. And, when the telephone message comes from Hoxton, we can turn on our heel and stride into the night, climb into the Rolls and head for trouble.

At whatever age we read thrillers, a necessary part of our pleasure comes from taking sides. The plots are struggles between Good and Evil. The author ropes us in, cunningly or blatantly, on the side of Good, and Good triumphs in the end. Our side wins.

The English schoolboy is expected to be a good loser. But this doesn't mean that he should enjoy losing in preference to winning. You're a good loser only if you've tried your hardest to win, if you have been beaten by a better opponent and if you acknowledge your defeat gracefully. If you have fought the good fight, you can go back to your House, wallow in a hot bath and put iodine on your bruises with a good conscience, whatever result the School Magazine prints for the match.

It is better to have been playing a team game. But if you have been playing a lone hand, say in boxing, rackets or golf, you should still be playing for some cause greater than your single self. Your House, your School, your club. And if you are good enough to play the game at the very top level, then you play it for England. Even if you are a professional boxer out for the biggest purses, the papers and other partisans will hold that you carry the honour of your country in your gloves. England will rejoice if you win against a foreigner. England will mourn, and the English papers make accusations or excuses, if you fail. Schoolboys, dissatisfied at heart that two masters of cricket such as Hutton and Miller should always be on opposing sides, make up teams to represent The World against Mars. In that way schoolboys can virtually be sure of cheering patriotically for the winning team.

Taking sides, and wanting to be on the winning side, are, if not matters of instinct, at least so much matters of upbringing that it requires a highly sophisticated training and mental discipline to be impartial in any study that interests us. The scholar should be impartial in his collation of facts; but the historian who writes without bias writes for a tiny public. The schoolboy wants all his History to be a contest between Good and Bad. He takes sides between Hector and Achilles, the Greeks and the Trojans, Athenians and Spartans, Jews and Gentiles, Romans and Barbarians, Christendom and Islam, Catholic and Protestant, Guelphs and Ghibellines, King and Baron, Red Rose and White Rose, Whig and Tory, Fascism and Democracy. And if, internationally, honours are easy, then he accepts patriotism as an absolute good, and, if he is English, backs England against the Rest. If he is French, he backs France; if American, America; if Russian, Russia. And the rulers of countries are glad that it should be so.

Whether our predilection for taking sides is a good thing or a bad thing, it is greatly encouraged by the authors of thrillers. Still, in my middle age, my first swaggering, quasi-instinctive attitude to all England's problems is that they are soluble, and will be drastically solved. Not by me perhaps, but by someone. On retrospection I attribute this swagger (I can't think of a word meaning swagger but without a connotation of good or bad; words take sides, too) to a wide youthful reading of Buchan, Sapper and Yates. Add, if you like, Stevenson, Kipling, Doyle, Anthony Hope, Ian Hay, Edgar Wallace and Dorothy Sayers. Their heroes were men who, generally without prayer, faced fearful odds and triumphantly solved their problems—which were often England's problems too. They were baffled, but only in the first chapters, and to fight better. No problem was too hard for them (or if it was, it didn't get written about). Having enlisted myself in their teams, I grew up with a feeling that England could always rely on some one person's, or some one team's, brains and bravery to pull it out of its perils. When I was a boy, and after I had grown out of imputing omnipotence to all grown-ups, I transferred my trust to the infallible English heroes of the English thrillers I read. If God came into it, then I felt that God was not only a Christian but, in the ultimate analysis, an English gentleman. He, naturally, took sides too.

I was building up to a let-down, of course. And this let-down is signified now in a vivid incredulity super-imposed on the natural uneasiness given to me by the newspaper headline problems of today. I wish it weren't so. I wish I could accept the appearance of Flying Saucers, and the disappearance of diplomats, as problems in space, without my thinking that surely some Hannay will be forthcoming to get the answers. Won't Arbuth-not settle the troubles in Malaya, Maitland the troubles in Kenya? Why didn't Drummond go and do something about Pontecorvo? Couldn't Jonah Mansel have found the Coronation Stone in a matter of days rather than distressing months?

These heroes gave me a taste for certainty. Life gives me dusty answers. It is a serious disenchantment. Of the free-lance British Agents of fiction, only Somerset Maugham's Ashenden could have prepared me for the continuous disappointments of real life today. As near as dammit the Ashenden stories ignore the two major, if latent, premises of the other books: that Good triumphs over Evil and that that one Englishman is worth four foreigners. I am not expert in the writings of Eric Ambler, Geoffrey Household's and those others who are carrying on the tradition. But am I right in suspecting that in today's thrillers the hero is no longer, because English, therefore automatically a much superior being?*

* Americans don't quite count as foreigners in Buchan, Sapper and Yates. Sandy Arbuthnot married an American, and Blenkiron, the

Am I right in thinking that the Good and Evil theme is less in evidence? If so, could it be because these authors have also had healthy, if dulling, doubts of the Englishman's innate excellence, and have to go more carefully therefore on the moral issues.

I have taken each author separately, followed by his characters. I have not had the privilege of knowing any of the authors personally, and I know hardly anything about any of them personally. I feel I do know, now, very personally, the characters they have written into life. And if I write about them in the following chapters with an annoyingly donnish display of factual knowledge (e.g. Berry getting his shoes from Nobb's, Hannay wearing a nightgown, the telephone number of Drummond's flat), it must be remembered that, long since my boyhood, I have re-read the books from first to last, from beginning to end. Where I have mentioned such detailed facts, I have done so airily as far as possible, without proliferating the footnotes, more donnishly still, with all the textual references. There is no reason why the reader of my book should remember, from his own less recent and more casual reading of Yates, Buchan and Sapper, a tenth of the trivia which I have accumulated and listed from my authors' books. But, if I say that Berry got his shoes from Nobb's, it means (for what it's worth) that I can give—or could when I was writing it—chapter and verse for the statement.

American, was a minor hero in several of the romances. There is no anti-American sentiment in Sapper. In Yates Adèle Feste of Philadelphia marries into the Berry and Co. group. In the Chandos books of Yates much of the adventuring is done in Europe and thus many of the beautiful countesses into whose castles, on rescue and treasure bent, the young English heroes storm their way, are necessarily foreign. Even so practically all of them have had English or, *next best*, American mothers; so that they are worthy to marry the Englishmen in the end. They come back to England in the Rolls, with Englishmen and treasures. They will soon have British passports.

I have started with Dornford Yates. He has two styles of story: the frivolous and the thrilling. From the ranks of the frivolous Berry and Co. group Yates took Jonah Mansel to be his main thriller-hero. Berry and Co. were often involved with crooks, but the stories in which they star together are not one-track thrillers. Berry and Co. were not strictly heroic. But they were very important to me. I have given them first place so that they may be granted their due before the shooting starts.

I have included a brief study of Carl Peterson, a villain to whom his author was deeply attached, and who recurred in person or in spirit through most of the Bulldog Drummond books. The Secret Service seemed to need general treatment against the background of the period and in the study of the formula.

But I am not trying to show that these three writers had much in common. Except for their period, they hadn't. They are brought together in the essays of this slim volume, without by-your-leave and in 1953, because they were my favourite reading in my boyhood and teens, and they have been a source of great pleasure to me since.

Popular Culture and the Romantic Heroine
Beatrice K. Hofstadter

from

The American Scholar, vol. 30, no. 1, Winter 1960–61.

Popular Culture and the Romantic Heroine

BEATRICE K. HOFSTADTER

Critics are rarely satisfied with pointing out that popular taste is bad; they insist that it is steadily getting worse. They assume that in the ideal world that existed before the mass media were devised, the popular taste was uncorrupted, and therefore necessarily better than that of our own time. Does this ideal cultural state of nature have any relevance to the problems of our world? Was a once pure taste seduced by the tricksters of Madison Avenue thirty or forty years ago, to be ever since the plaything of one manipulator after another?

This is not the story that a study of the popular culture of the last hundred years will tell. To take one example, American women have been reading love stories, and critics have been abusing them for doing so, for at least a hundred years. What may have been a waste of time for them is nonetheless valuable to us as a means of adding a badly needed historical dimension to the discussion of popular culture. The themes and characters that emerge and are transformed by successive generations of popular novelists have a surprising reality in the life of their own times, and a suggestive continuity with the themes that beguile popular audiences now. Perhaps popular taste has always been unregenerate; we can deplore it, but should we permit our distaste to deprive us of the light that may be cast on it by a historical examination of problems which are too often discussed as if they were wholly new?

❂ BEATRICE KEVITT HOFSTADTER lives in New York City with her husband and two children. This essay is taken from a book she is now writing, dealing with best-selling novels and their relation to American social history.

The theme I am concerned with here is romantic love, the most popular theme in Western fiction since the Middle Ages. English and American novelists have most often written this kind of story from the heroine's point of view; and in popular fiction particularly the woman is the central figure. To illustrate the development of this theme over the past hundred years, I have chosen the heroines of five American best-selling love stories published at approximately twenty-year intervals from 1850 to 1920, with some further consideration of a contemporary novel. My selection is random in the sense that no single book is uniquely important among best-sellers, but this is in the nature of the materials of popular culture.

Each of these heroines was immensely popular in her own time. The reason for such popularity lies in the rapport that existed, and must always exist, between a popular author and his audience. While it is not safe to assume that the reader of a best-seller agrees with everything in a book, neither does it seem reasonable to think that large numbers of people would acclaim and buy any book that did not fit in some way into their view of the world. For if it did not, readers would be irritated or bewildered rather than amused or thrilled or moved. Each of the authors of these books knew how to deal with his own world at the level of ordinary sensibility. We can accuse them of moral simplicity, but it is a simplicity they shared with their readers. A discussion of popular taste aimed at finding ways to study the development of popular sensibility, not merely to draw up an indictment against it, must take a historical point of view.

I

The archetype of all popular heroines is Samuel Richardson's Pamela, whose appearance in England in 1740 stimulated innumerable tyro-novelists to produce fair copies. It was nearly a century, however, before there was a large potential audience in America for a similar kind of fiction. Yet when Americans did begin to write for that audience, for reasons of both language and history they took as a model for their heroine the figure that had been evolved from Pamela into a popular convention by the English sentimentalists who exploited Richardson's creation.

One of the first American sentimental best-sellers was *The Wide, Wide World* by Susan B. Warner, published in 1850. Although it was a daring thing to be a lady author, it was hardly so bold as some of the other things American ladies had been doing. Two years before, a small number of women had held the first women's rights convention to protest against what Elizabeth Cady Stanton called "repeated injuries and usurpations on the part of man towards woman." The feminists who met at Seneca Falls were a small avant-garde whose opinions were by no means shared by all American women. On the contrary, their boldness shocked at least as many women as men. Nevertheless, the situation they were protesting against was one that nearly all of their sex had reason to deplore.

Miss Warner was no feminist, and her book at first seems to support the traditional pattern. Her heroine, Ellen Montgomery, is a reassuringly conventional creature, whom Pamela would have recognized as a sister. She is virtuous, modest, domestic and, above all, has the patent of gentility, a great sensibility which she displays in floods of tears. In one significant way, however, she does differ from the prototype. For Pamela duty was a moral imperative humbly and willingly performed, except when that performance would have been a crime against her virtue; for Ellen, who is exposed not to sexual but domestic tyranny, duty is a heavy yoke which she stubbornly resists.

She submits to authority after a struggle and only then because she comes to see her troubles not as acts of men but of God.

Thus, while Pamela was religious, Ellen Montgomery is pious. And what a weapon she, and a host of other heroines, can make of piety! Sinful man need but offer an injury; by raising her eyes to heaven, the pious female raised herself to the stature of a martyr. As *The Wide, Wide World* opens, Ellen's mother is taking leave of her daughter before going abroad for her health. She says, "Remember, my darling, who it is that brings this sorrow upon us—though we *must* sorrow, we must not rebel." It is not immediately clear who she means is the bringer of sorrows; but we know that her husband is forcing her to go away against her wishes, and he has refused to take Ellen. A few sentences later Mrs. Montgomery invokes God as the ultimate source of all trouble, but one does not miss the accusation that her husband is its proximate source.

Despite repeated protestations that God would ultimately settle all scores, genteel female authors could not resist giving Him a helping hand. They had a habit of killing off a heavy-handed father, and of reducing a lover to helpless invalidism before entrusting their heroine to him. Mr. Montgomery is pictured as being utterly unable to share or sympathize with his wife's distress at leaving their daughter. Later in the book, after Mrs. Montgomery has died abroad, the author sinks the father to the bottom of the sea in one short paragraph. His death brings not a single tear to the heroine's usually lavish eyes.

Susan B. Warner was born and brought up in an elegant New York City home, but when she was barely twenty her father lost his entire fortune. She and her sister were forced to retire from New York society to a dilapidated caretaker's cottage on an island in the Hudson River. They both began to write to support the family; and, although their books sold well and the proceeds should have supported them in comfort, their father so mismanaged the family finances that they lived all their lives at the edge of poverty. To kill off a heroine's father may have been small revenge, but they made what they could of it.

Despite her seeming conventionality, Susan B. Warner's books in fact made a subtle but far-reaching change in the accepted view of the tension between love and duty, between individual inclination and parental authority. Her heroine suggests that the docility of the Pamelas should be questioned. In principle, of course, submission was still acknowledged to be proper to females. Submission was written in the heroine's face—"There was in all its lines the singular mixture of gravity and sweetness that is never seen but where religion and discipline have done their work well" —as we can see it now in the faces of the pensive beauties so fashionable in the steel engravings of the period, smooth wings of hair modestly folded down over their cheeks. But to whom was submission unquestionably due? Is there an infinite chain of command? If parents are replaced by unwelcome guardians, the reader's sympathy then becomes available to an oppressed orphan, as it could never be to a daughter who did not honor her father and mother.

By removing Ellen's parents, Susan B. Warner was thus able to use her orphaned state as a vehicle of underground rebellion. After many trials under the guardianship of an unfeeling aunt, Ellen has a brief moment of happiness with a neighboring family who have befriended her. In this home she finds the sister she has longed for, and a hero whom she calls brother but who, it is hinted, may one day be something more. She is no sooner settled in, however, when wealthy relations in Edinburgh claim her and she must go, all unwillingly. Although her new guardians welcome Ellen and shower her with luxuries, they also insist that she obey them unquestioningly and forget her friends in America. She is a model of duty until they snub her religion and her country. Then she stubbornly goes to church against their express orders and defends her country against all comers. In time, the hero finds her in Scotland, still true to him in her fashionable home:

"I thought you would never come, John," at length Ellen half whispered, half said.

"And I cannot stay now. I must leave you tomorrow, Ellie." . . .

"O I wish I was going with you!" Ellen exclaimed, bursting into tears. . . . "I never thought you would leave me here, John."

"Neither would I, if I could help it; neither will I a minute longer than I can help; but we must both wait, my own Ellie. Do not cry so, for my sake!"

"Wait?—til when?" said Ellen, not a little reassured.

"I have no power now to remove you from your legal guardians, and you have no right to choose for yourself."

"And when shall I?"

"In a few years."

"A few years! . . . what shall I do?"

"What the weak must always do, Ellie, seek for strength where it may be had." . . .

"What will they say to you then, Ellie, if you leave to give yourself to me?"

"I cannot help it," replied Ellen,—"they must say what they please."

With this scene the book closes. Perhaps the actual leave-taking would have been too painful for Miss Warner to write. She does add a final paragraph "for the gratification of those who are never satisfied," which assures her readers that after three or four years Ellen did go home again, but which gives only the faintest clue to Ellen's final relation to the "brother" she treats with such tearful passion. Thus, without risking open rebellion, or disputing the weakness of women, Susan Warner was able to create a heroine with a new point of view, to oppose the moral sanction of parental authority with other sanctions as widely accepted, love of God and love of country.

This slight deviation from conventional obedience provides a clue to what *The Wide, Wide World* and other weepy tales of the 1850's were really about. As Mother, the American woman of the period shared with God and Home an official position in the sentimental triad of proclaimed American values. Yet her husband could treat her any way he pleased. In a society which extended its egalitarianism even to the rearing of children, women were superior moral beings with inferior legal and economic status. During the turbulent years of the mid-nineteenth century, when fortunes were as easily lost as made, a woman's position could suddenly become lamentable indeed. If a man went bankrupt in one of the recurring financial panics, he could lose his wife's money as well, without her consent. If a husband took to drink or to his heels, he could take with him everything his wife owned. A wife had no property rights, no recourse in the divorce courts, and no chance of earning any but the most meager living. There was no lady-like way out of her troubles; she could only bear them in the expectation that wrongs would be righted in Heaven. But the feminists could take heart from the example of their own country, founded in rebellion against tyranny in the name of the rights of man. To more cautious souls, Susan Warner and a host of other novelists could give hints that within the bounds of decency there might still be a way to oppose outrageous use of domestic authority.

II

By 1867, the feminist movement had gained considerable following, and woman's sphere was beginning to widen. The greatest gains were made in the field of education, and several women's colleges were founded in the 1860's. Even women who opposed political emancipation for their sex began to demand the right to be educated. Augusta Evans Wilson, a Southern gentlewoman and best-selling author, derided the feminist agitation for "the right to vote, to harangue from the hustings, to trail her heaven-born purity through the dust and mire of political strife" but claimed the right to be "learned, wise, noble, useful, in women's divinely limited sphere. . . ."

Mrs. Wilson had lifted herself out of her personal troubles by means of education, and each of her heroines put intelligence to similar use. Her father had been born into a wealthy planting family, but he lost his plantation before his daughter was four years old. By the time she was in her teens the family was penniless. Augusta wrote her first book when she was fifteen and be-

gan to make money before she was twenty-five. After the Civil War, she married a wealthy man older than her father, but she continued to write and to take great pride in presenting large checks—once an advance for $15,000—to her mother. Mrs. Wilson had no formal education. Her books are full of the pedantry of the self-educated; her prose is spread with a thick cultural pastiche. But her point is that women have minds and therefore ought to have the right to control their own lives; she is the first author to suggest that a heroine's destiny need not be a man.

There are, again, small but far-reaching differences between Mrs. Wilson's heroines and Miss Warner's. Edna Earl, the heroine of *St. Elmo*, published in 1867 and Mrs. Wilson's greatest success, is, like Ellen Montgomery, a precociously virtuous orphan. When she is fifteen, she is pulled from a train wreck by a wealthy woman who then takes the girl into her home. There she is educated, but the author continually points out that Edna owes her personal excellence to her own talent and determination. Her wealthy benefactress provides only the opportunity for the heroine's self-development. Unlike Ellen Montgomery, who is dutiful except on special points, Edna Earl cannot bear dependence, even on those she loves. She looks to education for economic, and therefore personal, independence. When she feels she is prepared to look for a post as a governess, she announces to her benefactress, "Much as I love you, I can not remain here any longer, for I could not continue to owe my bread even to your kind and tender charity." Despite the lady's tears and entreaties, Edna Earl persists in what she considers to be doing her duty. "I feel that when duty commands me to follow a path, lonely and dreary though it may seem, a light will be shed before my feet, and a staff put into my hands. . . . I feel assured that the chief of the 'Shrouded Gods' is Duty, veiling her features . . . whose unbending finger signs our way. . . . I shall follow that stern finger till the clods on my coffin shut it from my sight." Here is an entirely new version of the love-duty conflict. The center of duty has shifted not only away from parents but also, despite the piety of the heroine, away from God. Duty is raised to the grandeur of an abstract principle, a shrouded god whose sibyl is the heroine herself. That is, duty is no longer a social imperative, but by a rather clever shift has become a defense of individual will. In the name of duty, the heroine can assert herself against whatever demands may be made upon her. She is right to leave the luxurious home where she has been treated so kindly, but where she cannot be her own mistress. To underscore the point, several wealthy and desirable men propose marriage to her; she thanks them politely for the honor they bestow, but she refuses every one.

When Edna Earl does fall in love, it is with a cynical, dangerous man, St. Elmo, the profligate son of her benefactress. Although he loves her in return, she refuses him because of his sinister character. But under the influence of her pure example, he gives up his rakish ways, and unknown to her enters the ministry. While he is busy regenerating himself to suit her tastes, Edna has been earning her living as a governess in New York and also has become a famous writer. After many years, St. Elmo comes to see her and declares that "God has pardoned all my sins, and accepted me as a laborer worthy to enter His vineyard. . . . I never expect to be worthy of you! But you can make me less unworthy." Now that he is clay in her hands, she accepts him, although she faints at the wedding ceremony, presumably from joy but possibly overwhelmed by her own power.

Before his reformation, St. Elmo was a reincarnation of the eighteenth-century rake, but now how different a fate awaits him! Pamela had simply encased herself in the citadel of her virtue and held out against the siege. A proposal of marriage was her victory, but, hard-won as it was, it was also short-lived. As soon as she married, the rake regained the upper hand; as a husband Mr. B—— was unquestionably lord and master. Edna Earl, on the contrary, with her education to back her, does not marry except on her own terms. After the wedding she will continue to control her

destiny, and she will not become the domestic slave her predecessors were. She has insured a lasting victory by remodeling the hero to her own taste, removing the most threatening aspects of his masculinity and reducing him to pious jelly. Popular novelists in these times never discussed sex openly, but the sexual implications of Edna Earl's victory may well have been as clear to contemporary readers as they are to us.

III

After Mrs. Wilson, only the outward forms of the conventions inherited by the nineteenth-century novelist remain to the heroine; her moral forces have gathered strength, and with them her powers of self-assertion. Mrs. Wilson showed how she could use these powers to make life yield what she wanted. What would happen if her success with the hero went to her head, if, seeing how easily she had reformed one man, she set about reforming the sexual mores themselves? This was the task set for his heroine by E. P. Roe, one of the most popular writers of the Gilded Age. He wrote innumerable novels, several of which sold in best-seller quantities; but because they were bland, home-loving and cheerful in tone, he was dismissed even in his own day as an anachronism, a latter-day version of Susan B. Warner. He did not consider himself a writer of simple love stories; he meant to be a social reformer. Nevertheless, since his work was directed at moral rather than political reform, his intent was misunderstood by the political-minded generation that came after him. Still it was Roe who first gave voice in popular fiction to the reform spirit that was to swell into the ringing choruses of Progressivism.

Roe was a clergyman who was distressed by what he considered to be a growing spirit of materialism in American life. He wanted to revive the values of former days, to right a balance that had somehow been tipped. Cities were ugly and full of sin; the possession of money corrupted the soul; hard-hearted, empty women of fashion were neglecting their homes, and prodding their husbands on in ruthless, predatory careers that brought them not happiness but ruin.

Mildred Jocelyn, the heroine of *Without a Home*, published in 1881, is given the power to work those miracles Roe thought were within the capacity of a good woman. Her father, who has failed in business, has begun to solace himself with opium; her mother, pretty and affectionate but weak, is unable to prevent his dragging the family down from affluence to the depths of poverty. When the final disaster strikes, Mildred takes over and mothers not only her younger brothers and sisters but her parents as well. She superintends a move to the country, and here she meets the hero. He is no rakish St. Elmo, but an ignorant country lout. Under her gentle influence, he spruces up, and from wanting to better his manners and his appearance goes on to bettering his station. He leaves the farm and studies law, eventually becoming not only a moral but a financial success. But not for one moment does he forget that he owes everything to Mildred. Meanwhile Mildred has been too busy being the mainstay of her family to have time for love. The family moves back to the city, so that Mildred can try to support them by working in a department store. This episode nearly ends in disaster, from which the fledgling hero-lawyer saves the heroine. Emboldened by this success, he proposes marriage:

"Miss Mildred, you know that I have loved you ever since you waked up an awkward, lazy country fellow into the wish to be a man. . . ."

"Oh, my perverse, perverse heart!" wailed Mildred. . . . "How strange it seems that I can say from the depths of my soul that I could die for you, and yet I can't do just the one thing you deserve a thousand times!"

"I'd give all the world for this little hand, but I won't take it until your heart goes with it. So there! . . . As a woman you have sacred rights, and I should despise myself if I tried to buy you with kindness or take advantage of your gratitude. . . . I'd rather have an honest friendship than a forced affection, even though the force was only in the girl's will and wishes."

"Oh, Roger, Roger," sobbed the girl, "I can do nothing for you and yet you have saved me from shame and are giving us all hope and life."

"You are responsible for all there is good in me," he tried to say lightly, "and I'll show you in coming years if you have done nothing for me."

Mildred decides to take up nursing, by 1880 a highly respectable profession. Not until she has nursed the hero through a near-fatal accident—until in fact he owes his very life to her—does she realize that she loves him. In the time between, her self-sufficiency has saved her from what feminists in those days were calling "legal prostitution"—that is, marriage for support and protection, not for love. The hero, whom the eighteenth-century rake would hardly recognize as a fellow man, agrees that this attitude is right. So powerful is this heroine's influence upon her lover that he is as wary of physical love as she is; sex without love, the great sin of materialism, is as repugnant to him as to her. Theirs is a wholly spiritual marriage, the symbol of the better world Roe hoped for. Feminists since Mary Wollstonecraft had been arguing that chastity could not be required of women unless it were also required of men. This hero is willing to wait for his love with almost female patience, if need be, forever. And while he is waiting, his chastity equals hers. Roe advocates sexual equality of a special kind; he imposes on men the limitations traditional for women. Feminism can be a sword that cuts men down to women's size.

IV

No matter how appealing, as an ideal, equality in sexual morality may have been to an age infatuated with the very idea of ideals, it was too bloodless to have a wide appeal for long. By 1895 the sales of Roe's books had begun to drop off sharply. At the turn of the century a new heroine appeared, epitomized in the drawings of Charles Dana Gibson and hailed everywhere as the "New Woman." She was tall and active, she held her body straight and her head high. Her free and easy manners shocked her genteel mother, and her determination to live her own life appalled her father and his world of domineering men.

The American novelist Winston Churchill was one of the first to make the New Woman a heroine. At the center of his stories is a conflict, at once personal and ideological, parallel with that the Progressives were waging in the realm of politics. Churchill's heroines and heroes both embody social morality, civic virtue, personal integrity, and together they fight against businessmen fathers who represent the established order—money-centered, corrupt, powerful. In the sphere of family life Churchill tried to dramatize the other side of the coin of worldly success: the businessman as husband is superfluous, awkward, utterly banal; as father, he is both neglectful and autocratic.

Determined as he was to repudiate everything associated with the materialistic generation that had preceded his, Churchill tried to make his heroines entirely new. Victoria Flint, heroine of his best-selling *Mr. Crewe's Career* (1908), is, Churchill wrote, "not only of another generation, but might almost have been judged of another race than her parents. The things for which her mother had striven [money and social position] she took for granted. . . . She had by nature that simplicity and astonishing frankness of manner and speech which was once believed to be an exclusive privilege of duchesses." Victoria is, in short, that most exemplary democratic creature, a natural aristocrat. Moreover, she scorns as female weakness the kind of emotionalism that was so prized as a sign of sensibility and refinement fifty years before. In every situation she is calm and dignified, a model of self-possession. When the hero proposes marriage, she is controlled, he is emotional; his eyes fill, not hers. In moments of danger Victoria does not faint or yell for the hero's help; she springs into action, catches runaway horses, rescues children from the path of various vehicles, all without a tremor.

Armed with these multiple virtues, Victoria is not content to stay at home as her predecessors were; her interests range beyond herself and her family to the larger world of men, business and politics. Her father owns a railroad, and the hero, Austen Vane, is the son of one of the railroad's political agents. When they meet, they discuss not love, but railroads:

"I have been thinking since I saw you last— yes, and I have been making inquiries, I have been trying to find out things—which you will not tell me. . . . They say that the railroad governs through disreputable politicians,—and I— I am beginning to believe it is true. . . ."

Austen did not smile. She was speaking quietly, but he saw that she was breathing deeply, and he knew that she possessed a courage which went far beyond that of most women, and an insight into life and affairs.

"I am going to find out," she said, "whether these things are true."

"And then?" he asked involuntarily.

"If they are true, I am going to tell my father about them, and ask him to investigate. Nobody seems to have the courage to go to him."

Austen did not answer. . . . Suppose she did find out? He knew that she would not falter until she came to the end of her investigation, to the revelation of Mr. Flint's code of business ethics. Should the revolt take place, she would be satisfied with nothing less than the truth, even as he, Austen Vane, had not been satisfied. And he thought of the life-long faith that would be broken thereby.

When Victoria does find out that her father's business ethics are immoral, she never hesitates between morality and filial duty, not to speak of selfish considerations. So much does she disdain material things— her money is also involved—so devoted is she to truth and justice for all mankind that no other moral or human claims can influence her behavior.

Clear-headed and courageous as she is, however, Victoria feels the limitations her sex imposes upon her, and she wishes more than once that she were a man. The qualities Churchill prizes in his heroine, that proclaim her a New Woman, are masculine. Yet he does not wish to unsex her and, perhaps in compensation, places her even higher than her predecessors on the pedestal of Sacred Womanhood. Aloof and coldly virtuous, this heroine insists not so much on being loved as being literally adored. When Churchill proclaims her the "Goddess of Liberty" she seems to be indeed as unattainable as a statue.

But once Victoria has won her political victory and forced her father into the paths of economic virtue, she crumbles. What she really wants is not different, in the end, from what Ellen Montgomery wanted: not a career, but love and marriage. What seemed to be a break with the chains of the past turns out to be only a different sort of link. Like her predecessors, Victoria will not marry for money; money has made moral degenerates of her parents and has corrupted society as well. She accepts marriage only after the hero has proved he is as immune as she from these temptations and has a high-mindedness equal to her own. Churchill ends his novels with the promise to his readers that the ideal and idealistic couple he has just married off will not only live happily ever after, but will add to the world's happiness. They belong to a sort of moral elite; the example of their upright, selfless lives will, through some undefined process, improve the lot of the poor and the characters of the rich.

V

Sacred Womanhood was one of the first images to be shattered by the iconoclastic twenties. The feminist battle had been won; the prize of victory was the vote, which symbolized recognition of women's rights not only in the political but also in the economic sphere. But women had no intention of stopping there. No sooner had their political chains been struck off than they scrambled to throw away all the other signs of servitude—long skirts, decorous manners, prudential morals. The most advanced flappers did not want equality on the old terms; they wanted a single standard of moral behavior, but the other way round—not requiring men to be subject to female restraints, but allowing women male liberty. Marriage was no longer the life-and-death matter it had been. There were other roles for women now—career women, white-collar girls, bachelor girls. Who was to say what women could *not* do?

It was an Englishwoman, Edith M. Hull, who created in *The Sheik* (1921) the most popular heroine in America in the twenties. Diana Mayo is free, white, twenty-one and independently wealthy. Her parents are dead; her only living relative is a timid older brother, whose effeminacy presents a strong contrast to her boldness. Diana craves adventure, rides like a man, can handle a gun as well as a man, and has "the easy, vigorous carriage of an athletic boy." She will not tolerate love-making, not because she is a prude, but because she thinks it a waste of time; one of her admirers calls her "the coldest little fish in the world."

With a contemptuous sneer at her brother, and without a care in the world, she sets off to cross the Sahara, alone with a party of Arab guides. On the second day out the caravan is attacked by brigands, and Ahmed, their sheik, carries her off kicking and screaming. He is dashing and romantic-looking, a superman of the type created by Jack London, but, unromantically, he rapes her. She is not cowed but furious. Although she runs away, preferring the dangers of the desert to his attentions, when he catches her again she realizes that she loves this son of the desert. His primitive masculinity has awakened the primitive woman in her. Her happiness is unimpaired by her awareness that Ahmed does not love her, that she is nothing more than a female convenience to him. However, when a rival sheik steals Diana, and the hero rescues her from those greasy hands in the very nick of time, he too awakens to love. But love sobers him; Ahmed insists that he cannot ask Diana to continue to live with him this way, that she must go back to England. She rebels, she demands and then begs that he let her stay. When he still refuses, with her former courage she puts a gun to her forehead:

He turned like a flash and leaped across the space that separated them, catching her hand as she pressed the trigger, and the bullet sped harmlessly an inch above her head. . . .

She seemed only half-conscious, unable to check the emotion that, unloosed, overwhelmed her. . . . Gathering her up to his heart he carried her to the divan, and the weight of her soft slim body sent the blood racing madly through his veins. . . .

"You won't send me away?" she whispered pleadingly, like a terrified child.

A hard sob broke from him and he kissed her trembling lips fiercely. "Never!" he said sternly. . . . "Pray God I keep you happy. You know the worst of me, poor child—you will have a devil for a husband. . . ."

"I am not afraid," she murmured slowly. "I am not afraid of anything with your arms round me, my desert lover. Ahmed! Monseigneur!"

Probability is cast aside to make way for a happy ending. The sheik turns out not to be an Arab after all, but the son of an English lord and a Spanish lady. Diana can marry him not only without the disgrace of miscegenation, but even without the inconvenience of declassing herself.

This emancipated creature who roams the desert on her own seems at first glance to have little resemblance to the Gibson Girl who liked to shock people by riding alone over familiar country. The Gibson Girl prided herself on her superiority as a high-minded woman; when she married, it was because her lover recognized and paid tribute to that superiority. The flapper has jumped off the pedestal, and knows no ideal but physical equality and personal independence. Life seems to hold out only two possibilities to her: if she would be a woman, she must accept the age-old chains of domesticity; if she would be free, she must be a man. Despite the vote, at bottom the flapper felt she was not and could never be free as a woman; her sex itself made freedom impossible. Diana's mannishness is her way of refusing to accept the cruel fate of being a woman.

When she meets a man who is man enough to master her, Diana discovers that even for her woman's ancient role is the most satisfying. But just as she overplays one part when she starts on her daring adventure, so she overplays her metamorphosis. The height of happiness is not merely to be an awakened woman but a slave of her man. The freedom she had so boldly demanded nearly frightens her to death when she gets it. At the beginning of this story, Diana's great courage is continually commented upon; when the book ends, she is almost as fearful and tearful, almost as dependent on her lover, as Pamela had been so long ago. But not quite; the seducer has also changed. He admits that he has behaved like a devil, a beast; he wishes to undo the harm he has done and declares, "For your ultimate happiness I am content to sacrifice everything." Diana's victory is not the one Mrs. Stanton had fought for, but it is a distinctly female triumph. When Diana murmurs "Monseigneur," she has won exactly what she wanted.

VI

After thirty-five years of legal equality, thirty-five years during which many women have by choice or necessity made successes of nondomestic lives, freedom is still a dilemma for the popular heroine. A fling at equality sent Diana Mayo scurrying for safety to the arms of a man, proclaiming her essential femininity; Marjorie Morningstar rebels against the world of her parents and then recoils in a way very reminiscent of Diana's about-face. Marjorie's attempts to forget the Jewish traditions and sexual conventions of her middle-class parents, to be an actress, to have an affair, to be a free-wheeling individual, end when all she had longed for is offered her. Summarily, she rejects it. She wakes up to find that what she really wants is the time-honored safety of marriage and the family. "When Marjorie finally did get married, it happened fast."

Unlike Diana, Marjorie does not emerge from her adventures with a clear victory. True, Diana was raped and Marjorie was willing. But this is not the point so much as that Marjorie's attitude toward men and sex is confused, while Diana's is clear. Unlike the earlier heroines, who gave or withheld love with perfect self-assurance, who were secure in their female superiority, Marjorie is never sure of her attractiveness to the first man she loves, and then doubts her fitness to be a wife to the man she wants to marry. After a hundred years of an uphill fight, what are women's rights? Must women now prove they have not misused their freedom, and pass the tests once imposed on St. Elmo? Marjorie puts herself to such a test. She confesses her brief sexual transgression to her fiancé; she not merely submits herself to his judgment, she has prejudged herself by his standards.

All the time he talked she sank deeper into fear and misery. . . . It seemed impossible to break into this run of bubbling high spirits with the revelation about Noel. . . .
She had her rebellious moments during that sorrowful ride, behind the smiling face. This was the twentieth century, she told herself. He was an honor graduate of Harvard; he ought to know what life was all about. Obviously at thirty-one he himself wasn't a virgin. . . . She hadn't claimed to be one. Inwardly she raged at the injustice of his assuming that she must measure up to the standards of dead Victorian days. . . . Her guilt over having had one affair was childish. Everybody had affairs nowadays, the world had changed. . . .
In all these reasonable thoughts, however, Marjorie could find no trace of relief or hope. The fact was, she had passed herself off as a good Jewish girl. Twentieth century or not, good Jewish girls were supposed to be virgins when they married. . . . For that matter, good Christian girls were supposed to be virgins too; that was why brides wore white. . . .
Then all at once, at the very worst moment, just after the food was set before them, the story somehow broke from her in a stammering rush of words; every word like vomit in her mouth.
That ended the evening. . . . She had never seen such a change in a man's face; he went in a few minutes from happiness to sunken melancholy.

Still, Milton Schwartz decides to marry her. "But she never again saw on his face the pure happiness that had shone there during the drive. . . . He took her as she was, with her deformity, despite it. For that was what it amounted to in his eyes and in hers—a deformity. . . ." Marjorie, like Diana, has found freedom wanting and reestablished the double standard. But Marjorie never wanted to be a man; for her the choice was to be either an actress or a "fat housewife." Nevertheless her dreams of a career turn out to be a trap; even though she tries to compete in the world of men as a woman, she is unable not to violate her womanliness. When Marjorie finally chooses domesticity, she overplays her new role much as Diana overplayed femininity. She limits herself to prudential morals and home-centered goals as rigid and circumscribed as Ellen Montgomery's. What looked like confines to the nineteenth-century feminist, however, look like safety and the resolution of an impossible conflict to the twentieth-century female.

Refurbished domesticity—"togetherness" —is once again a central value in American life. Once again girls go directly from their parents' homes to their husbands', no sooner cease being children than they become parents. An independent life, or even postponement of marriage and motherhood to gain some experience of the larger world, get less and less sanction from our popular writers. They are no longer occupied with the restraints of authority but with the dangers of freedom. On the level of the popular novel, at least, we seem no nearer than we were a hundred years ago to finding a working answer for women's opposing needs—fulfillment as women and as autonomous individuals.

Literature and the Historian
Walter Laqueur

from

Journal of Contemporary History, vol. 2, 1967.

Literature and the Historian

Walter Laqueur

Historians sometimes forget that they have no monopoly in their own field of study. The reading public, perhaps unfortunately, has a preference for amateurs over professionals, and outsiders over academics. The book trade is hardly likely to agree with Ludwig Borne's dictum (admittedly 140 years old) that no one ever profited from the study of history with the exception of some publishers and booksellers. Novels not merely sell better; *War and Peace* and *Le Rouge et le Noir* ought to figure at least as prominently in the education of the student of Borodino and Waterloo as the works of Kolyubakin, Horsburgh, or Navez. The writings of Balzac and Dickens do not abound in statistics, but they are as essential for an understanding of nineteenth-century social history as even the best conventional histories. Eugene Sue and Spielhagen are not in the same class and their rating in the annals of literature is not now very high, but they remain invaluable for understanding the *Zeitgeist* of the eighteen-forties. About the life of the proletariat around the turn of the century there are now many interesting monographs. Does anyone give a fuller, a more gripping picture than Zola and Gorky, Andersen Nexö and Blasco Ibanez? No period in recent history has been more thoroughly studied by historians than the first world war. There are military accounts, diplomatic analyses, and economic surveys, many of them of the greatest value. And yet, to realize what the war meant for millions of participants, to understand the quality of life during those years, teachers will refer their students above all to Barbusse and Remarque, to Siegfried Sassoon, Jules Romains, and the dozens of others who took it as their theme.

The historian, by a venerable tradition, used to be a man of letters: 'History begins in novel and ends in essay', Macaulay wrote. True, the number of badly written histories is legion. But the Muses had *one* father; and Calliope and Erato were Clio's elder sisters. If tragedy was born out of the spirit of music, history descends from epic and lyric poetry, from tragedy and comedy, not from Euclid. The relationship between Clio and her sisters in the age of quantification has become a distant and tenuous one, but it ought to be recalled from time to time as, so to speak, part of the family genealogy.

The strict division between writers and historians occurred only in the second half of the last century. Before that, historians had often dabbled in *belles lettres*, and poets were not disqualified from writing history. Schiller wrote 'straight' history, but this is not what he is famous for. Of the well-known historians of the pre-scientific age, many were by modern standards profligate characters; their extra-curricular activities would do them little good now in terms of academic promotion. Gibbon wrote on the theory of literature, Guizot on Shakespeare, Michelet on nature and nightmares. Voltaire could be classified both as a historian and as a writer, and what about Carlyle and Macaulay, Renan and Taine? The literary approach came under attack following the growth in influence and prestige of the German school of historians – not only in Germany, but also in England, the United States, and elsewhere. Later this trend was reinforced by the emergence of the scientific school of historiography. This was the era when many historians felt they were on the verge of some discovery that would do for history what Darwin had done for nature, as a famous president of the American Historical Association once observed. The breakthrough, alas, never came. The historical school stuck closely to the sources and hardly ever went beyond preparatory spade work, as some of its earliest critics had predicted. Imagination became a dirty word, though it was later brought in through the back door as 'associative imagination' – in contrast to poetic fancy. Some brave attempts were made to restore Clio as a Muse. The belief in scientific history waned, but there was no revival of the literary school in the academies. Of the new technical historians some wore their learning lightly and were blessed with grace in expression; others less gifted produced papers and monographs destined to be read by a small circle of professional colleagues only. The whole trend was not conducive to books of wide appeal; the progressive specialization characteristic of industrial society was reflected in the universities in a strict division of labour according to which every scholar was classified and put into a compartment. There was an unwritten convention as to how history should be written, and it became unwise to stray too far from it. Unwise from the academic point of view, but not if the taste of the reading public was considered; they continued to ask for readable history. The great historians of the eighteenth and nineteenth centuries had produced best-sellers; none of their successors (with the exception of Toynbee and one or two others, similarly suspect in professional circles), had done so. The average scholarly work became more and more specialized or esoteric; the appeal of even the best books of this kind was in inverse ratio to the critical acclaim they received. As Goethe said about Klopstock: Everyone praised his books but who bothered to read him?

It was not however only a matter of style and literary approach. The public was deterred by the reluctance of many historians to deal with broad and important subjects, by the perverse attraction that historical footnotes held for the professionals. The image of the ivory-tower historians emerged, 'the rag pickers of Clio who take their subjects from the garbage heap, who make napkin rings to pass the time like a retired customs official' (Lucien Fèbvre). 'We protest when the public takes XYZ for historians. But what do we offer them to read that is readable?' XYZ have been doing well in recent decades. For if the historians have not produced best-sellers, the appetite of a public, much larger in numbers than in the last century, for historical literature has grown by leaps and bounds. Lytton Strachey and Emil Ludwig had their vogue in the twenties; there has been a whole spate of literature, much of it of value, in our own time. Mr Shirer's book on Nazi Germany has sold many hundreds of thousands of copies despite the almost universally negative attitude of professional historians. More recently Mr Cornelius Ryan has done even better. The comments of the historians did not greatly matter; this literature answered a definite need which the historians had been unable or unwilling to satisfy. In France there is a whole galaxy of highly successful journals devoted to popular history of the *histoire historisant* kind; *History Today* in Britain (a journal by no means popular in character) succeeded beyond all expectations. This great interest in history, biography, the historical novel, has not diminished even under the impact of a new literary genre, science fiction. Technical history could not compete with popular biographies and instant history – these are legitimate activities moving on different levels; to this extent the relative unpopularity of the professional historians was inevitable. But was it not at least in part often due to a deliberate neglect of style and an absence of imagination on the part of the academic historians themselves?

Style and imagination are the great preservatives in history, and the world at large, as a contemporary historian has reminded us, will sooner forgive lack of scientific solidity than lack of literary charm. Competence, scientific solidity, should be a prerequisite for writing history, not a synonym for boredom. A limpid style is invariably the result of hard labour: 'The idea that histories which are delightful to read must be the work of superficial temperaments and that a crabbed style betokens a deep thinker or conscientious worker, is the reverse of the truth. What is easy to read has been difficult to write' (Trevelyan).

Writers of historical novels – and what nineteenth-century author did not try his hand at this genre at one time or another? – have had it easier than the historians. They can pick and choose, extracting the most dramatic incidents, ignoring everything that lacks wide appeal. They are attracted by great men and women, their ambitions, intrigues, confrontations. Above all, they search for the motives behind the action: why did Philip II kill Don Carlos? Why did Peter the Great have his son Alexei executed? What was the real identity of the false Dimitri and of Kaspar Hauser? What made Thomas-à-Becket act as he did? What impulses motivated Jeanne d'Arc and Mary Stuart? Was Masaniello a criminal or a patriot? Who is more worthy of our sympathy – Charles I or Cromwell? These and other heroes have attracted hundreds of writers and playwrights over the years and, to a certain extent, continue to do so. In a few decades a more sophisticated Lanny Budd will no doubt report his meetings with Hitler and Goering. Where historians feared to tread writers of historical fiction have moved with far less restraint, unfettered by any of the rules and taboos which historians have to observe. There have been novels and plays that merely transfer into the past contemporary problems and conflicts. In the medieval romances Charlemagne or Edward IV appeared as living characters; in the modern psychological novel Julian the Apostate and Antigone become twentieth-century figures. It is interesting, but it has nothing to do with history. But there were others, the purists of the historical novel who, like Walter Scott, based their work on solid historical research, retracing the course of events with much insight and knowledge. Their reconstruction of the past may often be, for all we know, as near the historical truth as the work of the professional historians. Even so, historians have usually regarded the historical novel as unfair competition and have not, on the whole, taken it seriously. Were not the heroes of even the most successful historical novels like guests at a masked ball – contemporaries of Bulwer Lytton, Sienkiewicz, or Manzoni in Greek, Roman or Papal garb? Were not most of these novels *romans à clef* in which prominent contemporaries appeared and could be identified without undue difficulty? But the same charge can frequently be made against eminently academic historiography, in the sense that all history is contemporary history. There is not that much difference between the historical novel and orthodox historiography where the assessment of key figures is concerned. Surely it is no coincidence that in the struggle between Charles I and Cromwell the sympathies of almost all the historians and the writers up to the early years of the nineteenth century were on the side of the King. There is a similar parallelism in the approach of both historians and novelists to Charles XII of Sweden; the adventurer of the eighteenth century became the great romantic hero of the nineteenth. Napoleon, so bitterly attacked during his lifetime outside France, after his death was presented by historians and writers alike as a genius to whom ordinary standards could not be applied.

History and literature meet on many different levels, and there is a large area of no-man's-land into which both sides have made forays. Some of the writers who have written history have already been mentioned; there were many more who had no intention of writing history, but have done so if only indirectly, and often unconsciously. For their works reflect the issues of their times, and thus constitute a source of great importance for the historian. An account of the *Vormaerz* that does not refer to Heine and *Das Junge Deutschland* is at best incomplete; a survey of the Second Empire that omits Victor Hugo is unthinkable. A discussion of the politics of Thomas Mann and Sartre, of Graham Greene and Roy Campbell are relevant (as essays in this volume show) to the understanding of the *Zeitgeist* of the twentieth century.

Lastly, there are those writers who from time to time have not only written or reflected history but have made it. Some historians have belittled their importance for roughly the same reasons that made Stalin enquire about the number of divisions at the disposal of the Pope. But is political power really measured that way? The 'literary intelligentsia' has been prominent in all political movements of the past two hundred years; they have played a decisive role in revolutions even if their function usually extended no further than blazing the trail.

Neither as individuals nor as a group have intellectuals held political power for long. Usually they are in opposition; indeed, it is widely thought that to be outsiders is their historical mission. To their political allies they may not be of great help, but as opponents they can be dangerous. More and more of them, as the articles which follow show, are politically committed.

On the news of the death in 1841 of Diego Leon, a now forgotten Spanish general, the German revolutionary poet Ferdinand Freiliggrath wrote a poem that shocked and disturbed many of his friends: Whatever I wrote, he asserted, I wrote freely. The poet does not and should not care whether his verses please everyone. He knows that there has been evil in the world since the days of Troy. The poet bows to the hero Bonaparte, and is angered by the Duc d'Enghien's death cry, for he views the world around him from a higher vantage point than that of a political party:

> Er beugt sein Knie dem Helden Bonaparte,
> Und hoert mit Zuernen d'Enghien's Todesschrei:
> Der Dichter steht auf einer hoeheren Warte
> Als auf den Zinnen der Partei.

Georg Herwegh, Freiliggrath's friend and his rival in popularity among the German left, answered almost immediately in a poem called simply 'Die Partei'. Who could refuse to join the great movement in these stirring days? Who could shirk the question: Slave or Free? Were not the poets in duty bound to act, to break their lyres and to lead the people in the struggle for a better future? Not for poets the Olympian detachment; and had not the gods themselves descended from Olympus to take part in the partisan struggle? Poems are swords, poets are called to action.

> Ich hab gewaehlt, Ich hab mich entschieden,
> Und m e i n e n Lorbeer flecht ich der Partei.

(I have chosen, I have decided, and *my* laurels will be woven for the party.) This controversy in the poetry columns of German news-papers more than a century ago anticipated in its main arguments current discussions about commitment and *littérature engagée*.

Individually, writers and poets have always participated in the political and social struggles of their time. But the idea of literature as a political force and the poets as the unacknowledged legislators of their age appeared only towards the end of the eighteenth century. It originated in France, where men of letters without wealth, social eminence, or the responsibilities of official status (as Tocqueville notes in a famous passage) took the lead in politics, as they were the only ones to speak with the accents of authority. The political ferment was channelled into literature, 'the result being that our writers now became the leaders of public opinion and played for a while the part which normally, in free countries, falls to the professional politicians'. These men of letters were now in charge of the political education of the French nation, shaping the national temperament and outlook on life. It was a great movement and it had a great impact. But was the importation of literary propensities into the political arena an unmixed blessing? Tocque-ville, at any rate, did not think so; he did not like the broad generalizations coupled with contempt for hard facts, the abstract words, the gaudy flowers of speech, the sonorous clichés: 'For what is a merit in the writer may well be a vice in the statesman, and the very qualities which go to make great literature can lead to catastrophic revolutions'. It is almost literally Monsieur Raymond Aron castigating Sartre one hundred years later.

The French revolution marked the great divide; ever since the literary intelligentsia has made a great and growing impact on politics; 1848 was the revolution of the intellectuals *par excellence*. This involvement did not proceed everywhere in equal measure, and it was not to everyone's liking. Least of all to Goethe's, who wrote to his friend Luden that it was not necessary for him to take up public affairs when they were adequately handled by excellent men, 'and so I could stay in my closet and think of my innermost self'. On another occasion, to the same correspondent: 'Let the world go its way, and do not mix yourself up in the quarrels of kings'. And when his advice was ignored and Luden decided to go into politics after all: 'I hate all bungling like sin, especially bungling in affairs of state, from which nothing but misery results for thousands and millions'. Goethe's reasoning is unexceptionable – the effects of bad politics are usually more fatal than those of a bad poem. But the men of letters in France and Germany, in Italy and Austria, were convinced that affairs of state were not in the hands of excellent men, and that the bunglers at the top needed to be replaced by intellectuals.

England was the one country where these ideas had no impact; it was teeming with revolutionary ideas but there was no revolution. It has been argued, by Belloc for example, that in England at the time literature and the arts were far more extreme and revolutionary than on the continent – Blake's and Turner's paintings, for instance, in comparison with David's pseudo-classicism, 'Kubla Khan' and Shelley in comparison with André Chenier: 'English Romantics, English Liberals, were not public men making a republic but poets, each seeing a vision'. In the Victorian age even the visions disappeared; social criticism there was, but on the whole the divorce between public affairs and writing became more pronounced. The aftermath of the first world war caused despondency and withdrawal but no major call to action as on the continent. The great debate about commitment and literature came to England only in the 1930s, almost a century later than to the continent.

Russia, on the other hand, was the country of *littérature oblige*. When Chernyshevsky wrote that novels, essays, and poetry 'have a far greater significance for us Russians than they have in any other country', this was a statement of fact, not merely the credo of the extreme left. As in eighteenth-century France (only more so), literature was the only outlet into which revolutionary energies could be channelled. It had replaced religion as the main inspiration of the intelligentsia, and since the censorship made open discussion of political questions impossible, literature became the obvious forum for such debates. Philosophical, aesthetical, literary essays and surveys were almost invariably political tracts in disguise; indifferent novels like *What is to be Done* educated generations of revolutionaries. The Russian *littérateurs* in their enthusiasm were all in favour of abolishing literature; when Bazarov said that he believed not in principles but in frogs, and that a decent chemist was twenty times more useful than a poet, the caricature was uncomfortably close to realities. The leading critics at the time wanted to ban private, individual problems from the novel and from poetry, for were not public issues much more important? The extremism, and above all the nihilism, of some of these enragés annoyed even Herzen in his London exile:

> What struck me about them was the ease with which they despaired of everything; the ferocious joy of their denial and their terrible ruthlessness. Despite their excellent spirits and noble intentions, our 'bilious ones' can by their tone, drive an angel to blows and a saint to curses. They exaggerate everything in the world with such aplomb and not as a joke but out of such bitterness, that they are quite unbearable.

These observations refer to young mid-nineteenth-century Russian bohemian revolutionaries; it is purely accidental if they have a familiar ring on some university campuses in the western hemisphere.

The nineteen-thirties were the classic age of political involvement, of writers' congresses, manifestos, and politico-literary tracts. The social convulsions in the wake of the world economic crisis, the rise of fascism, the emergence of Stalinism, brought home the lesson that politics did matter. There was much talk about the responsibility of the writer, his obligation towards society, his duty not to withdraw into the proverbial ivory tower. The idea of the writer as a man of action was not altogether new; in practice most of such adventures after the first world war had not been successful, whether on the right (d'Annunzio in Fiume) or on the left (Eisner, Toller, Muehsam in Munich). But in the thirties there was a collective call to arms; a partial retreat from politics came only in the fifties with the emergence of a new literary generation.

The responsibility of the writer is twofold: as a writer he has, if he is any good, a wider forum and more authority for his views than most other men. But is he always aware of the responsibility which such a position implies? Would the political views of Thomas Mann or of Sartre have attracted the same measure of interest but for their eminence in the field of *belles lettres*? Would the leaders of the extreme right in France have found enthusiastic followers for their ideas but for the fact that many of them had a witty, elegant, and effective style? Have we not seen playwrights of genius in whose expert hands a primitive political message assumes great sophistication, in which perverse moral judgments become a new categorical imperative? There is a danger of eminence in one field imparting more or less automatic authority in another – politics in this case; if here we are concerned with letters, the danger is no less great in the case of physicists, theologians, and above all television personalities. If historians had a wider public they would probably be faced with the same dilemma.

These then are some of the questions discussed in this issue of a journal which tries to take a broad view of its field of study. The choice of subject may invite criticism. A discussion of the views of Chernyshevsky in a Russian historical journal of the eighteen-sixties would no doubt have encountered criticism by its contemporaries – what has this to do with history? A great deal, even if it was not always immediately obvious. History will never be the exclusive preserve of the historians; literature should not be the monopoly of the literary critics. Poetry is under no obligation to take notice of diplomatic or economic history. But in a wider sense history and literature need each other. They must make constant forays beyond the borders established a long time ago by well-meaning pedants.

Psychology of War Literature
Joseph Remenyi

from

The Sewanee Review, vol. 52, 1944.

by Joseph Remenyi

PSYCHOLOGY OF WAR LITERATURE

WAR is apt to cripple the creative spirit (*inter arma silent Musae*) but, considering the output of warbooks today, it does not seem to diminish the quantity of writing. In fact, one must be resigned to the frantic and pragmatic attempt of many scribes who devote much of their time to the issues of war. However, in the flood of words that confronts the contemporary reader, it is important to differentiate between timely works and works, though timeless, that are also very timely. Man is prone to waver in his wrestling with destiny; this is also characteristic of many writers. Novels, for example, do not cease to be pot-boilers because "noble intentions" stir the heart of the authors. To recount episodes or events that show the selfadmitted stalwart disposition of the writer in the service of democracy, might reveal a span of months or years that are interesting or frightful interruptions of peace; yet such works, with all their actual or assumed documentation, are not necessarily literary attainments. A drummer might be needed in an orchestra, but he is not the orchestra itself. So many of the novels or plays, inspired by war or by the ideological expediency of war, seem to invalidate the principles of literature. They are clever, often not even clever; they are sensational, but often boring; the writers of personal narratives are inclined to be garrulous or champions of "thrillers" that make of facts rivals of unrestrained imagination.

Aristotle said that the supremacy of poetry over history consists in higher truth and higher dignity. No view is final in its infallibility; not even that of a Greek philosopher. The Greek sage evidently thought of the relationship of the word to a complete fate; no doubt, in terms of a complete human fate, the "personal history" of many writers in connection with the global war or with the preliminaries of the war is fragmentary indeed. Such recollections show that the authors were witnesses of certain events, but that they were not creative writers who knew how to concentrate on essentials and how to express these essentials. *Universal conflagration suggests an interaction of forces which, in a sense, expects writers to be poets.* The accuracy of note-books is not sufficiently impressive. In relating experiences, the chiaroscuro method of interpretation is often used; black and white seem the only symbols born of this modern cataclysm. E. M. Forster remarks in his *Passage to India* that "it is not when we examine life, it is when we are examined by life that we become real persons." Thus the English novelist pays homage to inner discipline and humbleness. I am not underestimating the difficulties that a correspondent experiences when he writes about the collapse of civilized values with the horizon of immediateness. It is also comprehensible that in giving account of extraordinary events, despite the writer's scrupulousness, the temptation for sensationalism is almost unavoidable. Having been close to the scene of action interferes with the perspective of expression. Nevertheless Antoine de Saint Exupery's *Flight to Arras,* a story of a reconaissance flight in France, indicates that it is possible to combine observation and expression without sinning against truth in relation to the essence of an experience.

There is value in the well organized accounts of correspondents like Lochner, Shirer, and a few others; their principles of qualification as to the material about which they wrote is more or less that of good journalists, probably offering future generations the kind of information that one sometimes finds in Plutarch, Livy, and Sallust in regard to ancient Rome. They are primarily concerned with the mobile elements of an experience; and though lacking, for instance, the unusual gift of character-delineation of Plutarch, (and I assume they themselves recognize their own limitations) there runs through their reports a thread of symbolized actuality that seems to connect the pre-war conditions of Germany, the war-conditions of Europe and those of the world with the possibility of a basis for a sensible interpretation by future historians.

Of course, the ghastliness, sadness and heroism of war are recorded in novels, plays, and poems that have a certain literary merit. The perplexed, frightened or fearless human spirit, occasionally related to a concept that suggests the perfectibility of man, finds expression in novels written about the first World-War, as, for instance, in Vicente Blasco Ibanez's *The Four Horsemen of the Apocalypse* or in Henri Barbusse's *Under Fire*. The second World-War gave us Eric Knight's *This Above All* and John Steinbeck's *The Moon Is Down*. A much longer list could be enumerated, but the impression that one obtains from these novels would not be modified. The writers pour out words that show firmness, in some instance objectivity, or resentment against satanized humanity. They try to stir imagination through creative indignation. Such works contribute to the understanding of the complex problems of man in wartimes, but fail to reach the core of the problem. Like novelists who fictionize biographical topics, they fictionize war in obvious symbols. For example, John Steinbeck's central theme, that men want freedom, (naturally a very desirable attitude) is not adequately visualized in its psychological motivation. One senses that the writer was determined to prove his point; so he wrote a didactic novel in disproportion with his artistic ability, though in proportion with his moral and social intentions.

It is the creative approach to war that makes struggle in a profound psychological sense memorable. In great literary works puny or wicked humanity is not excluded from deep sorrow and nobility. It is the glory of the creative spirit that informs humans how to barricade themselves against their own smallness. Euripides's *Trojan Women* is a study in war, but also in feminine psychology. The plight of the Trojan women cries for pity and compassion, and it is understood by an Athenian audience of Pericles's time as well as by a modern audience. Great writers are always contemporaries.

In literary masterpieces one discerns the miracle of the umbilical cord; it is the memento of man's individuality, of his organic self. Sentimental, moral, or cynical generalizations cannot replace this fact which is the connecting force between honesty and utterance in genuine literature. It is the psychology of this fact which triumphs. Abstract grief is a contradiction in term. Grief and joy must be concrete. The *ad hoc* necessities of war can make humans anonymous as soldiers, but they cannot destroy the symbol of human entity. Unless it is the testimony of total man, war literature is merely a documentary expression of feeling and intelligence, indifference and mental inferiority, related to social, political, economic problems. War is life in the grip of death. *This is the real issue of war literature.* Great writers know how to re-echo the Bible's statement that "man's conscience is the lamp of the Eternal, flashing into his inmost soul." Because great writers know how to give form to distress and relief, the magic of their own ability enters into our own life when we understand their works. Poems or tragedies written 2,500 years ago or written day before yesterday whisper or sing to the man the mystery of life. Thus war, of which so much is sinister or confusing, achieves grandeur through expression.

II

While most warbooks of today affect one like marginal notes of contemporary destiny, real literary works, produced in the past or in modern times, point out the highways and sideroads to an understanding of man's place in the universe. There were too many depressing periods in the history of mankind when not merely sense but the yearning for sense deserted the human soul. Yet even then there were poets who fought the demon of life, though their own private lives showed a dangerous disbalance. The creative mind may be unfaithful to experiences, but cannot be untrustworthy to the need of expressing them. Neither wars, nor the indifference of the public, allows honest poets or writers to gamble away their ability. In carrying out their part of responsibility, works of classical or romantic value become correlated with man's permanent problems, independent of the time-liness of the subject. There are examples of unchangeable human traits in Aeschylus's *Agamemnon* or in Vergil's *Aeneid* which expressed in a poetic language, preserved for posterity a *feeling of actuality,* despite difference in time and space, taste and be-havior, conception of simplicity and complications.

It does not require much effort to be an amateur-Jeremiah or an imitation—Cassandra. It is plain that the arid or wrecked human spirit rarely, perhaps never, realizes the boldness and courage of the creative mind when it introduces meaning into the seeming or real meaninglessness of things and events. Much of war literature is *histoire scandaleuse* in its private reference. Talleyrand's versatility and uncanny adaptability revealed the spirit of a diplomatic Proteus; his clerical and anti-clerical activ-ities, his adjustment to Napoleon and then to the Bourbons, his success at the Congress of Vienna showed the absolute un-scrupulousness of an engaging personality. Unfortunately much of war literature, especially under the surveillance of certain interests, has the same flexibility that was the secret of Talley-rand's career. Meaning, thus obtained, places expression on the level of a principle which refuses to recognize truth, and ac-centuates man's lasting relationship to corruption. "Official" biographies of Frederick the Great in Hohenzollern Germany or Empress Catherine in Romanoff Russia, the interpretations of their relation to war, stress an attitude which is, as a rule, unaided by truth or by a desire for truth.

When, however, the creative spirit is aroused by the form and externals of warfare, the urge to expression has the conscience of a dream and not of a scheme. It follows from the very nature of creative expression that it must conquer formlessness. When a poet lies, which he is apt to do, he must lie for the sake of truth. Lieing in such instance is identical with unlearning the lessons that facts bring home, in order to arrange the pattern of experiences, so that their symbolism should unfold the essence of the struggle. According to Christian views man is charged with a duty that should be the glorification of God. The value of this glorification is in direct proportion to the symbol that the value of man's life suggests. The poet's battle with love through self-love, this strange fusion of selfishness and disinterestedness, indicates a position in regard to the universe that does not accept dullness, dreariness or disaster as the only answers to the enigmatic question whether there is purpose in life. Creative integrity cannot be entranced with Machiavellism, or with strife that is politically or commercially capitalized. Creative expression begets meaning, which pragmatism might exhaust, but vision sustains. It pays homage to the essence of existence by obeying the maskless demand of imaginative awareness.

Without this concept of creative function it would be impossible to understand the clarity or the controlled complexity of great poetic works, thematically related to confusion, bloodshed, barbarism, lamentation, active shrewdness and slyness. Expression and form, as understood by Benedetto Croce, are knowledge obtained through intuition and representation. But the words of the Italian philosopher affirm a will that transcends the practical spirit, though he himself associates will with the practical spirit. If it is true that the activity of judgment that criticizes and recognizes the beautiful is identical with what produces it, then it should be also true that creative activity which recognizes and expresses a new experience, is beauty itself. Consequently beauty, being form, compels destruction or disintegration to possess meaning that a self-evident plot, not expressed artistically, does not possess. For instance, distinction must be made between war which agitates the human spirit because of its heroism or horror, and between an artistic interpretation of war which interests the human spirit because heroism or horror were made universally significant.

Cartesian philosophy attributes imagination to man's animal emotionalism. This implication is only then valid when it recognizes imagination's relationship to the intellect, the latter functioning as an aesthetic disciplinarian of feeling integrated by imagination. Poetic communication is an utterance of the spirit that knows no substitute for this particular activity. It has meaning by being what it is, regardless of what view the poet takes of the action or of the character that he describes. Achilles is a glorified bully; Homer made him significant through characterization that awakened our understanding for the primitive Greek concept of heroism. No rational explanation could replace poetic revelation. Tolstoy's Napoleon in *War and Peace* is less omnipotent than history has made him. In the Russian writer's extraordinary psychological portrait he is a man of obnoxious principles obsessed with a sense of power which made of him an undesirable phenomenon of human history. Literary genius challenged history in exchange for truth.

Life and death are appearances. Of course, there are scientific, imaginative, and purely human adventures from which life and death emerge as a symbol of myth or purpose. It is desire for meaning that makes us cross the boundaries of appearances. One cannot, however, stress sufficiently the view that imagination in itself does not signify meaning; this task is performed by imagination creatively used. It is for this reason that a creative assimilation of war-experience is more than a report of war-activities; it is psychology aesthetically made authentic.

III

Scholarly works about history, hence about warfares, have values which no one of common sense will deny. For instance *The Decline and Fall of the Roman Empire* by Edward Gibbon or *The French Revolution* by Thomas Carlyle are the kind of interpretation that are symbolic of a powerful arranged material of history. Erudition and selection make them effective. They bring forth informations in a manner of factual authenticity that one misses in imaginative works. They are able to move and to enlighten the reader. They seem to encompass the universe with chains of factual intelligence within which humanity must confess its imperfections and ambitions. In contrast to the disorganized character of many everyday experiences they show order, concentration, symmetry.

Yet the *living voice* of human destiny is not made audible through them. Unlike history, imaginative literature takes care of human traits which, in an ironic sense, scholarliness could not consider of enough importance to be included into historical works. "Military glory" interpreted by a historian is quite different from the rapture or resignation of man in relationship, let us say, to the solitude of his own soul. Aristotle's dictum as to the superiority of poetry over history might be too strong a statement, but it suggests a demarcation line between these two expressions which is an occasion for trying to understand the reason, if not the quality, of difference. It is the difference of accent. History is the outgrowth of a need for information. It is also the outgrowth of an unemotional (scientific) wish to penetrate into the past and by projecting historical facts to extend understanding to other nations, besides our own. There are philosophical views which maintain that man is history.

Imaginative literature is as old as the first song of man, whereas history is as old as the first theory that man evolved. Evidently the source of songs is older. The basis of every creative expression is the song; the lyrical cry of man, his naïvete and undeveloped curiosity. The song is man's expression of an organic union between the joy of living and the fear of death. A song is vaster than the universe and more permanent than theories. It grows from inside and recalls experiences which the singer may not have ever had, and yet they seem familiar. A song is the religion of the senses. It diminishes the importance of facts and increases the importance of sympathies or antipathies. It is relentless in its strength and softness. Imaginative literature does not know more about life than history, but it suggests more. It is the symbol of the perpetual revolution of the spirit; it appropriates the cosmos in praising leaves of grass or falling in love with the infinite.

There are the attributes of poetry, behind which history seems to trail with an intellectual and factual conscience, sometimes generous and sometimes less so with poetry. Man does not ascend as a new being from the ashes of war. The wonders of life, the simplicities of living, the monstrosities of life, the atrocities of living establish a variety of metaphors and conclusions in their creative presentation but never a withdrawal from the essence of human nature which is the eternal trail of the good and the evil before the court of destiny.

Man does not change, notwithstanding apocalyptic or other unusual experiences. This is one of the lessons, *this painful platitude,* which warliterature teaches. It is said that war leads to new inventions, that business gains, that it advances medical science and influences social structure. True. But the guiding principle of man remains his ego, infected, sometimes affected, by progress. The latter seems like a thrust of energy into inevitable inactivity. The dominant evidence of man's unchangeableness seems his willingness to succumb to slogans, implying mystical roots or the warmth of the herd instinct. Environment, climate, ruling views, the power or lack of power of the elite, et cetera, are, of course realities that cannot be excluded from the psychological atmosphere of warliterature; but in the strict sense of the word they are externals, without profoundly affecting the central disposition of man.

But the sameness of the human spirit as revealed by warliterature does not preclude faith in progress. Despair is not more legitimate than hope. The sameness of human nature is not analogous to immobility. Growth and development are not incongruous terms applied to the *homo sapiens.* Man can learn how to restrain himself; he can learn how to lean on reason; but substantially he cannot be anything but what he is. In every major literary work, inspired or irritated by war, one sees a renewed attempt to show man's inconsistency to nobility and ignobility. In the *Greek Anthology,* in certain plays of Shakespeare, in Rabelais's *Gargantua and Pantagruel,* in Swift's *Gulliver's Travels,* in Stephen Crane's *The Red Badge of Courage,* in Thomas Hardy's *The Dynasts,* in Leonid Andrejev's *The Seven Who Were Hanged,* in Andre Malraux's *Man's Hope,* in M. A. Solokhov's *And Quiet Flows the Don,* (despite its "collectivism") and in other literary works, entirely or partly affected by war, one marvels at the recurring motives of human behavior. Man is a miracle, unwilling or unable to respond to change in matters of fundamentals; man is a creature who echoes institutionalism, but never with such force as he echoes his unchangeable traits. War does not convert man to peace; peace does not convert man to war. The universalities and particularities of man, enacting their function in relationship to war, do not attain a nobler pattern because of social or technical progress. Granted that the tradition of Socratic awareness demands attention; granted that awareness enriched the nature of living; nevertheless, the psychology of war literature assures us that widened adventures and widened outlooks are determined by the qualities of human organism which stood the superstitions and tribulations of ages with fear, intelligence, and courage, but could not change the essence of their being.

Man's ghost is ignorance. War literature, while it is not promoting belief in man's essential change, supports the idea that knowledge assimilates ignorance. In a psychological sense war commands man to discipline fear through consciousness. War thus becomes awareness in action, by compelling action to be aware of its own purpose. Man's capacity to endure pain is immense. Embittered and tormented humans meet blind fate with defiance and fortitude. Man does not change, but war literature celebrates man's braveness and sorrow in proportion to ideals and interest that man is capable of understanding and fighting for. In mediocre or bad imaginative works the theatricality of plot and characterization or of bombastic lyrical outbursts is observable without any special effort; in good imaginative works we follow man's actions and reflections as an expression of his total being, regardless whether he gives way to feeling of a particular hatred or whether he reveals particular gallantry. Knowledge obtained thus brings a mental picture to the reader, resulting in a emotional identification with human valor and human suffering.

Whether one is interested in the Irish world of the *Cuchulain Saga* or in the Christian and Mohammedan world of *The Song of Roland*, whether one reads modern novels, like Jules Romain's *Verdun* or Ernest Hemingway's *For Whom the Bell Tolls*, the war-atmosphere of these creations helps retain one's sense of value that ridicules absolute indifference or absolute futility. Man is shown as an agent of his own will, or as a puppet of forces which he could not control, even if he would have the desire to control them. Man is exposed in his tireless integrity and in his selfish pettiness, in his enormous unimportance and in his important self. In epics of ancient times there is, of course, less rationalization than in modern fiction or plays; but good war-literature impresses upon the reader the magnificence and wastefulness of human energies. Great literary works related to war touch the innermost existence of man, and defy the nothingness of human life with a full and rich expression of actions and aims which are organically attached to the will to live and to the will to die.

Meditations on the Literature of Spying
Jacques Barzun

from

The American Scholar, vol. 34, no. 2, Spring 1965.

Meditations on
The Literature of Spying

JACQUES BARZUN

A s I BEGIN these notes (midsummer 1964), the American public
is making into best sellers two works of light literature:
Candy[1] and *The Spy Who Came In From the Cold*.[2] The one is
supposed to be a parody of the modern novel of sex; the other is
held up as a really real realistic tale of modern spying; and there
is evidence from conversation and printed comments that readers
who usually scorn the best seller are giving these books their attention. I suspect that something important but unspoken links
these two efforts and also attracts the consumer of so-called serious
novels.

I do not know what that something is, but I do know that
Candy and *The Spy* are dull and, under their respective cloaks of
gaiety and of sobriety, affected. The point of *The Spy* is that he
wants to quit but is impelled to go on by professional routine. This
is enough, I imagine, to make him congenial to all of us. He does
not believe in what he is doing; he is anything but a hero; he is a
good deal of a masochist. And being a spy in the field, indeed a
potential martyr to an unfelt cause, he entitles himself to certain
low pleasures—despising his associates; having, skill apart, a poor
opinion of himself; sinking morally and physically into degrada-
tion almost beyond control; falling in love listlessly, like a con-
valescent; and, after being betrayed in action by headquarters for
double-cross purposes, making a sacrifical end. Death, we are to
think, is the only "coming in from the cold" there is.

I am sure that this melodrama played in iron curtains corresponds to something older and deeper than our anxieties of the

⊙ JACQUES BARZUN's most recent book is *Science: The Glorious Entertainment*.
Mr. Barzun, who is a member of the Editorial Board of the SCHOLAR, is Provost of
Columbia University.

cold war. The soul of the spy is somehow the model of our own; his actions and his trappings fulfill our unsatisfied desires. How else explain the stir caused, also this past summer, by the death of Ian Fleming? Ten books about James Bond, published in a little more than ten years, do not justify the front-page laments, and even less the studies by academic critics who have argued over Fleming's morals and political philosophy. No, there is something here like earlier ages' recognition of themselves in the pioneer, the warrior, the saint or the poet. We are the spy—an agent, mind you, not a man—hiding behind the muffling zeros of 007 which mean: the right to kill *in the line of duty*.

The advertisers, who always know the color of our emotions, rely on our being good Bondsmen. Leafing through the *New Yorker,* I am told by a travel magazine: "Come to Beirut and see spies. Real spies . . . with shifty eyes and tiny cameras." In *Playboy,* cheek by jowl with a discussion of the "cultural explosion," I am invited to examine a dinner jacket and to "ask Agent 008, the one for whom survival often depends on the smallest detail." These hints play on the surface and suggest the depths. As technologists we love that tiny detail, that tiny camera. As infidels without purpose, we attach a morbid importance to survival. Yet our aplomb is restored by the possession of cosmetic virtue: with those faultless garments on, we would be content to let our eyes shift for themselves.

The spy story does this for us, then: it permits us not to choose, we can live high and lie low. Since Graham Greene no longer writes "entertainments," read Eric Ambler's *The Light of Day*[3] and see how the ironic title is brought down to mean simple survival for an outcast in a dirty raincoat with a mind to match. We are on his side, for as with the cold spy in his Skid Row phase, we relish the freedom that exists at the bottom of cities. And we know that in exchange for a few dirty tricks there is also power and luxury, cash and free sex. True, even James Bond marries while *On Her Majesty's Secret Service,*[4] but the wife mercifully dies within a few hours. They had been lovers, so all is well.

જ

The advantage of being a spy as of being a soldier is that there is always a larger reason—the reason of state—for making any little scruple or nastiness shrink into insignificance. But I want to leave the question of morality to a later place. At this point I am still curious about the satisfactions that the tale of espionage affords Western man in the afternoon of this century. As always in trashy literature, it is the satisfactions that produce the illusion of reality: man despising and betrayed, listless in his loves, dying pointlessly every second, scared, scared, scared—this is, if one may so speak, the life existential. But in the portraits and myths of that life what calms our fears is that dangers and difficulties yield to technique. The spy is imperturbable not by temperament or by philosophy, but from expertise. He is the competent man. Whether the need of the moment is to play bridge like Culbertson, speak a Finnish dialect like a native, ski to safety over precipices or disable a funicular, he comforts us with his powers no less than with the pedantry of the subject. He makes mistakes, of course, to keep us in countenance, but they are errors of inattention, such as killing the wrong man. We respond to this agreeable image of our scientific world, where knowledge commands power, where facts are uniformly interesting, and where fatalities appear more and more as oversights, professional *faux pas*. These results constitute the romance of the age; why should they not be translated into stories—spy stories especially, since what we know as science comes from ferreting and spying, and since we care so much for truth that we are willing to drug and torture for it?

One stumbles here on a preestablished harmony: the novel as a genre has been prurient and investigative from the start. Growing out of the picaresque adventure, which is high life seen from below stairs, the novel does not merely show, it shows up—and what a mountain of discreditable information it has unloaded into our eager minds! What pedantry! What snobbery! At first, simple encounters and reversals kept the reader going; lately it has been character and relationships; but it is all one: from Gil Blas to Henry James's "observer" somebody is always prying. From Scott to Dreiser we take a course in how some other half lives, how fraudulent men and their society really are. The novel is dedicated to subversion; the novelist is a spy in enemy country. No reason, then, to be surprised that his ultimate parable should be the tale with a declared, certified spy in it, one who like the original *picaro* sees society from below, and resentfully.

ह्ॐ

Mr. Matthew Head, who has written a dozen good detective stories and whose name conceals a well-known art critic, gives in one of his books what might be called the moral strategy of the novel-bred mind. His archeologist hero confides that "the first thing I always wonder about new people is what they manage to do for a living and how they arrange their sex life, because it seems to me that those two activities plus sleep and a movie or two account for most people's twenty-four hours a day."[5] This is the brass-tacks appeal, and it goes well with our primitivism, our reliance on formulas, our fatigue at the thought of understanding "new people": there are so many of them, thanks to immoderate prenatal care.

And the wish to invade the privacy of sex gives a clue to the kinship I suspected between the two best sellers with which I began these notes: spying and pornography are related through the curiosity of the child about the mystery of sex. Perhaps the relentless curiosity of science has the same root; certainly our fiction does not neglect the fundamental needs, only the fundamental decencies. It neglects, that is, the difference between recognizing the demands of the body under the elaborations, softenings and concealments of civilized society and thinking that one is very sharp to have discovered them and made the rest negligible.

The genuine primitive has another ring to it. The *Iliad* is about "Helen and all her wealth"—money and sex if you will, but like other national epics it is also about war and the gods, human character and the sorrowful brevity of life. The novel is about malice domestic, and this is what ends by stunting our souls. I reread *Clarissa Harlowe* during a recent bout of illness, and I was shocked by the orgy of violence—of action, language, feeling— that it comes down to. The rape of Clarissa is only the fit gesture to symbolize the concentrated fury that animates all the characters

—friend against friend; man against woman; parents, children, relatives against one another. All this hate, like a contagion, made me want to annihilate the lot.

The cold-spy, cold-war story presumably expresses and discharges the tension of violence under which we have lived since 1914. But that expression is rarely touched with regret or remorse. Only occasionally, as in William Haggard's story *The High Wire*,[6] is the theme in contradiction with the mode of life depicted. The main character here is a peaceable, middle-aged engineer who is catapulted into espionage and finds in it only horror, helplessness and torture. He manages to live and marry the heroine, an agent who is—or just has been, for purely professional reasons, of course —the mistress of an opposing agent: again, the true romance of our times. It almost makes one prefer the moral of Cyril Connolly's now famous parody of James Bond, in which 007 must in the line of duty impersonate a homosexual and finds—but the surprise ending must not be told.

An uncommonly deft practitioner, Hubert Monteilhet, gives us another singular version of this romance in *Return from the Ashes*,[7] which tells how a woman survivor from a concentration camp attempts to regain an old lover who may have betrayed her to the Gestapo. She has to turn spy, privately, to achieve her ends, and in so doing she destroys others as well as the hopeful part of herself. At one point she defines the embroidering of sentiment over brutality as "the work of a tragic Marivaux, one to suit this century." But why blame the century? Why are we told over and over again, as by Raymond Chandler in his masterpiece *The Lady in the Lake*: "Doctors are just people, born to sorrow, fighting the long grim fight like the rest of us"?[8] Or in reverse, by one of Chandler's imitators: "She was really a rather naive and inexperienced little girl. She apparently still believed in things like love and hate and gratitude and vengeance, not realizing that they had no place in this work, where your enemy one minute is your ally the next—and maybe your enemy again a few minutes later."[9] The speaker of this maxim, the tough spy Matt Helm, acknowledges that ours is "not a chivalrous age, nor is mine an honorable profession." The excuse, it appears, is necessity.

Chandler's indestructible hero, Philip Marlowe, who crystallized a good many of these poses, declares: "However hard I try to be nice I always end up with my nose in the dirt and my thumb feeling for somebody's eye."

Obviously the reason why these things occur and are bewailed is the way men choose to take life, and modern men take life in the way of sophistication, that is, universal suspicion, hostility, fear of being taken in. People who read only "noteworthy" novels do not know how far the second- and third-hand fiction has copied and exploited the disillusioned stance of the masters. At times one could imagine that it was Somerset Maugham who had decanted into all the lesser works the sour wine from the great vintage casks: "His intelligence was obvious . . . he never quite gave himself away. He seemed to be on his guard. . . . those eyes were watching, weighing, judging, and forming an opinion [sic]. He was not a man to take things at their face value." This is Maugham's Dr. Saunders, the hero-observer of the well-named *Narrow Corner*.[10] To know in advance that everything and everybody is a fraud gives the derivative types what they call a wry satisfaction. Their borrowed system creates the ironies that twist their smiles into wryness. They look wry and drink rye and make a virtue of taking the blows of fate wryly. It is monotonous: I am fed up with the life of wryly.

ॐ

One reason for my annoyance is the contamination that the sophisticated and the spies have brought into the story of detection. Mr. Le Carré himself began with two attempts at the genre, in which his talent for situations is evident and any interest in the rationality of detection altogether missing. Under a surface likeness the purposes of spying and criminal detection are opposite: the spy aims at destroying a polity by sowing confusion and civil strife; the detective aims at saving a polity by suppressing crime. Thanks to our literary men we have been made so much at home with crime, we have found the spy's "unobserved shadow world which is nevertheless starkly real"[11] serving us so well as a sort of subconscious of society, that we readily agree with the head of the French Secret Police who said no man "could fully understand our age unless he had spent some time in prison."[11] Logic thus compels the writer to turn detective fiction into the domestic branch of espionage.

In consequence the murders that do not arise from the drug traffic arise from the enchanted realm of "security." And so an excellent story such as Val Gielgud's *Through a Glass Darkly*[12] seeks the solution to a London murder simply by turning inside out the lives of the wife, the friends and the business associates of the victim. In place of the classical observation and inference, there is snooping, which also obliterates action. Simenon's Maigret, whom many innocent readers take for a detective, is but a peeping Tom. He is praised for his patience in looking out of windows across a road, but his "psychology" is a mere offprint of Dr. Saunders': "He took an interest in his fellows that was not quite scientific and not quite human. . . . it gave him just the same amusement to unravel the intricacies of the individual as a mathematician might find in the solution of a problem."[10] In short: the mathematical interest that a Paris *concierge* takes in his lodgers and finds rewarded by the Sûreté.

The great illusion is to believe that all these impulses and enjoyments betoken maturity, worldliness, being "realistic." The truth is that Maugham's observer and the ubiquitous spy are bright boys of nine years. Nine is the age of seeking omniscience on a low level. The spy's ingenuity (why not ship the fellow in a trunk?), his shifting partisanship without a cause, like his double bluffs, his vagrant attachments, and his love of torturing and of being tortured are the mores of the preadolescent gang: they yield, as one storyteller puts it, "the joys of conspiracy—all the little thrills and chills that go with being secret and devious."[18] For adult readers to divert themselves with tales of childish fantasy is nothing new and not in itself reprehensible. What is new is for readers to accept the fantasy as wiser than civil government, and what is reprehensible is for the modern world to have made official the dreams and actions of little boys.

ह

There is a further sense in which the philosophy of the spy is childish: at the critical moments it does not work. On this point the authoritative theorist of espionage, an American agent who writes under the pseudonym of Christopher Felix, leaves us in no doubt. He tells us in his *Short Course in the Secret War* that "during World War II the German High Command had at least three reliable reports stating the date and place for the Allied invasion of Normandy," and believed none of them.[11] Again, the Russians had daily reports of German battle plans straight from headquarters, and disregarded them all. In the same happy vein of skepticism, Stalin disbelieved Richard Sorge's information from Tokyo that Germany would invade Poland in September 1939 and would attack Russia itself in April 1941.[14]

These failures supply their own moral, although not in the way a moralist would prefer. The moral is that nothing in this world can be accomplished without trust, however rudimentary. You cannot buy a box of matches without your entering into a tacit trust agreement with the tradesman to the effect that when you have handed him the coin he will hand you the box. Deception and ruthlessness are not "Machiavellian" wisdom as the vulgar think; they overshoot policy and recoil on the user. The modern spy, being sophisticated, works for both sides—a double agent—is therefore trusted by neither side and thus loses his only value. Similarly, in literature as in life, the double bluff wears out and can only be succeeded by the triple cross. It is an endless series in which agent and principal are both likely to lose their wits. Who is fooling whom and when? In the end, espionage modern style is like advertising: the participants deploy their gimmicks and make their shifty eyes at one another exclusively. The lack of *pragma* throughout is as shocking as the reckless expense.

੪৽

As for the game, one can understand why the reader and the spy relish the permissible depravity that goes with it. But why insist that the spy take sides and risk life without conviction? The only answer that suggests itself is that the lukewarm agent can avoid being torn between his conception of his own cause and the acts of his own party. No need to wonder why their enemies hanged Major André and Nathan Hale so reluctantly and unavoidably. Indeed, one need not go back as far as the American Revolution to find out what preceded the universal loss of honor and conviction. From medieval chivalry to Elizabethan times, the spy was a "base fellow," known as such to others and to himself. This notion survived from then to within recent memory: when Henry Stimson, as Secretary of State, was shown the progress of code-breaking, he pushed the documents aside and said curtly: "Gentlemen do not read each other's mail." Now, we hear, every citizen has a democratic chance of serving as a spy. Housewives, students on their travels, foundation officials, merchants, scientists, exchange professors and visiting virtuosos are eligible. Only the *New York Times* protests, on the antiquated ground that duplicity may damage the once trustworthy professions.

The most that can be said in extenuation of the citizen-spy's bad taste is that it corresponds to the decline of a world system. The phases are: 1900, 1914, 1945. At the turn of the century, when Erskine Childers wrote *The Riddle of the Sands*,[15] no one could mistake the amateur spy for anything but a patriot, and the professional on the "wrong side" was partly excused by a mixed ancestry aggravated by private misfortune. Even after the *Götterdämmerung* of the First World War, John Buchan could make his hero pursue espionage and chivalry without a split psyche. If today *The Three Hostages*[16] were by a fluke to reach the screen, Richard Hannay would be hooted at by every thirteen-year-old of either sex. His soldierly attempt to save the life of his deadly enemy while chasing him across the scree and gorges of Scotland would seem puerile; and the valuing of every man in the tale, not by his ruthlessness, clothes, or sexual potency, but by the pain it causes him to be a spy, would be adjudged the improbable invention of a maiden aunt. This contrast in conduct and instinct reminds one of the fate of the old German army in the face of Hitler's shirts. This is but another way of saying that we live in times like those that led Thucydides to make one of his tyrants say to his victims: "We give you joy of your innocence, but covet not your silliness."

&

But let us be careful. Let us not put this love of spying—one might almost say this love of dishonor—to the sole account of the dictatorships. It grows just as naturally in the soil of democracy; for it has something to do with equality and the confused emotions relating to class. Few people, no doubt, remember James Fenimore Cooper's early and internationally popular novel, *The Spy*, which dates from 1821. I had to refresh my vague memories of a French translation to find that Harvey Birch, the spy who mysteriously helps George Washington, was no hero but a frightened, mean and mercenary character. He was moved by patriotism, to be sure, but also by a restless envy. This was a shrewd insight of Cooper's. Kill the patriot by sophistication and what is left is the competitive egalitarian, the status-seeker powered by envy.

Out of envy and the will to arrive comes the whole apparatus of personal, industrial and governmental spying. Mr. Richard Rovere has written with justified passion about the multiform attack on privacy that implements this vast jealousy and fear. When no one can take his own merit and place for granted, no one can look upon the world with that "well-opened eye" which Conan Doyle ascribes to "a man whose pleasant lot it had ever been to command and be obeyed." Whatever bad things went with the system that produced such men—and these bad things are many— it did not lead to prying. The Henry Stimsons refrained from reading others' mail, not because they controlled an itch to do so, but because they were not interested. By contrast, the great democratic virtue is to be "interested in people," which undoubtedly fosters sympathy and helpfulness. But it also fosters mutual surveillance and social tyranny.

True, in Flaubert's *Dictionary of Accepted Ideas* the entry "Spy" reads: "Always in high society." But that is the spy of the Age of Reason, polite and cosmopolite, who comes historically between the base fellow and the modern Every Man His Own Secret Agent. E. Phillips Oppenheim gave the ultimate renderings of that delightful intermediate type, a suave habitué of the Orient Express and a willing prey to the svelte seductress whose prerogative it was to transfer the naval plans from his well-marked dispatch box to her bosom, no less well marked. Protocol required these trappings, and this too rested on presumption.

So far from presuming, the democratic character, for all its uneasy claims to equal rewards, is not quite sure of its own existence. Psychoanalysis has taught even the common man that he is in some ways an impostor; he has spied on himself and discovered reasons for distrust and disgust: in all honesty he cannot turn in a good report. Nor do his surroundings help to restore his confidence. The world is more and more an artifact, everywhere facsimiles supplant the real thing—the raucous radio voice, the weird TV screen. Just to find his bearings he must fashion a computer simulation of his case. So mimicry, pretending, hiding, which are part of the child's first nature and used to be sloughed off as true individuality developed, now stay with us as second nature, and indeed as the only escape from the bad self and the bad world. Or as a tough dick in a crude story tells another: A false name, a false address "gives them an immunity from the dreadful actuality of being themselves. . . . Perfectly respectable people, too."[17] Which is to say: for "privacy" read "secrecy."

ह•

But I must close with literature, for heaven knows it is literature—the best and the worst—that our feelings have had to imitate in order to make our world what it is. The petering out of an era, the grubby romances of the envious and the blasé, mirror themselves in the mechanical moves, aggressive and sexual, of Candy and the Cold Spy. But there is more than one underground and one resistance, and here and there one hears echoes of Conrad's dictum that "it is conscience that illumines the romantic side of our life." Any other point of view, he goes on, is "as benighted as the point of view of hunger."[18] Thus in effect speaks also the late Arthur Upfield after some violent doings in the bush: "No, I tell you. It's loyalty. Only the basest of us are not actuated by loyalty."[19] And in a remarkable story to end all spy stories, that unfailing virtuoso Andrew Garve winds up a harrowing scene in which is disclosed a spy's lifelong deception of his daughter as to all his beliefs and all their circumstances, by saying: "I'd been *too* fair to Raczinski. No one had the right to do what he'd done to Marya —not for any reason on earth."[20]

NOTES

1. Southern, Terry and Hoffenberg, Mason. *Candy*. New York: Putnam. 1964. $5.
2. Le Carré, John. *The Spy Who Came In From the Cold*. New York: Coward-McCann. 1964. $4.50.
3. Ambler, Eric. *The Light of Day*. New York: Knopf. 1963. $3.95.
4. Fleming, Ian. *On Her Majesty's Secret Service*. New York: New American Library. 1963. $4.50.
5. Head, Matthew. *The Devil in the Bush*. New York: Avon Books. 1964. 50 cents.
6. Haggard, William. *The High Wire*. New York: Ives Washburn. 1963. $3.50.
7. Montheilhet, Hubert. *Return From the Ashes*. New York: Signet Books. 1964. 50 cents.
8. Chandler, Raymond. *The Raymond Chandler Omnibus*. New York: Knopf. 1964. $6.
9. Hamilton, Donald. *The Ambushers*. New York: Gold Medal Books. 1963. 40 cents.
10. Maugham, Somerset. *The Narrow Corner*. New York: New Avon Library. 1944. 25 cents.
11. Felix, Christopher. *A Short Course in the Secret War*. New York: Dutton. 1963. $5.
12. Gielgud, Val. *Through a Glass Darkly*. New York: Scribners. 1963. $3.50.
13. Stein, Aaron Marc. *Days of Misfortune*. New York: Collier Books. 1963. 95 cents.
14. *New York Times*, September 5, 1964.
15. Childers, Erskine. *The Riddle of the Sands*. London (1903): Penguin Books. 1952. 65 cents.
16. Buchan, John. *The Three Hostages*. London (1924): Penguin Books. 1950. 65 cents.
17. Roeburt, John. *Triple Cross*. New York: Belmont Books. 1962. 40 cents.
18. Conrad, Joseph and Hueffer, Ford Madox. *Romance*. New York: Nelson. $1.25.
19. Upfield, Arthur. *Bushranger of the Skies*. New York: Maxwell. 1963. $3.50.
20. Garve, Andrew. *The Ashes of Loda*. New York: Harper. 1965. $3.50.

The Secret Service: a Period Note
Richard Usborne

from

Clubland Heroes by Richard Usborne. Constable, London,
1953.

Reprinted by permission of Barrie and Jenkins Limited.

The Secret Service

A PERIOD NOTE

I HAD my first instruction in Secret Service work at my mother's knee. She was a keen player of *L'Attaque*. *L'Attaque* was a board-game that worked on a mixture of the principles of chess and Pelman Patience. On a board that my mother kept remarkably steady on her lap, we arrayed our armies, all with their backs to the foe, all our pieces mobile except *Le Drapeau*. The object, if you were in an aggressive mood (my mother was always aggressive, and her defence was bad), was to probe around for the enemy *Drapeau*, and say '*Attaque!*' If you attacked in sufficient strength, and with the right pieces to get through the minefields, brigadiers and rivers, you might be lucky and bump the enemy *Drapeau* before your own got bumped. *L'Attaque* was a good game and, by my mother and myself, cleanly played. Why our armies were French, with French terminology, I don't know.

One man in each army was in mufti, *L'Espion*. He was a very valuable piece, and I think he could only be annihilated by the other *Espion*. I have long since forgotten the details and the features of the other ranks. But *L'Espion* remains clearly in my memory. He was standing in high grass, which, like a bird-watcher (perhaps he said he *was* a bird-watcher if challenged), he had slightly parted to get a better view. He had an expression, again like a bird-watcher, of mixed calm and cunning. He was a man used to working alone. He was not afraid of seeming to be afraid. If a platoon of enemy *sapeurs* had bicycled past, he would have drawn the grasses together in front of him and lain doggo. He would not have sprung out and offered battle. If he carried incriminating papers, he was prepared to eat them. If he was caught, he died with the same calm, cunning look on his face, refusing a bandage round his eyes. You loved your own *Espion*, hated your opponent's.

I doubt if any mere writer, of fact or fiction, has improved on that picture. Many have complicated it. Some have amplified it. But for the war-time spy, the cardboard *Espion* of my mother's favourite game is the pattern. The complications and amplifications begin when the brave (or, if he is on the other side, devilish) gentleman has to operate in peace-time. Since authors must live between wars, so must their spies.

The fact is that in romantic fiction espionage in peace-time is Not Done. When peace breaks out, the brave Englishman, lately an *espion*, must make do with being a *contre-espion*. The hero should be the saviour, not the disturber, of peace.* If the clean-limbed Englishman goes on perilous journeys, it is not to plant a bomb in a palace, or to steal the Secret Treaty. It is to dish the devilish Ruritanian who is preparing to plant a bomb in Buckingham Palace, or, by stealing the Treaty, is pushing England into war.

The terminology changes. 'Spying' and 'The Secret

* But Buchan (*The House of the Four Winds* and *The Courts of the Morning*) and Sapper (*Tiny Cartaret*) cheerfully sent their heroes to embroil themselves in the domestic politics of foreign sovereign states in peace-time.

Service' begin to sound pejorative terms, even in an arm-chair in the 'Rag'. The word for your own side now is 'Intelligence'. ('Intelligence' in war-time is such a wide service that there is no glamour in the word, unless you speak it in French.) When Peace begins, ostensibly England draws in her pickets, pensions off her war-time agents (venal foreigners) abroad. Official Intelligence in peace-time comes home to roost in Whitehall, and is an office job.

By all accounts there are a lot of Army Colonels in peace-time Intelligence. They can be tired men who live cheaply in hotels off the Cromwell Road, or spruce men who live in the Albany. That depends on their private means. There is no real money in the job. There is still a little glamour, and some foreign travel. The work has to go on. But there are no D.S.O.s gazetted on vague citations. Civilian clothes are no longer an intrepid disguise. The man who is caught is not shot at dawn. It is no longer a matter of life and death. It is, most of it, an exchange of files between the Foreign Office, the War Office and Scotland Yard.

In *Greenmantle* and *Mr. Standfast* Germany was the declared enemy; there was a war on, and the boundaries of Tom Tiddler's Ground were clearly defined. Since nations were fighting against nations, and the broad principles of enmity were not in doubt, Buchan could at moments even make his enemy villains (Von Stumm, Hilda Von Einem, Moxon Ivery and such) human; indeed, in their patriotism, almost noble. But in peace-time the villain tends to become a stateless, probably Jewish, venal personal menace, a bad man disturbing the peace for his own pocket or to increase his own sense of power (Medina, Castor, d'Ingraville).

There is generally, in conditions of world peace, one

nation which can be fairly safely suggested as having villainous intentions towards England at the period of writing. But it is seldom more than a suggestion, and the easy-going author prefers to leave the villainous nation vaguely defined or pseudonymous. Russia has been a good stand-by for daring authors over the peaceful periods of the last seventy-five years. Russia was the threat on the North-west Frontier in Kipling's *Kim* and *The Man Who Was*. Russia was the threat in Buchan's *The Half-Hearted*. Russia was the threat in almost all Sapper's Bulldog Drummond books.

But you will notice that the pointing of fingers and the naming of names in these books is, even so, rather discreet. The extent to which a nation in peace-time can be called a villain even in fiction depends to some extent on the distance by which it is separated from England geographically; but largely on the pulse-beat of international affairs of the moment of publication, and the candour of the author and his publishers.

In peace-time, then, nations and national ideologies tend to recede in the plots of thrillers, and personal villains come forward. Only the best authors can play The Game against such a drab backcloth of peace. And they have to pile on the personal devilishness of their foreign villains to make their capture, by the heroes, seem worthwhile. If the chase is confined to the English scene, it has the air of a drag-hunt rather than of the real thing. The English police, that fine body of men, are immanent, at least in the reader's subconscious, to help and protect the Right. It pays dividends in action to send the hero abroad to get his man. Abroad there are ravines and dungeons. Abroad the police are mercenary, and few and far between. Abroad there is reason to let the Bentley blind, the Rolls rip. The war-time *espion* may have, for the sake of The Code, to become a *contre-espion*. But there is nothing against his going into the badlands to do his stuff.

Perhaps we ought to define the term 'Secret Service', even at the risk of rubbing some of the romantic bloom off it. I take it to be a phrase never officially used, but fully understood, by the governments of such sovereign states as bother about national defence at all. A State may be said to have a Secret Service if it spends secretly any funds on the collection of secret information about another State, with the object of discovering that other State's secret doings or intentions. Ruritania may collect some such information about Bessonia's secret national intentions by secretly watching Bessonia's secret agents inside Ruritanian territory. That could be called counter-espionage. But if the money Ruritania spends on its sleuth-work is public money deceptively accounted for, then the operation comes under the heading Secret Service.

The sanction of Secret Services is war, or the preparation in case of war, or the prevention of war, or the prevention of severe damage to the State by any means just short of war. If the British Treasury sets its sleuths to rumble the forging of British banknotes by a French gang, that is not strictly Secret Service in the best and most glamorous sense of the word acceptable to us readers of thrillers. But if the French gang is encouraged by the French Government, and the basic purpose of the French malfeasance is national, with the intent to wreck England's economy, and thus soften England up for a possible future attack in war, then it is up to the British Secret Service to get to work. At a lower than national level, and with no threat of war on the horizon, the counter-measures may be given to a Special Agent to handle, and by any Whitehall Office. If it is a national peril, then the Foreign Office or the War Office, or both, will put their Dick Bartons on the job; and the Dick Bartons then will be Secret Service men.

I never did quite understand what Medina's purpose was in Buchan's *The Three Hostages*. Although no war seemed to be threatening England from Medina's machinations, Medina was apparently heading a group of anti-British agents whose object was not their own personal gain so much as the softening up of England. So the planning of counter-measures came into the province of Lord Artinswell (Foreign Office and Secret Service proper) as well as of MacGillivray (Scotland Yard).

I wonder whether Switzerland, Iceland and Panama have Secret Services. Do they have agents abroad, ostensibly business men or charwomen or waiters in cafés, but coming home in the evenings to mutter coded messages into radio transmitters? Does Luxemburg have its Ciceros photographing secret treaties in the Chancelleries of Europe? How big or important does a sovereign State have to be before it starts secretly buying information? Does it, when it is small, rely on Big Nation A giving (not selling) it scraps of secret information about the secret machinations of Big Nation B? Do neutral countries such as Turkey and Portugal like, in war-time, being full of Hannays, Arbuthnots, Standishes, Ashendens, Von Papens and Canarises, to say nothing of hosts of their eager juniors? Is there then a premium on the price of valets (who are good photographers), concierges (who can read any foreign language, albeit coded, blurred and upside down, on blotting pads), *femmes fatales* (who can slip a Top Secret document out of the pocket of a coat on a bedrail) and waiters (who can intercept glances and interpret sharp intakes of breath)? Do their prices go up, and does their country prosper on its exciting *entrepôt* trade?

During the last war I was briefly in Syria and Lebanon. It was the first time I had had to use extensively my preparatory school French. When asked by Arabs what my job was, I said '*Intelligence*' with all the French accent I could manage. What my prep. school hadn't taught me was that the French equivalent for our Army 'I' was *Service de Renseignements*, and that when I said '*Intelligence*' it was the accepted French for the dread British Secret Service. The sharp intake of breath by Arabs who had read their *romans policiers*, and knew the omnipotence, omniscience and ruthlessness of the British Secret Service, was flatteringly audible. Some Arabs instantly asked me if I was a lord. Others came snaking round to my hotel room after dark, desiring me to take them on as highly paid agents. Others, more sophisticated, suspected that my alleged job with the British Secret Service must be a cover for something else, and they paled beneath their tan wondering what. Long afterwards, when my French improved and the penny dropped, I looked back, nostalgically, to those days of false glory, of gazelle-shoots with Emirs and of baffled looks from Free French officer allies; and I wondered how many other English officers were blissfully making confusion worse confounded in the Near East with their schoolboy French.

I only once met a man who, to my certain knowledge, was a career officer in the British Secret Service. Appropriately, he wore a monocle. It was during the war, and we met in one of the countries that changed hands and was liberated by both sides. I had some work to do which in this one instance necessitated my being in the picture about this man's activities and background. And

I had to tell him I knew. Spoon-fed on Buchan and Sapper, I ought to have had the right sophisticated words with which to convey the information. Perhaps I ought to have imitated the hoot of an owl or the bleat of a snipe before entering the man's office. As it was I blushed and tittered, 'You, I gather, are in the—er—Secret Service'. He sized me up pityingly for the sort of man I was, i.e. spoon-fed on Buchan and Sapper; and he said, 'My dear chap, my job is simply to buy information'. His eyelids were a little weary. Perhaps he had been trafficking for strange webs with Eastern merchants that morning. I know he had had a tiring game of golf that afternoon with the Inter-Nuncio from the Vatican. There was presumably little information on sale that evening, so we sat and drank tea in his office while he told me of his difficulties.

'It's all right in war-time, and for you chaps,' he said. 'But I was here five years before the war, and, unless I'm lucky, I shall be here for five years after it's over. The military barges in, with no thanks for the information I had sweated to collect for them in the previous five years. Their damned Security boys imprison half my best agents, and employ the other half for their own dirty work without telling me. And when the war's over, they'll clear out, leaving everybody handsomely *brulé*. I've got to work to get things organised now so that we can go on doing our job after the war. It's hell. Have another cup of tea.'

If that is the problem—the enduring qualities of the basic British Secret Service against the temporary and *ad hoc* war-time alarums and excursions—it is justification for the Secret Service's use of Hannay, Drummond and Mansel whenever possible for its active jobs of derring-do. They are free-lance. They are brave and will not count the cost. They do not have to be given the complete picture. When the job's on, they cannot give the whole thing away under torture. They are men of means; so that, when the job's over, they will not come whining around asking for salaried office jobs to keep their mouths shut. They are mobile, but they can usually be contacted at their West End Clubs.

In war-time the heroes are in uniform, and can be taken out of the front line, bravely protesting, and sent off through Switzerland in bowler hats. It is practically an order. In the period between the wars Whitehall and the career Secret Service has excellent free-lance helpers.

'This time we are up against the real thing.' Sapper's Secret Service operatives, career and free-lance, are constantly assessing each new assignment in some such words as these. How much did Buchan, Sapper and Yates know of the real thing? We know less than they did, probably. But what do we deduce that they knew? Each would be likely to disguise his knowledge the more, the more he knew. What is the picture each author gives? How much does he give away? And, if you had read them all in the days of your impressionable youth, what would have been the overall picture you retained of the British Secret Service in the days before the Hitler War?

Dornford Yates is the least interested in the British Secret Service as instituted to protect England against her national enemies. In his thrillers it is a world of civil, private torts. His crooks are peace-time jewel-thieves, fences or just plain murderers. Jonah Mansel, the scourge of these rotters, was only once in peace-time working to a Foreign Office brief, and therefore presumably for the Secret Service. That was when he was watching, in France, the villainous villainess Vanity Fair in *She Fell among Thieves*. Of Jonah's war-time Intelligence work we know nothing. His peace-time expeditions were in defence of The Right, as interpreted by the Police. The details of such international political plots as he bumped into he could have written on a post-card to Chief Inspector Falcon of Scotland Yard, and rested content.

If Dornford Yates was the spokesman for a group, that group was the English squirearchy. The group's enemies were the people who were after its private property, the jewel-thieves, and, by extension, the social have-nots who wanted the squirearchy levelled down through taxes and socialism generally. So the enemy in Yates might be English or foreign. But he did not represent a nationality.

Sapper was not contented with mere jewel thieves, or even Napoleons of private-enterprise crime. His villains in nine cases out of ten had aggressive national or ideological affiliations. Their first object may have been to make a few millions of pounds for themselves. But if these millions were to be made by bringing England to her knees under the bayonets and bombs of Bolshevism, so much the more exciting and worthwhile. In Sapper the Englishman's enemy is the foreigner; and, by extension, the enemy of England is the lesser nation that does not speak England's language and is jealous of England just for being England.

Sapper implied that it was the soldier-men who ran The Game. Certainly in the areas of the world abroad coloured pink in the Atlas it was the soldiers who officiated. Maitland's secret reports were presented to the soldiers in Cairo, not to the Oriental Secretary. According to Sapper's books, the Whitehall offices involved were the Home Office, Scotland Yard and the War Office. Not the Foreign Office. If there was a single man who was head of the British Secret Service (and it would be a terrible disappointment and disillusionment to all readers of thrillers to think that there wasn't), where did he work?

The nearest thing to a salaried, full-time Secret Service Agent hero in Sapper's books is Ronald Standish. He is very near the top in The Game. Find his boss, you think, and you may have the head of the British Secret Service. But Ronald Standish has several bosses. At least three of them. They are all soldiers. One of them (Colonel Talbot, 'The Chief') gets shot dead with a silenced rifle in Hyde Park, and there seems to be no difficulty about finding his successor. It looks as though even these gallant colonels are peripheral officers, and not at the plum centre of the web.

It would be intelligent to guess, from Sapper's books, that the British Secret Service is run by the Military. Blow up the War Office any day, and you would (except at lunch-time: then blow up the Service Clubs) probably blow up the head of the British Secret Service.

Buchan's Secret Service was based on the Foreign Office. Sir Walter Bullivant was the Head Man as early as 1914, and he was still Head Man fifteen years later, as Lord Artinswell. MacGillivray of Scotland Yard kept close official contact with Bullivant in his peace-time schemes. When MacGillivray wasn't reading Homer with his feet on his Mount Street mantelpiece, he was ready to go and talk secrets with Bullivant at the Rota Club. But the official head of the British Secret Service was the Foreign Office man, the Permanent Under-Secretary. It was to the Foreign Office that Blenkiron, the American millionaire, reported. It was to the Foreign Office that Hannay and Arbuthnot reported.

One wonders how Blenkiron fitted in with the British Foreign Office picture in 1916, the date of *Greenmantle*.

America wasn't in the war then, but Blenkiron was working flat out for the British already. Did Washington know? Blenkiron was working for the Americans and the British in *Mr. Standfast* (1917). He was working for the Americans in *The Courts of the Morning*. Although in that book he roped in Sandy Arbuthnot to lead the revolt against Castor, dictator of Olifa, Olifa was a direct threat to America, not to England. Arbuthnot sealed the Atlantic pact by marrying Blenkiron's niece, an American. From Buchan you gather that the American and British Secret Services were pooling their secrets amicably, certainly through Blenkiron, possibly through Embassies, from 1916 right through to 1939 (*Sick Heart River*).

Compared with the known factual standards of the Second World War period, the fictional standards of Security in the pre-1939 fictional British Secret Service were rotten. When we read Buchan and Sapper today, we are struck by the way their heroes discussed their secrets and their missions with people whose credentials they had no reason to trust. No owl-hoot, no secret hand-clasp, no snipe-bleat.

Hannay was inclined to Tell All to anybody who had an honest face. He and Lancelot Wake, both in The Game in *Mr. Standfast*, had every reason to distrust each other. But, after a fight, they had quite a heart-to-heart discussion of their secrets on a Scottish hilltop. By the 1939-45 war-time code both should have been drummed out of the Secret Service for that. Hannay, on the run, would stumble into a country house, be well treated by its surprised owner, and very soon be telling his host the whole story. When he was searching for the three hostages, it was as near as a toucher that he roped in Dominick

Medina to help him. And Medina was, in fact, the king villain of the piece.

When Bulldog Drummond was in The Game, he spilt the beans with considerable insouciance. In *Challenge*, the best of the Secret Service books that Sapper wrote, Drummond goes with Standish to a hotel in the South of France where a (recently murdered) young British Secret Service officer had been staying. They question the proprietor about his recent guest. The proprietor says, 'Yes, Mr. Latimer told me he was working for the British Secret Service . . .', and Drummond and Standish say, 'So are we.' Not good Security by our Hitler War standards. It is amusing, later in *Challenge*, to watch Drummond, now in Switzerland, pump questions at a young English diplomat in our Berne Legation. The diplomat says to Hugh, 'Why should I answer these questions? I don't know you.' In another mood, and in one of the less good novels, Drummond might have slapped the young puppy down with a ham-handed buffet. In *Challenge* he says, in his kindly way, 'Well done, youngster. I was just testing you out.'

We have tightened our ideas about Security since these good books were written. Another World War has made us unfairly critical, not only about Security, but about Disguise, Anti-Semitism, Wealth, Leisure, Privilege—and a lot of other things on which between-the-wars thrillers grew fat and prospered.

Notes Towards the Analysis of the Bond Stories
Tim Moore

from

Occasional Paper no. 4, Centre for Contemporary
Cultural Studies, Birmingham University, 1969.

Reprinted by permission of the author.

1. The Licensing Operator

A community must to some extent limit and direct the actions of its members. In a large and complex society, this is a difficult matter. Not only do bureaucracies grow, but means of control multiply and become institutionalized. We have permits, orders, authorizations, qualifications, licences; old words like "title" and "command" fall out of use with increasing differentiation between various forms of permission and obligation.

Living in such a society, we remark the appropriateness, in a myth of our society (assuming it to be such), of the role played in Ian Fleming's novels by the episodes in which instructions and permissions are given.

It is an important role. Not only is Bond's double—O number a "licence to kill", but all the Bond stories, with the exception of three which are not spy-stories (i.e. 'Quantum of Solace' and 'The Hildebrand Rarity' from *For Your Eyes Only*, and *The Spy Who Loved Me)* are started and sustained by at least one licensing episode, in the form of an interview with M.

A "licensing episode" is one in which an authority gives an agent instructions, vests him with powers or privileges, subjects him to some hazard, endows him with some prize. It is the structure of such episodes which we must now determine. The method will be to hold M the authority, Bond the agent, and X the action authorized, as constants. Then we shall ask through what permutations the authorizing goes when M authorizes Bond to do X.

A first question is: who formulates the order? The *authorization,* of course, invariably comes from M (on the present abstraction), but M and Bond may each be either active or passive in the formulation of the plan. We may derive the following matrix.

(authorization)

M ——→ B
+   −

active +

(formulation)

passive −

Here, the counters M and B (Bond), are both variable in the vertical plane, and both invariant in the horizontal. There are, therefore, four possible cases:

+
−

which could be drawn more simply as follows:

+

−

Which of these patterns holds in the books? In nineteen cases out of twenty four, M formulates the order, Bond merely receives it, and the following pattern therefore holds: as these brief summaries will show:

Casino Royale
Chapter III: M puts over the plan; Bond expresses misgivings; but "M knew all this already"; M assigns him an assistant; Bond would have preferred to work alone, but "one didn't argue with M".

Live and Let Die
Chapter II: No clear assignment is stated; but M gives all the information on Mr. Big; describes the task as a joint CIA and FBI job; and says "Be ready to start in a week".

Moonraker
Chapter IX: A new security man must quickly be appointed to the Moonraker project; M proposes Bond at Cabinet level; informs Bond of his appointment. Bond's reaction is surprise and resentment.
Chapter XXV: Bond is instructed by M to leave the country.

Diamonds are Forever

Chapter II: M describes a diamond smuggling racket;
                Bond "Where do I come in?"—
                M "We put you in the pipeline".

Chapter XXV: M: "I want you to get Jack Spang".—
                Bond: "Yes, sir".

From Russia With Love

Chapter XI: M sends Bond a "sharp note" appointing him to a committee of
                enquiry.

Chapter XII: M instructs Bond to go to Istanbul for a cypher machine and a
                Russian girl, and to meet the girl's romantic expectations about
                him.

Doctor No

Chapter II: M orders Bond to change his gun;
                Bond agrees reluctantly.

Chapter II—   M gives Bond a personnel problem as a soft assignment; Bond ac-
Chapter III: cepts reluctantly.

Goldfinger

Chapter V: M puts Bond on night-duty; Bond argues unsuccessfully against
                this.

From a View to Kill

                Cable from M to Paris instructs Bond to investigate killing and
                robbery of a SHAPE dispatch rider; Bond: "Bloody waste of
                time!"

Risico

                M puts Bond on narcotics job in Italy, to buy off the
                racketeers; Bond: "Why are we taking it on?"

Thunderball

Chapter I: M sends an incredulous Bond on a nature cure.

Chapter VIII: M sends Bond to track down SPECTRE in the Bahamas; but
                "in Bond's opinion, for he didn't give much for M's guess, he
                had been relegated to the back row of the chorus".

On Her Majesty's Secret Service

Chapter II: The letter of resignation which Bond is thinking about refers to
                M's instructions to track down Blofeld, and to his view that
                these instructions were foolish.

You Only Live Twice

Chapter III: M gives a disintegrating Bond a surprise job in Japan.

The Man with the Golden Gun

(Note the initial inversion of the normal M episode, when Bond tries to kill M)..

Chapter II—
Chapter III: M decides on Bond's mission; the orders are passed on by the
                Chief of Staff.

Chapter XVII: M in a cable encourages and expects Bond to accept a knighthood.

It may be objected that these nineteen so-called licensing episodes are not really homologous at all; some of them do not concern Bond's professional assignments; in some of them M is himself the recipient of instructions from on high; some of them are presented in direct narrative, others are presented indirectly or suppressed; in some, M gives a direct order, in others Bond seems to have a choice whether to take the job. It is true that there are these differences between the episodes; but to claim that they are not therefore homologous is to misunderstand the method being used. The method is to find homologies only as defined by certain abstractions or matrices. Indeed, there is no other way of finding them. And in the present case, we are considering the episodes only as licensing transactions between Bond and M, and as ones in which either Bond or M or both may be active in formulating the action to be licensed. Now the licence may be strong or weak (an order or an optional assignment); M may be a counter in another licensing matrix in which he receives the orders; the assignment may be minor, inconsequential or stupid. But none of these variations is relevant to the matrix now being considered. And so far as this matrix goes, the nineteen episodes are perfectly homologous.

However, as has been mentioned, there are five other episodes in the books which are not. In two of them, both M and Bond are active in formulating the plan; in three, Bond is active, and M passive:

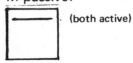 (both active)

Moonraker
Chapter II, IV: Does Drax cheat at cards? M suggests that Bond watch him; Bond later suggests a way of warning him off.

For Your Eyes Only

A murderer and gangster cannot be touched through the normal processes of law. M has a personal interest. M and Bond together agree on an "eye for eye" mission.
(Bond active, M passive)

Goldfinger
Chapter VII: M accepts Bond's plan for getting at Goldfinger with resignation and sarcasm.

On Her Majesty's Secret Service
Chapter VIII: M accepts but regards as stupid Bond's plan for tracking down Blofeld.

Chapter XXII: M accepts but does not officially sanction Bond's plan for ex-
terminating Blofeld.

We have now isolated three different armatures: an active M licensing a passive Bond, a passive M licensing an active Bond, and an active M licensing an active Bond. How are we to read them?

One coding is in terms of the opposition between individual and society. Can we read these armatures as manipulated to give coded messages on that plane? There is one simple way in which we can. For the episodes with the armature ⊠ are those in which society has the upper hand. M, an agent of society's authority, is using Bond as a tool. The reading is confirmed when we notice that Bond is often resentful of this passive role. Conversely, the episodes with the armature ⊡ ought to be those in which Bond has the upper hand.

However, let us look more closely at these three cases. In the last, M does not officially sanction Bond's plan. Thus, such approval as he gives is not as an agent of society; and Bond does not have the upper hand over society. Moreover, the other two cases are examples where M has given Bond an official mission not determined by Bond, and where Bond is active only in formulating particular plans for executing the mission. Accordingly, Bond does not have the upper hand in these cases either.

What then of the two episodes with the armature ▯ ? These ought to be, following the code for the first armature, examples where Bond is on an equal footing with society. But again, in both these episodes (about Drax cheating at cards, and in *For Your Eyes Only*) M has stepped down from his office.

Thus, if we had the three armatures with the same code, the messages would be different (Bond sometimes losing to, sometimes winning over, sometimes drawing with society); but as it is, the code differs, and the message is invariant: society has the upper hand.

We must ask a second question, already hinted at: is the licence positively or negatively given and received? That is, is it a strong licence (an order) or a weak one (a request); is it received positively (with enthusiasm) or negatively (with resentment)? The question yields a matrix formally similar to the previous one:

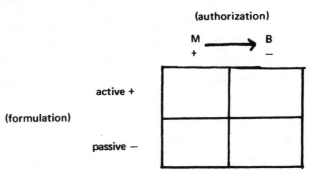

And from this matrix, we obtain as before a fourfold range of possible cases, varying this time not according to activity in formulating the plan, but according to positiveness in issuing or receiving the licence.

If, for the sake of simplicity, we confine ourselves to the fourfold matrix, and apply it to the cases already enumerated, we find ten cases with the armature ⧄ , ten with the armature ▭ and four with the armature ◸ ; sometimes Bond receives positive orders with enthusiasm, sometimes with resentment; in the case of reluctantly given licences, he is always, though not always unequivocally, enthusiastic.

The results of applying the two sets of matrices should be coordinated. I find the following results. For episodes in which the first matrix gives ⧄ , the second gives ⧄ or ▭ , for those in which the first gives ▭ , the second gives ▭ , or 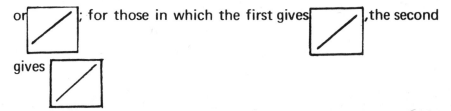 ; for those in which the first gives ,the second gives

If we read this back, it comes out as follows: when M is active in formulating the orders and Bond positive, then M issues them positively or negatively; when both are active in formulating the plan, then Bond is positive in receiving the licence, and M either positive or negative in issuing it; when M is passive and Bond active in formulating a plan, then the licence is issued negatively (i.e. reluctantly or unofficially).

Thus out of the nine possible double armatures, only the following five are found:

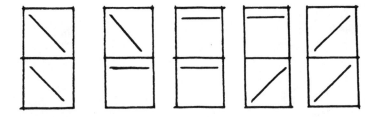

If as before we try to interpret these five in terms of the opposition between individual and society, we find that the original interpretation is merely expanded: society has the upper hand, *whether Bond likes it or not.*

Interpretation aside, however, we can now derive a consolidated matrix on the two planes, of activity in formulating the plan, and positiveness in issuing or accepting the licence. The new matrix will therefore be three-dimensional, retaining the horizontal as the dimension in which licences are issued irreversibly from left to right, the vertical as an active/passive dimension, and the third dimension as negative/positive.

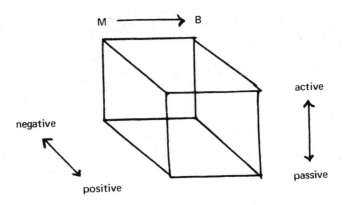

This structure is what we describe as the "licensing operator". Let us now observe the rules for its operation. Restricting ourselves to the material so far considered, we have four possible positions for M and Bond in their respective planes, as follows:

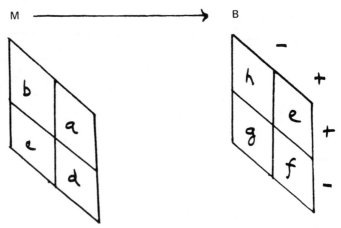

However, as has been seen, only three positions are permitted to either counter. M cannot be at position d (is never both passive in formulating and positive in issuing an order), while Bond cannot be at position h (is never active in formulating and negative in receiving an order). Moreover, not any combination of positions is permitted. A licence starting at a can emerge at e, f or g, but a licence starting at b or c can emerge only at e (an actively formulated and positively issued order may be received positively or negatively, and may or may not have been jointly formulated; a passively formulated or negatively issued order can only be actively and positively received).

The licensing operator can be regarded as the means by which a society ordains or permits various actions. Writing L for the operator, then, we shall have: such and such a society—L—such and such events. However, no society, and not that in the Bond books, operates only the M/Bond L—operator. There is, for example, a parallel set of operators with M and other agents. Moreover, M himself is sometimes at the receiving end: we occasionally get a Prime Minister/M L—operator. Bond himself is sometimes in charge of other agents, giving us a Bond/other L—operator. Then there are other systems not operating through M at all, but for example through Vallance of the Special Branch; and other hinted at in the CIA or the Deuxième Bureau.

But this is not all. Hostile societies have their own licensing operators, which play an important role in the books. A great deal of space is taken up in establishing a Russian licensing operation for the plot against Bond in *From Russia With Love*. Equally, we find L—operators at work in criminal societies like SPECTRE. Now in describing such proliferation of L—operators, based on different societies, and having different licensors and licensees, we should not have said nearly enough about the operator. For it can itself be put through at least three transformations, depending on the sort of event which is put as its right-hand terminus.

In the cases which we have actively considered (interviews with M), the events are taken to be wanted and ordained by the society (usually the curtailment of the activities of an enemy). But the matter is not as simple as that. It is not enough for society to ordain: someone must carry out the ordinance (hence the possibility of the Bond stories, since Bond is the executive par excellence). And to carry it out, various appropriate actions must be performed, some of them outside the law, or outside the conventions of the society. Thus the society, in ordaining x also and thereby licenses the means to x. The goals aimed at by Bond are ordained, and the means which he adopts may be licensed.

Further, as Bond pursues the ordained goal by the licensed means, he is exposed to various hazards. Are we to say that society is not responsible for these hazards, that it does not ordain that Bond should undergo them? We are not; and this is frequently recognized in the books by references to the provisions made for agents who are wounded or killed.

Thus the L—operator under these three transformations may be an instrument of command, licence, or jeopardy. This completes a sketch for that enormous formal complex which has been named the "licensing operator". We have approached it where it is nearest the surface in the Bond stories. But the rules governing the structure in the interviews with M may be changed as the L—operator goes through its various transformations. This is a matter for enquiry.

II. The Individuator

However, the licensing operator is not the means to a sufficient analysis of the myth. For the Bond stories are not just about the goals of various societies. Indeed, these societies and their goals are rather dimly depicted. Thus, though the licensing operator denotes a necessary framework for the actions of an individual, and indeed is explicitly concerned with the social licence for those actions, it tells us nothing about the individual.

We have already been led to interpret the licensing operator in terms of the opposition between society and individual. It was not an arbitrary interpretation. For when the society's means of control over the individual proliferate in the way mentioned at the outset, the problem of conflict and interaction between individual and society is sharpened. In more than one way. It does not need a McLuhan to tell us that society invades the individual with the complexities of its technology more subtly than by its permits and licences.

Appropriately, the story of this invasion is another important topic of the myth. The question to be asked here is: does Bond defeat society? And there are various axes along which the conflict takes place. Some of them are already embedded in the

licensing operator. There Bond is characteristically given instructions, put in jeopardy, and so forth, sometimes to his
resentment. To this extent, society defeats Bond. But of course
there are several "societies" in the stories, some criminal and
hostile. Thus Bond's conflicts with these enemies, in which he
sometimes is victorious, can be read as transformations of the
Bond/society conflict. Here Bond sometimes wins. Again, we
find in the stories what I have called "licensed outrages". Bond's
special mission sometimes entitles him to do things which would
not normally be acceptable to the society. He may kill in cold
blood, cheat at cards, gamble several years' salary, and so forth.
On one dimension, these are victories for Bond over society.

Again, technology figures in the books. As we have seen, this
may be read as an instrument of the society against the individual.
On this axis, Bond sometimes masters the machine, and the
machine sometimes wins. Another axis of the Bond/society
conflict is displayed in Bond's brand-name expertise. The victory
here is Bond's. In a multiplicity of consumer goods which might
baffle choice, and so quell the individual, Bond knows just what
he wants, by name, and knows why. It would be unfitting in the
compass of these notes to pursue this analysis. But by now the
techniques should be clear.

We construct the following four-position matrix:

	society	Bond
victory +		
defeat −		

We then show that it operates in five different dimensions (at least), as enumerated above (instructions, licences, jeopardy, technology, brand-names). A five-dimensional consolidated matrix is established. We then apply this to the stories, and discover the rules according to which it operates. Generally we should find, to anticipate detailed research, a victory for Bond.

It is to be noted that what was formerly treated as a *message* encoded in the licensing armature, namely defeat or victory for Bond against society, has now itself become the *armature* of a new structure. So we can ask what message is encoded in this new structure, the structure which we call "the individuator", since one of its functions is to transpose action from the social to the individual plane.

III. The Bond Armature

One message to be read there is the important one of Bond's prowess. Prowess is a mixture of natural endowment, practice and luck. We may construct a general matrix for prowess as follows:

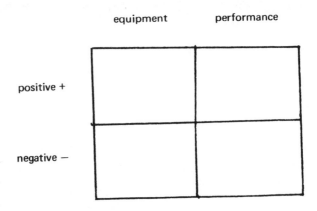

This takes different forms for the three components of pro-wess. In the case of natural endowment, Bond is typically positive in equipment (e.g. he is attractive to women, he is courageous), and positive in performance (e.g. he gets the girl; he doesn't falter). But, of course he sometimes fails, typically through ill luck. Thus in the case of luck, Bond may be positive or negative in equipment (i.e. lucky or unlucky); if he is lucky, he is typically positive in performance, if unlucky, he may succeed or fail. But practice, as well as fortune, contributes to success; and Bond often practises, with a gun, with a pack of cards, by physical training, and so on. In this case, he is typically positive in equipment (i.e. he does practise), but may be positive or negative in performance, according to luck.

This structure could be discussed in much more detail, in its application not only to Bond, but to other characters. Moreover, the "Bond armature", like the licensing operator before it, goes through three transformations. One extreme is where Bond is faced with what are often described as fantastic or impossible tasks, in which he typically succeeds. Then he is faced with practicable tasks, in which he may succeed or fail. If these two cases, we have to do with Bond's official assignments. But he has also his own life, for instance with women. In these cases, he typically fails (at least on some levels: e.g. the girl marries someone else, his wife is killed, and so forth). This would be the place for a detailed working out of the formal structure of the operator, and for an enquiry into its application to the text.

But given this armature, what message should we see encoded in it? A ready answer is that it should be read in terms of the Bond/society conflict. For it is in Bond's official missions that he is most successful, and outside them that he is least successful. Thus the Bond armature may be decoded as reading once more: *society has the upper hand.* Thus the third abstraction leads us back to the other levels of analysis, and we have described a closed system which can be regarded as generating the Bond myth. It may be easier now to see what Levi-Strauss meant when he wrote (CC 346) that myth may be regarded as "a matrix of significants arranged in lines and columns, but in which each plane, however it is read, refers always to another plane".

IV. The Permutability Maxim

It may seem that this bare sketch of an analysis belies its promise. For the purpose of taking the Bond stories as an example was that they seemed to be social phenomena, manifestations of a contemporary mythology. At what other points in our culture, then, do permutations of the Bond myth appear? This is the sort of task at which Lévi-Strauss exclaimed "God forbid!". I shall do no more than hint at some of the answers.

We might start near at hand, with le Carré's spy-stories. The easiest way of expressing the relation between these and Bond is to say that le Carré transposes Fleming down a tone. Whereas Bond, in the "individuator" cycle, breaks away from the upper hand of society, this never happens in le Carré's world. The upper hand of authority is attached to a much longer arm. Correspondingly, the le Carré agent never displays fantastic prowess, but sometimes (as in *The Looking Glass War*) fantastic lack of prowess. Again, he totally lacks Bond's brand-name mastery. Luck is typically eliminated.

If we could discern in the two cases systematically different armatures, we should be able to read off different messages, given the same code. It might seem that in Fleming the individual has his field of freedom from society, while in le Carré he doesn't. But this is too simple. For while in Fleming the licence-issuing authority (M) is solid and single, in le Carré, the licence-issuing authority is fragmented and indeterminate.

Thus, as the individual is "transposed down", so too is the authority of society. The result is that while Bond freedoms are denied to the le Carré agent, new freedoms are open to him, even if only deceits and disobediences.

The transposition is achieved in le Carré mainly by the manipulation of a dimension to the licensing operator which is held virtually constant in the Bond stories: what we might call the "briefing dimension". In effect, Bond is always fully briefed, and always keeps M briefed; but a mark of the le Carré situation is that the various protagonists are variously and often minimally briefed. It is thus that the licensing authority is fragmented, and that the agent, by being put at a greater distance from the authority of the society, is less in conflict with it.

The "briefing dimension" may recall the "briefing column" of the Observer: and it is not quite an accidental association. For the Sunday newspaper sociology and other features marking that newspaper are cultural phenomena which may be susceptible of the same sort of analysis. Its species of "briefing" gives the illusion that it is a means of activity (corresponding to the "Bond armature"), and a means of redress against the powers of society (corresponding to the "individuator"). Features of the society can be pilloried, castigated or casually reported; the myth associated with such activities is that engaging in them is itself a way of freeing oneself from society. But reading Nora Beloff no more annuls bad legislation than a Union Jack shirt or shopping bag eliminates the power of the establishment. They do these things magically: that is the myth.

We have now set down some intuitions about other cultural phenomena where transformations of the Bond myth might be discernible. They in turn might be suspected to lead on to considering political ideologies which form part of our culture, liberal and fascist ones. In all these cases, we see certain of the themes that figure in the Bond stories, and transpositions of the Bond structures of the kind hinted at for le Carré.

Such intuitions should be the cue for research. They are confessedly no more than the vaguest hints at some of the myths in our culture which might turn out to be permutations of the Bond myth. The hints must be made, since permutability is a maxim in the structural study of myth. But the task of following them is forbidding.

V. The Myth and Society

A final and important topic is the relation between the myths and society. A condition of treating it is of course an independent study of the relevant social phenomena. Here we can do no more than repeat the suggestion already made that the themes of the Bond stories are particularly appropriate in our manner of society. In some respects, then, the Bond stories may be said to mirror our society. But we also find systematic divergences which are no less significant: notably, the oversimplification of authority (Bond is responsible only to M and nothing ever overrides this authority), and the idealization of prowess (Bond survives any danger). The myth, then, presents a magical solution to a set of problems lived in our society, and—as has been remarked—themselves requiring independent analysis, problems, for example, like those we try to meet in practice by appointing Ombudsmen.

But the magical plane of the Bond myth is securely anchored by two devices which we have discovered playing other roles as well, namely, brand-name mastery, and technological mastery. Bond's feats are tied down to reality by a sufficiently realistic and carefully labelled and documented collection of machines. It is here that the weakness of the films is most clearly displayed. For in the films of the Bond stories, the linking function of these devices is ignored. The machines cease to be sufficiently real to connect fantasy and reality, and become a fantasy in themselves. They are thrown away. The films cease to be myth and become a joke. Confrontation of society and individual no longer occurs; we are left with passing extravaganzas, reaching a high-point of foolishness and tedium in the film Casino Royale. We are left agreeing with the brain-washed Bond in *The Man With The Golden Gun,* when he said to M: "You've been making war against someone or other all your life. And for most of my adult life, you've used me as a tool". If we agree with this, the myth of liberation from society is destroyed, the winning magic becomes an empty gesture.

Breaking a Culture — a Theme of Science-Fiction
T.A. Shippey

Revised version of an article originally published in *Alta*, vol. 2, no. 9, 1969.

Reprinted by permission of the author.

BREAKING A CULTURE -
A THEME OF SCIENCE-FICTION

T.A. Shippey

As a form, science-fiction conceals homogeneity beneath apparent diversity. The diversity can be seen by looking at the range of paperbaacks in any bookshop. One finds lumped together 'end of the world' stories, galactic empire stories, stories of the near future and, via time-travel, of the very far past, as well as stories which have nothing to do with science at all but depend on magic or the fantasy-type known as 'sword and sorcery'. One might well think that the inclusion of all these under one heading is just a mistake, that the diversity is real. But most of the material now appearing in paperbacks has appeared first, as short-story or serial, in one of a comparatively small number of *magazines*; it is their existence which demonstrates, and may cause, the in fact striking homogeneity of most SF. Even the layout of one of these can suggest how close-knit the field really is. Each editor has his stable of writers, whose names appear fairly regularly and who do not write for other magazines all that often; he imposes his views also by regular review columns, and by editorials, frequently long and argumentative. But his authority is not quite tyrannical, because a fair share of time and space is also given over to readers' letters, while - in one magazine at least - authors' pay depends partly on a bonus scheme tied to a published analysis of readers' reactions. In any case the writers are often not professionals, but readers who have gone over to a more extreme form of participation, so that the triangle of writers, editors and readers is mutually supporting in all directions. Inside the field, the influence of fans and magazines is immense. It is not commonly recognised by those who read a little SF in book form, and who may feel inclined to despise the garish covers and aggressive titles - *Astounding, Fantastic, Galaxy, If, Fantasy and SF* - but it is important. And the magazines bring up the problems of homogeneity and definition most acutely; for though they specialise a little, it is still clear from any one of them that the same people both write and read all the various sub-types listed above, and that very often the true fans do not read anything else. But what similarity is it that they see in this diversity, and that they do not find anywhere else? The answers are surprising and not easy.

    To find some answers, I intend in this article to use mainly material from the magazine *Astounding/Analog*, partly because I have an uninterrupted run of it for the past 13 years, partly because its editor, John W. Campbell jr., is himself one of SF's most conscious and deliberate analysts. His awareness of readership problems can be seen in the change, nearly nine years ago, from the name *Astounding Science Fiction* to the name *Analog: Science Fact and Fiction*, a change supported by great alterations of format and by the monthly inclusion of a factual article, sometimes related to the fiction. It is perhaps significant that the name-change cannot have been entirely successful, since the price has continued to rise, and a British edition has not been printed since August 1963, presumably from lack of demand. But the standard of fiction has remained high; and the magazine has kept a reputation for being 'harder' and more technical than its competitors. This only makes more surprising the fairly complex relationship between science and fiction in its stories.

One might have expected *ASF* (the usual abbreviation covering both names), to have stayed fairly close to the rigorous and non-fantastic defi-nition of SF given by Kingsley Amis in his *New Maps of Hell*: Science-fiction is that class of prose narrative treating of a situation that could not arise in the world we know, but which is hypothesised on the basis of some innovation in science or technology, or pseudo-science or pseudo-technology.

The 'innovation' in technology; this is certainly what *ASF* is often interested in. But what is one to make of such stories as the lead novel-ettes of November 1964 and November 1965, the 'Gunpowder God' stories of H. Beam Piper? In these the hero is shifted from the contemporary world to an 'alternate' one, in which the racial movements of our history have taken a different path, so that the present United States is inhabited by an archaic people living under something like feudalism. Admittedly the stories are set off by an accident caused by superior science; but the interest is not on that at all, but on the changes the hero tries to make in the 'alternate' world as a result of his own knowledge - a process which turns out to be surprisingly difficult, but does not involve anything that is an 'innovation' to us. This case is not picked out merely to cavil. The point is that SF authors very frequently show a tendency towards archaism rather than futurism, that a favourite device is the 'alternate' world or planet on a barbarian level, which just happens to be reached via superior science, and that in any case the scientific developments allowed may well be, as Amis says, pseudo-scientific, so that one runs into telepathy, ESP, and conscious developments of witchcraft rather than physics. Very rarely does the interest of an SF story depend on simple marvelling at technology - that is now more character-istic of the spy-story or thriller.

What is the mainspring, then, of SF? What causes the interest in the man with the 'wild talent', that least expected but most prevalent theme? A view aired in the readers' columns of *ASF* itself is that it is just a case of wish-fulfilment, the 'security device', everyone wanting to be a superman and taking this way of indulging it. But the features of archaism and pseudo-science seem to me to be only the tip of a comparative iceberg of beliefs, which the SF fan is likely to acquire as an adolescent and which enable him to read many stories in a way almost denied to the common reader. One story may help to illustrate this - the lead novelette of *ASF* October 1958 (British edition), Jack Vance's *The Miracle Workers*.

In it we find ourselves as so often on a barbarian planet, Pangborn, watching the feud between two local castellans, Lord Faide and Lord Ballant. But there are several complications to their mediaeval tactics. One is that these people are clearly the descendants of marooned or exiled space-travellers; they preserve heirlooms of ancient days, like the gun on top of each keep, and the ancestral car of Lord Faide. But they have lost all knowledge of science, so that the guns fail to work and the car is in fact barely more efficient than a horse, or its local equivalent. Moreover, their ideas of science are re-placed by a scheme of magic, so that Lord Faide's most important striking force is the corps of 'jinxmen', headed by Hein Huss and seconded by Izak Comandore, whose respective interpretations of magic take up much of the story. A third complication is the existence of the First Folk, the aborigines of the planet, long since driven into hiding but not entirely spent. These three factors interlock to provide a narrative on more than one level.

Military, the pattern is this. Lord Faide marches to attack Ballant Keep and subdues it, thus for the first time becoming effective ruler of the planet. But on his way there and back he meets resistance from the forest-dwelling First Folk, which angers him so much that he determines to subjugate

them also. Hein Huss, Izak Comandore and the bumbling apprentice who becomes
the real hero, Sam Salazar, attempt to gain information about the First Folk,
but do not entirely succeed. A jinxman attack on the natives merely provokes
them, and, using specially-bred animals, they besiege and almost conquer Faide
Keep; the situation is only saved by Sam Salazar who, in spite of all dis-
couragements from his superiors, has been patiently trying to invent chemistry,
and who finds that vinegar is an effective neutralising agent to the natives'
foam. Put this way, the story sounds obvious, as it is on plot-level. But
the real theme of the story and the main point of its interest for all readers,
is the idea of Belief. It is belief which is the secret of the jinxman's
success. This is hinted at by the importance of simulacra or mannikins in
casting hoodoos, for they remind one of the (apparently effective) death-spells
of Australian aborigines, and the author uses the word *mana* to point out his
allusion. Furthermore, one of the more fascinating jinxman discussions concerns
the technique of demon-possession, in which it is agreed by those in the secret
that the demon itself has no validity, and that the commodity actually traded
among jinxmen is public acceptance. And there are other examples of belief -
Lord Faide's quite unfounded belief in his ancestral heirlooms, for example,
even though he does not know how they work, and in the end they prove not to.
All these combine to point out the essential irony of the title. Who are the
'miracle workers'? Clearly we, the readers, must regard the jinxmen as archaic
barbarians who nevertheless perform miracles. On the other hand, it is equally
clear that the inhabitants of Pangborn regard their ancestors as barbarians,
and wonder also about *their* undoubted ability to perform miracles. Several discussions help us to reverse our normal views and see science as irrational and
magic as rational. In one scene the hankering after the old days is dismissed
ironically as a Security Device, the wish to be a superman: 'There is an aura
of romance, a kind of wild grandeur to the old days - But of course ... mysticism
is no substitute for orthodox logic'. In others we see the random nature of
scientific experiments, for Sam Salazar forgets to take notes and so cannot
repeat his actions, adding to the disgust of his superiors; while the First Folk also
develop a concept in their breeding of animals, which they call 'irrationality'
and which Hein Huss translates as 'a series of vaguely motivated trials', but
which we recognise as science or experimental method, the root of the miracles
of the ancients.

This continuous reversal of logic provides the amusement and much of
the action for the story. But it is not a point which is meant to be taken
entirely comically. No modern man, who uses every day half-a-dozen devices
of whose operation he knows nothing beyond a few simplifications, should doubt
how much science is supported by popular belief. And one of the favourite
themes in *ASF*'s science-fact pieces has been for some years the discovery of
engineering anachronisms, discoveries made ahead of their time but apparently
shelved because they did not fit in with accepted opinion. In March 1965, for
example, *ASF* printed a genuine US patent, dated 1930, which appears to describe
a transistor; other finds concern early steam cars and the spread of the nickel-
cadmium battery. The points may not be important in themselves, but from them
John W. Campbell, the editor, has developed a considerable theory of learning,
always liable to be expressed fictionally by writers under his influence. An
example could be his distinction between scientist and engineer, in favour of
the latter; in matters of complete novelty, he argues, the scientist can be
handicapped by attachment to system, theory and explanation, while the engineer
is useful under any circumstances, preserved by careless pragmatism.

So *The Miracle Workers* presents a theory which is in a way relevant to
contemporary readers, even though there is no 'innovation in technology' which

we can recognise, and the only links between us and Pangborn are the spaceships
of the ancients, 1600 years from the story and unguessed time from us. Something like this theory lies behind many of the apparently cranky and implausible
tales of telepathy and ESP so frequent in modern SF. But there is another
common theme present in this story which may cast some light on the genre -
that of the 'end of the world'. For the natives of Pangborn this is not a
material disaster; it occurs instead at the victory-banquet after the capture
of Ballant Keep, where the five jinxmen of the two sides meet, and Hein Huss
reflects, after his demon-combat with Izak Comandore, that:

> tonight sees the full amplitude of jinxmanship. I think that never again
> will such power and skill gather at the same table. We shall die one by
> one and there shall be none to fill our shoes.

It is in recognition of this that Hein Huss takes over Sam Salazar the apprentice from the troop of Comandore. We are meant to see his perception that for
the jinxmen there is no way but down, for the practical bungler no way but up.
The scene is a good one, for in it we see the death, not exactly of a world,
but of a system of belief, also related obscurely to Lord Faide's political
decisions. It is this inevitable failure in victory that causes Lord Faide's
hinted regret for his enemy and victim Lord Ballant; we realise that both men
were dedicated to the same purpose, that the emergence of the winner ends an
era, and that it is for this reason that laughter at the expense of Lord Ballant
is discouraged. The whole story, in fact, gives us a pattern of groups united
by a belief and seeing nothing outside themselves; only Huss and Salazar have
power to change their worlds.

Again, relevance to contemporary life could be asserted. But it is
worth noting how abstract the application is; Vance has no satiric targets
and makes no particular references. Indeed *The Miracle Workers* and its like
are in some ways completely opposed to those stories which deal, not with the
end of *a* world, but with the end of *our* world - the (sometimes satirical)
disaster-novel as pioneered by H.G. Wells in *The War of the Worlds* or *The War
in the Air*. It seems significant that this latter is a determinedly English
phenomenon, for while it would not be quite true to say that all English SF
writers write disaster novels, or that all disaster novels are written by
Englishmen, neither generalisation is very far wrong. John Wyndham is the
most obvious example. But one can note also how both John Christopher and
Brian Aldiss have abandoned their American-style short stories for novels
like *The World in Winter* (a new Ice Age), and *Greybeard* (universal sterility),
and how the newer writer J.G. Ballard appears to be going the same way, as he
works through the possibilities of flood, drought, hurricane and even crystall-
isation. Minor writers add themselves quickly - Edmund Cooper, Charles Eric
Maine - and even 'mainstream' novelists venture into the well-trodden path,
as Nevil Shute did with *On the Beach*. All this could be seen as oddly parochial,
but there is no denying its popularity. For many Englishmen end of world
novels represent SF in its entirety, and one does not know whether to be more
surprised at the acceptance of so many variations on the same theme or at the
effect which single examples, like Nevil Shute's, clearly have on the general
public.

What is the secret ingredient? Political moralising appears in some
cases, such as *The Day of the Triffids*, and indeed it is this which helps to
mark off the English type from American post-Bomb novels, like Poul Anderson's
Twilight World or Algis Budrys' *Some Will Not Die*, both of which are far too
concerned with their new societies to bother about the ruins of the old. But
even politics is not common to all English examples. What is common seems to

be this. In all cases one ends up with the average Englishman, probably married, trying to make his way in a ruthless and insecure world which is nevertheless still familiar — robbing supermarkets and fighting his way towards Westmorland (Christopher's *The Death of Grass*), the West Country (Wyndham's *Triffids*), or Norfolk (Cooper's *All Fools' Day*). Clearly there is a strong element of *Robinson Crusoe* in the percentage of these stories, but there are other repeated features which are not so cosy, e.g. the scene of rape (*All Fools' Day, Death of Grass, A Wrinkle in the Skin*), or of gross sexual humiliation (Maine's *The Tide Went Out*), along with reversals of sex-dominance, and the curious inversion of white and Negro (Christopher's *The World in Winter* and Aldiss's *Earthworks*). From these characteristics one might conclude that the English disaster novel exists to feed the wish-fulfilment of aggression against a familiar society, with overtones of guilt and masochism. That may be too strong. But there is one important point. In contrast with most SF, this English variety sticks close to the reality of here and now, changing only one element at a time. But though this makes it more acceptable to critics by bringing it closer to conventional realism, it does not make it less escapist! Instead, its indulgence of a *possible* mediaevalism conceals a far closer connection with the longings of the reader than the relatively pure fantasy of *The Miracle Workers* ever has, and includes far less in the way of rational criticism; these novels are so close to our own society that they illustrate it and pander to its fears more than they comment on it.

Not that I wish to argue that SF *should* avoid fantasy and provide rational criticism. It is, after all, one of very few forms now left which are read for entertainment only. But this type of English SF, with its itch to be easily credible, seems to lack novelty; and it lacks also a certain cultural detachment. For my next, and main point is that the key to the great body of SF is that it encourages a detached presentation of cultures which should be different from our own, separate worlds like those of Lord Faide and Hein Huss, presenting on the face of it great strangeness but concealing a system of *logic* which must in the end be capable of comprehension. Only this interest unites the apparent disparity of the space-exploration story, the mythical-past story, the quasi-historical story. It explains the phenomenal success of J.R.R. Tolkien's *Lord of the Rings* trilogy, with its almost insanely detailed background — though this book and its readers are scowlingly dis-avowed by some SF purists. It explains also why more conventional SF satire is so reluctant to pick out present-day institutional and political targets, and why the American post-Bomb story rarely gets round to allocating blame. Unlike Wyndham, Christopher and the rest, these authors are frankly not interested in any reflection of the culture of today, because it is familiar and carries in any case an immediate emotional charge hard to use directly. Thus, in Pohl and Kornbluth's *Gladiator-at-Law* we are offered an extrapolation of business control coupled with juvenile delinquency which may (in 1955) have had some topical force. But we are also made to accept the institution of gladiatorial games — something which has no parallel in contemporary culture, in spite of the gesture towards American football, but which is nevertheless common in SF. (See Mack Reynolds' *ASF* serial *Sweet Dreams, Sweet Princes*, Oct.-Dec. 1964) The fact of the matter is that the authors and readers enjoy gladiatorial games as something undeniably possible, since they existed, but still inexplicable in our terms; with much the same mixture of modernity and archaism Walter Miller ignores all questions of atomic war to give us future monks illuminating the incomprehensible 'blueprints' of the ancients in *A Canticle for Leibowitz*. It would be wrong to say that the interest is in the results of change rather than the process of change, for very often we are given societies in the moment of their alteration or dissolution; but again in contrast with the English type of SF, that change is more likely to be *towards* what we can recognise as civilisation than away from it. Many SF authors maybe have a feeling that our society is at its peak, likely to go down rather than up, but if that is so, it is clear that most writers outside England are more concerned with rebirth of any kind than extinction, even if they have to travel great distances in time and space to find an appropriate setting.

But has the story concerned with culture rather than character any literary potential? Several critics and reviewers assume superciliously that SF is going through some kind of adolescent phase, prior to becoming aware of social problems, discovering character, approaching "mainstream" literature and producing Great Books; some would even say that a New Wave of writers is at the moment starting on all these tasks. One wonders how far this is simple failure to understand practice without an approved theory. Sam Salazar, the sorcerer's apprentice, is put forward boldly, even memorably, but in terms of actions alone, with the abstract thoughts which lead him to those actions. Could much be gained by inviting the reader to sympathise with his individual and emotional peculiarities? They might well require too much explanation in terms of different *mores*; and such explanation would itself lead away from a normal type of literature. It is better to admit that SF is already going quite well in its own way. The sort of success attained can be shown, again, by picking out two *ASF* novelettes, which also point out a representative story-pattern.

Both stories, *Wherever You Are* (*ASF* June '59) and *The Three-Cornered Wheel* (*ASF* May '63) are by the same author, Poul Anderson, though the first appeared under his pen-name 'Winston P. Sanders'. One of its more interesting features is the cover which illustrates the story, and which shows a large, blue, taloned, scaled, fanged monster with claws raised. Since the magazine was still then called *Astounding*, one imagines that 99 per cent of those who saw the cover would feel immediately confirmed in their view of SF as childish pseudo-Gothic. Only the odd few who read the story and were probably fans already would see the joke. For on closer inspection the monster can be seen to be slightly overweight, to be wearing a little hat and in any case to be in a position, not of menace, but of fear – naturally, he is frightened by the horrible Flat-Eyed Monster, the human being. The joke in fact is on the accepted convention of SF; and the whole of the story is further planned to illustrate this.

In the stock SF situation there ought to be three parties, the girl (A), the man (B), and the monster (C), while their relationship should be that A hopes that B will save her from C. Yet clearly other permutations are possible, and this is what *Wherever You Are* sets out to give us. The immediate situation is that the two humans, man and girl, are stranded on the planet of Epstein by the breakdown of their ferry. There is a human base on the planet, but it is on an island, and they will have to persuade the natives to take them there. Fortunately the saurian natives have a primitive steam-boat; but unfortunately they are not themselves at their home, but are on an exploring voyage – it is as if extraterrestrials had contacted a party of Europeans in the 1830s in the China Seas. To add to the complications, the saurians have a strict caste-system and are under the orders of the noble, Feridur. And while the lower classes are mild, peaceful and interested in technology, Feridur is a lizard with an *idée fixe* – he collects skulls, and with his monocle, his ideals of sportsmanship and his genial understatements, clearly parodies the English hunting lord. One problem is to prevent him from insisting on a sporting duel to add a human skull to his collection. The other problem, briefly, is that the humans no longer know where they are and so cannot even give a compass bearing on their base. The title refers partly to that, but partly, no doubt, to the odd humanity of the Epsteinians.

The two humans, then, go about solving their problems in separate ways. The man, B, timid, small and bespectacled, is called Didymus Mudge, comes from Boston and teaches high-school physics. During most of the action he appears to be worrying about his watch, put out of exact order by the crash, and trying to hang up a large copper ball full of sand, with the assistance of the lowlier Epsteinians. His attempts to explain are invariably cut off by the wrath of A, an Amazonian lady called Ulrica Ormstadt, major in the military service of New Scythia, who spends her time with the upper-class monsters, trying to learn the language and get into a position where she can give orders. Eventually she has no recourse left but to challenge Feridur to a duel, which, if she wins, gives her full control of his property and skull collection. However, as anticipated, she is losing until the two lines of action finally intersect, when Mudge asserts himself and shouts to her to lure Feridur on to a convenient patch of ground, where he is promptly flattened by the mysterious copper ball. This seems an elementary story on the bottom level of a comic human situation, the man bullied by the girl but turning the tables on her. It gains more interest from the permutations of one character saving another from a third. There are six possible, but two clearly cannot appear, since nothing would ever need to be saved from Didymus Mudge, and the typical case, the man saving the girl from the monster, is only present for a moment and then in a comically cowardly way. The story moves round the other three, beginning with a lower-class monster running down a path and hoping the man will come to save him from the girl (CBA), moving on to the man cowering with his Epsteinian friends and hoping the girl will save him from Feridur (BAC), and ending with the man shrinking back from the now-amorous Major Ormstadt, and hoping the monster will somehow be able to save him from the girl (BCA). Obviously the story was planned, like the cover, in exactly this frame. Still, the real interest comes from another typical pattern. There are two problems to be solved by the humans, and one is technical while the other is cultural. No doubt many readers spent a lot of time trying to work out what Mudge was doing, and solving problem 1, i.e. finding one's latitude and longitude from observations of the sun and a set of tide-tables. The explanation, I should point out, takes two pages, but briefly Mudge has to carry out one series of experiments to correct his watch, so that he can then identify the tides from his table and work out his longitude, but he needs the massive Foucault sphere to find his latitude, of which the sphere's turning path is a sine function. But this problem is not adequate on its own; it is a mistake to think of SF as a series of technical posers for junior scientists, though it can work like that for short periods. Even Hal Clement, that most relentlessly technical writer, has to show the effect of his imagined environments on the thought-systems of other intelligent creatures; and in this story the second problem is to find the weak spot in the Epsteinian culture, clearly the caste-system and duel-convention. It may be simple enough, but a lot of tiny observations help to build it up – Epsteinian honorifics, for example, their equation of nobility with 'sporting blood', their automatic assumption that Mudge is a slave, and the captain's feeble attempts to get past his owner's obsession with craniology to discussions of science or trade. The parallel with 19th century Europeans is also almost explicitly made, though there are continual reminders of what is out of place – the lack of firearms, the 'barbaric' thatch hut that serves as a cabin. On top of this, there is the obvious clash between the different human cultures of the man and the girl, with their respective strengths. Mudge and the low-class Epsteinian captain appear in the end to be the winners, a decision often reversed in other stories in favour of anthropologist as hero rather than engineer; but there is no attempt in this story to evaluate the cultures present. They exist only to be understood, to form the rules of the game within which a solution has to be found.

Much SF indeed seems to be almost purely in the spirit of a game with complex rules. (Two common minor themes, for example, are societies based on variations of chess, and stories based on variations of Sherlock Holmes, both exercises in pure reason with strikingly unfamiliar rules.) However, the second story chosen, *The Three-Cornered Wheel*, leads on a little further to more ethical questions. It is again a problem-story; and once more the situation is a barbarian planet with a transport difficulty. A merchant spaceship has come down on the planet, out of fuel, and in need of an atomic generator left in the unmanned repair-base a thousand kilometres from their point of landing. The natives, previously contacted, are quite friendly; but there is an absolute taboo in their culture on any form of the Wheel, a sacred symbol. So there is no prospect of bringing the generator to the ship, while the ship itself is unable to take off. Again, there are two problems, or at least two possible avenues of solution. First, can one find a way to move a heavy generator a thousand kilometres, assuming a Dark Age technology and no wheels? Second, is there any way to find a weak spot in the natives' culture, exerting no pressure from outside, but mining from within according to the culture's own system of logic? Only one method needs to be solved; but in fact both are.

The action runs like this. At the start, one of the crew members has ridden off to meet the local chief in whose area the repair-base lies, in an attempt to get co-operation from him rather than from the ruling central theocracy. The chief, like Feridur a character with archaic earthly traits, this time those of the mediaeval English Marcher lord, naturally has to refuse in spite of a certain practical sympathy and dislike of his own priests. And on his way back the crew-member, Falkayn, is ambushed by priestly attendants wearing the Circle. This is the violent level of the story, though still re-deemed from being updated cowboys and Indians by a series of reflections on the motives of all concerned, and by references to the various sub-cultures of the natives and indeed of the merchant crew; even while under fire Falkayn takes time to consider the effects of the natives' *quicker* learning time on their handling of elementary tactics. It is during this ride that Falkayn works out the solution to problem 1, solving it in proper melodramatic fashion simultaneously with his winning of the skirmish. As usual, the wagon arrangement finally arrived at would take half a page to explain, but suffice it to say that it is based, like our new 10 shilling coin, on the realisation that a circle is only the limiting case in the class of constant-width polygons, any of which will roll better than, for example, a 12-sided threepenny bit. Falkayn uses the one nearest to a circle and still theologically permissible, a fact learnt earlier in a discussion of bridges.

But meanwhile his captain, Schuster, has been busy with problem 2. His two solutions to the problem of breaking the alien culture's taboo are, first, to introduce differential calculus and second, to begin teaching Kabalistic philosophy. The first provides the bait, for the native priests, of a more accurate astronomy, and conceals the hook of Newtonian physics, specifically the law of gravity and the forced abandonment of the theory of cycles and epicycles, so reducing the validity of the Circle as a universal

principle. The second more subtly invites both reader and native to see the
beauty of unbridled logic acting on false premises, with all its mediaeval
concomitants of angelology, numerology, letter-arrangement and allegory. It
is hoped by Schuster that this will produce a situation of conflicting schools
and a break-up of the political hold of the theocracy. But it should be noted
that he is not in any way trading on the natives' stupidity; we are told
several times that they are 'intrinsically more gifted' than humans. In fact
he is trading on their intelligence, the whole argument depending on the point,
common in SF, that individual intelligence can be completely subservient to
the seemingly-accidental development of culture.

What this story, like *Wherever You Are*, asks one to admire is the
elegance of solutions to technical and ideological questions; these are seen
not in individual terms, but as a fairly abstract manipulation of forces;
human beings are seen as data for a problem. Some may find this cold-blooded.
If that is a literary criticism, it becomes largely a matter of habit and
opinion. If it is raised ethically, rather more can be said. For Schuster's
plans have to meet two objections raised by the crew and by Schuster himself.
His machinations may help marooned spacemen in fifty years, but they are of
no use straight away. It is Falkayn who has to solve the immediate difficulty. So why should Schuster try to break the natives' culture? And,
since it is a stable one, has he any right to? It is significant here that
Schuster, far on in the future, is still a Jew, and so attached to a stable
culture of his own with great experience of persecution. Why should he, above
all, want to break the aliens' monotheism? No firm answer is given. But the
question lies behind a good deal of SF. One could look, for example, at any
of the following *ASF* serials, all now out in book form, to see it treated
very clearly. - Robert Randall's *The Dawning Light* (July-Sept. '57), Poul
Anderson's *The Man Who Counts* (May-July '58), Harry Harrison's *No Sense of
Obligation* (Jan.-Mar. '62). Even the titles are indicative of their rather
grim contents, which perhaps explains why they usually get new names for appearance in paperback. But for a good short presentation of the problem on its
own, one might look at another *ASF* lead novelette, Robert Silverberg's
Precedent (April '58).

This is really a sequel to a much more liberal story, *Earthman's
Burden*, reprinted in the English magazine *New Worlds* in February 1959 and
also in a recent paperback collection by Sphere publishers. In that earlier
one a human commander handed over one of his men to an alien court for an
accidental violation of taboo, thus setting the 'Devall Precedent' - though
Silverberg skipped the moral question there by allowing the human to escape
in his trial by pursuit. But in the *ASF* story the precedent is intended to
bind a much more Machiavellian human commander, Colonel Norden. He agrees to
its letter while challenging its spirit by handing over one of his men for
another violation, this time of a temple, committed deliberately and insult-
ingly. The man is condemned to death by flogging, but - coached by Norden -
appeals for trial by combat. Then, because even the art of hand-to-hand
fighting can be developed by a technical society as much as any other, he
easily beats his much larger opponent and so proves his innocence in almost
miraculous fashion. Yet all the aliens know he *is* guilty, and he admits this
publicly after the trial. The resultant paradox leaves the theocracy again
with a problem; the moral being that one should not claim equality unless
genuinely equal, while differences in culture are unlikely to result in
equality under any objective standards.

All this may seem grossly illiberal. But it should not be confused with the illiberality caused by thoughtless self-confidence, belief that one's own way is right and all others are wrong. Though the stories chosen so far show superior humans and inferior aliens, the converse situation can be taken just as seriously. *ASF* has repeatedly printed stories showing the disastrous impact of a superior alien culture on even the self-confident societies of the West, e.g. George Whitley's *Familiar Pattern* (Jan. '60) or Seaton McKettrig's *A World by the Tale* (Oct. '63). Nor is the destruction in those just a matter of force; as with the Silverberg story, what affects the humans is the existence of a culture demonstrably more powerful than their own but not to be reached by human methods. People are then torn between their own beliefs and the realisation that other beliefs are stronger and truer, ending up in the situation of the traditional 'Marginal Man' - the Red Indian, for example, drunken and despairing because he cannot understand what has conquered him. There is no self-confidence here. Though the paradox is noted that no-one inside a working culture is likely to see much of its weaknesses, it is freely admitted that contemporary Western society must have just as many as the societies of imaginary aliens. One could generalise fairly that SF writers as a whole have less belief in the absolute validity of their own *mores* than writers of almost any other possible group.

Yet their political attitudes are those of hawks rather than of doves, for distrust of oneself does not imply confidence in anyone else! John W. Campbell's early editorials on Vietnam illuminate some fictional situations, and show what is and what is not likely to be treated. In them his attitude was from a very early date that the Americans should not be there, and that there would be no harm in letting the South go Communist. Yet he thought this without the least personal inclination to Communism or even Socialism; his point was merely that the U.S. had in this war put itself in the foolish position of a do-gooder - SF's typical villain - who tries to impose his beliefs and solutions on other people, thinking they must be universally valid. Campbell argued that this is ridiculous; forcing democracy on the East is as absurd as forcing Communism on the West. As a result he appears to be left-wing in practice and right-wing in theory, and in fact avoids the whole right/ left polarity altogether. Something like this is what we find expressed by Silverberg's Colonel Norden and Anderson's Captain Schuster. Neither has any wish to make his own beliefs universal, but both feel capable of deciding at least what is inferior, and are ready to cause hardship and death to destroy it. They decide not entirely on the basis of human progress or 'the greatest good of the greatest number', but on an ideal of truth. Granted, everybody including the judge makes mistakes. But if those mistakes can be exposed, they should be. If humans at some time meet a superior race - a possibility very present to Silverberg's Norden - then however painful the exposition of faults might be, they should in the end be grateful. Willingness to learn precludes many perils. The real enemy is not any single belief but rigid and inappropriate beliefs.

Again, one can read SF without sharing this attitude; there are even a few authors who do not share it, and a good many who do not go out of their way to express it. But it is one of the slants which help to give the form homogeneity, and can be seen underlying such familiar themes as the unfolding of cyclic history in Asimov's *Foundation* trilogy or A.E. van Vogt's *Voyage of the Space Beagle*. That idea of course leaves one with no final goal except the theory that it is better to travel hopefully than to arrive. But the confidence and decision of so many SF characters does rest on the exposition of three levels of humility from which, I imagine, most Europeans and Americans still rather shrink.

The first is the much-stressed weakness of the individual himself. It should be remembered that in both the problem-stories just discussed the protagonists are at the start bound to die unless they can enlist the *voluntary* help of others. Their only tools are their minds and their knowledge of science, and it is often pointed out how weak the latter is without a supporting industrial base. In a recent short story, Jack Wodhams' *Handyman* (April '68), the hero is unable to make himself even a cup on his unsettled planet, because he has not the skill, in spite of his theoretical knowledge. But he ends by developing a ceramics industry for his descendants, who take a coconut for their trademark because, as they explain, if they had had that in the first place they would never have gone any further. Strength is acquired; but it has to come from weakness. A second, and parallel, level of humility is the awareness of a society's weakness, applied not only to imaginary savages but also to SF authors and their readers. Again, if this is accepted, a compensating strength emerges. Poul Anderson's 'man who counts' is significantly not the scientist or even the engineer, but the man who can understand others' logic. To do this he has to submerge his own beliefs at least for a moment; but it gives him control over others, and makes him personally free of prejudice. A final humility, though, is the awareness of the vulnerability of both individual and society to the disruptions of technical discovery; the 'man who counts' has to have an engineer in close attendance. Christopher Anvil's short story *Gadget versus Trend* in *ASF* Feb. '63, with its ironic picture of a baffled social scientist, makes the point very nicely, but it is not uncommon, and far pre-dates Marshall McLuhan. But here the contrast with the English disaster novel is once more very marked, for Christopher, Shute and Ballard appear only to fear the effects of science; so perhaps, do Anderson, Anvil and the rest, but they at least hope to avoid total collapse, if necessary by abandoning their most cherished social habits painlessly as soon as they prove outdated. On all three levels the only force that survives is a kind of ruthless pragmatism that continually calls itself in question, and has no doubts because it has no faith – something closely akin to Sam Salazar's attempts at chemistry in *The Miracle Workers*.

To sum up: the common element in the great body of science-fiction is an interest in cultures, in the ways in which intelligent beings could live and think, as dictated by circumstances, their technical ability, their systems of thought. Though it borrows its plots and characters from older and more conventional literature, the form is as a result a curiously modern one; nothing like it could have existed before the present era and the discoveries of anthropology; it is not very similar to either of those two older forms, the didactic Utopia or the spectacular 'fantastic voyage'. Its modernity lies in outlook as well as in subject; and so SF can be recognised even when the apparatus of science is absent, as in the fantasies, the ESP stories, the stories of alternate worlds.

But interest in contemporary society is not very present. It may be too complicated for treatment in such mechanical terms, or just too emotionally loaded. The general absence of strong appeals to sentiment perhaps accounts for the depressing unpopularity of SF among educated readers in this country. It is noticeable that the few books to have been picked out for filming like Bradbury's *Fahrenheit 451* and what became Clarke's *2001*, are untypical in that they fix on dangers already well-publicised and perhaps no longer present. The challenge they present to thought is flattering rather than painful. In the same way the film *Soylent Green* preferred to exploit the horrid titillations of cannibalism rather than consider the real dangers of population growth as did its source, Harry Harrison's novel *Make Room! Make Room!* Can 'hard' SF then ever be anything but an Opposition? Possibly not; but at least it runs little risk of becoming the mouthpiece of accepted opinion in science or literature, and so becoming subject to the tyranny of whatever it is that is expected *now*.

On all its levels it is a form which assumes change - and unpredictable change, not just 'revolution'. It deserves more consideration than it gets. Readers might do well to cure their shyness or disdain and discover SF, not only through the paperback publisher or anthologiser, but also where it originates, in the ironic and polemical context of the magazines.

Review of 'The Fantastic in Literature' by Eric S. Rabkin
Peter Miles

from

Trivium 13, St David's University College 1978.

The Fantastic in Literature, ERIC S. RABKIN.

Princeton University Press, 1976. Pp. xi + 234. $12.50.

The Fantastic in Literature investigates a field which has long had its defenders, but which has seldom been the subject of sustained critical enquiry. Nevertheless, Rabkin's study comes hard on the heels of two other recent works, C. N. Manlove's *Modern Fantasy: Five Studies* (Cambridge University Press, 1975) and W. R. Irwin's *The Game of the Impossible* (University of Illinois Press, 1976), which display a similar critical, methodological, and pedagogic concern with the need to describe or define the nature of fantasy as a literary genre. Each recognizes British fantasy of the late nineteenth and twentieth centuries as the seminal area to be explored, but while such practitioners as Charles Kingsley, George Macdonald, C.S. Lewis, Tolkien and Peake are accorded separate chapters by Manlove, we find Irwin, and more particularly Rabkin, extending their exploration to many periods and countries, clearly reflecting that their major priority is the establishing of the genre rather than the evaluation of particular works. The irony, however, of this sudden wealth of studies in fantasy is that due to their timing none has had the opportunity to take formal stock of the arguments of the others. This is unfortunate, since stimulating differences of position and approach characterize the three books.

I think it was Northrop Frye who remarked that the endemic disease of generic criticism is hardening of the categories, and to this disease discussion of the fantastic is by no means invulnerable. Manlove sees fantasy as "a fiction evoking wonder and containing a substantial and irreducible element of the supernatural with which the mortal characters in the story or the readers become on at least partly familiar terms" (p. 1): this is a rather narrow, content-orientated definition, highlighted as such when contrasted with Irwin's presentation of supernatural fantasy as one of no less than five observable kinds. However, for both Irwin and Rabkin it is the psychology of response rather than the description of content which must provide the fundamental criteria of fantasy, and this involves the critic in making formulations in terms of the reader's sense of the probable, improbable, possible and impossible (terms, incidentally, which Borges has previously used to differentiate between the writings of Jules Verne and H. G. Wells). The broad difference in strategy between Rabkin and Irwin is that while the former first attempts to isolate observable signals *within* the text which indicate the presence of the fantastic and, by extension, fantasy, the latter firmly deduces its presence by examining the terms of confrontation *between* the text and the reader.

Irwin's is a simpler if more obviously questionable position than Rabkin's: for Irwin, "a fantasy is a story based on and controlled by an overt violation of what is generally accepted as possibility ; it is the narrative result of transforming the condition contrary to fact into 'fact' itself" (p. 4). The keystone, then, of Irwin's definition is impossibility intellectually perceived by the reader but accepted by him under the sway of that rhetorical function which Irwin sees as integral to fantasy, and which causes the reader to suspend his desire to resolve the paradox of what he knows to be possible (his contingent world) and what he knows to be impossible (the world of the fantasy). In consequence, excluded from Irwin's genre of fantasy proper are those works which do not satisfy Huizinga's *homo ludens* by persuading him to walk in the labyrinths of intellectual paradox ('the game of the impossible'), but instead only offer mere improbability or emotional rather than intellectual play: ghost stories, fairy tales, gothic romances, beast fables, detective fiction, pornography, and, with grudging support from Kingsley Amis in *New*

Maps of Hell, science fiction. But are there not difficulties in establishing that consensus of what is deemed impossible and what merely improbable, on which Irwin's isolation of fantasy depends? Irwin finds that consensus in what he terms man's common 'sense of fact', a faculty which enables human beings to pronounce consistently and uniformly, and without reflection, upon what they regard as possible and impossible. This might be reasonable if all readers of fantasy belonged to one place and time, but the problem of the cultural and historical relativity of concepts of the impossible does arise: these must change in time (especially within a technological society) and space, so that Irwin's faith in a yard-stick provided by an immutable human nature as the arbiter of the possible is by no means a satisfying foundation for his thesis.

The fantastic, as much as the genre of fantasy, is Rabkin's focus of attention. For Rabkin, the mind which perceives the fantastic reveals something about its own perspectives, and this observation serves as the basis of his contention that the study of the fantastic may provide a coequal complement to the study of the normative in arriving at a sense of the perspectives, or world-view, of readers and writers. Moreover, by indicating how quickly that which was once regarded as fantastic can become reality within our present culture, he effectively crystallizes one's doubts about identifying the fantastic simply by testing the world of the fiction against the reader's experience. Ideal would be a definition which would continue to identify a particular work as just as much a fantasy even when the status of possibility of the original fantastic elements (say, space-travel or solar energy) had changed in the reality and consciousness of the contingent world.

Promisingly, Rabkin first descends inside the whale to direct our attention towards the manipulation of the ground rules of a narrative as a possible index of the presence of the fantastic. This is typical of Rabkin's greater preoccupation with the structural (Vladimir Propp is an influence here), as contrasted with Irwin's concentration (in the fashion of Wayne C. Booth) on the work as rhetorical communication between author and reader. Thus for Rabkin the fantastic does not so much mean impossibility as the contradiction of an established perspective within the fictional world. When Alice, in *Through the Looking Glass,* wishes that the Tiger-lily could talk, she is endorsing a ground rule (to which we readily accede) that flowers can not talk. But when the Tiger-lily replies, that established ground rule is reversed, and for Rabkin the fantastic is in evidence. This is achieved by the use of the anti-expected (which Rabkin distinguishes from the expected, the unexpected, and the disexpected), amounting to a 'diametric reconfiguration' of the ground rules of the narrative world. Local occurrences of the anti-expected thus signal the fantastic, an effect which may occur in works other than fantasies proper, whereas a continued use of this technique in a work enables us to talk of a fantasy. To cope with these degrees of the fantastic Rabkin proposes a 'continuum of the fantastic' on which individual works may be charted, the demonstration of which occupies much of the study. Other internal indications of the fantastic may be found in the statements of the narrator or in the astonishment displayed by characters at their situation, though these are not as dependable signals. All in all, the employment of such criteria suggests ways of detecting the fantastic that are not affected by progress or the passage of time, but even more constructively Rabkin uses Roland Barthes' concept of *écriture,* or grapholect, to sketch the mechanics whereby a reader distant in time from a work absorbs something akin to the original structure of feeling, including expectations of the possible different from those normally his own, by responding to the language of the text. One imagines that some development of this line of thought may also be necessary to cope with those works which are less concerned to signal the fantastic than to lull the reader into an acceptance of the normality of the bizarre. Admittedly these considerations move us away from the formal to the rhetorical aspects of the work, but in doing so Rabkin preserves both work and reader as historically and culturally defined factors—something which Irwin's arguments do not. Today's reader of *The Time Machine,* no less than the hero, is a traveller in time. This being so, we are happier to allow Rabkin, then, to acknowledge the interplay between work and a particular reader's concept of the possible (moulded by culture and history, tempered by his response to the grapholect—and not a simple reflection of human nature), amounting to what Rabkin terms 'the armchair perspective'; he writes of Michael Frayn's *A Very Private Life* that it can 'lead one from darkness to light; [it] creates *in the mind* a diametric reversal and opens up new and fantastic worlds' (my italics). This is akin to the way Irwin sees fantasy functioning and the way most readers of fantasy would describe their experience of it; but the issue is whether that experience can practically provide (as Irwin wishes) the objective criteria for generic classification, or whether Rabkin's more cautious approach is the wiser.

The flexibility of Rabkin's approach to genre is evident in the way that he does not insist upon an autonomous, exclusive genre called fantasy, but instead explores the possibility of creating hierarchies of usage of the fantastic within such genres as westerns, adventure stories, detective fiction, science fiction, pornography and fairy tales, ranging from works with little of the fantastic to those where its use is so intensive as to warrant the term 'fantasy'. This is done by comparing representative examples from each genre. This means that David Lindsay's *Voyage to Arcturus* is no less of an example of science fiction for being also described as a fantasy, nor Julio Cortazar's *Continuity of Parks* any the less a thriller. Establishing a model continuum of the fantastic for a number of these recognized genres, Rabkin suggests that works within different genres occupying similar positions on the continuum promise fruitful cross-comparison, perhaps more fruitful than comparison with works within the same genre. Use is made of a number of diagrams to illustrate such relationships, but nowhere is his procedure more elegant than in his handling of the tricky overlapping relationships between satire, science fiction, and utopian/dystopian fiction: here Rabkin proposes a super-genre which will accommodate those works with allegiances to only one of the genres (say, Asimov's *I, Robot,* to science fiction), or to two (say, *Animal Farm* as satire and dystopia), or indeed to all three (say, Zamiatin's *We.*). This liberal approach to genre avoids the distortions that occur when works are too enthusiastically despatched to exclusive pigeon-holes, and instead we are offered both clarity and the possibility of new analytic insights.

From synchronic study Rabkin moves on to diachronic and suggests how examination of the fantastic may provide new perspectives on literary history, demonstrating how particular genres (his examples are detective fiction and Gothicism) have developed through time by modifying their conventions by reversal, even creating by that process new genres, themselves similarly to be modified in due course. For Rabkin, as he makes clear in his last chapter on the scope of the fantastic, 'Fantasy represents a basic mode of human knowing; its polar opposite is Reality', and the claims that he makes for fantasy and the fantastic are hence large and dignified. One's only regret is that in a work which offers so many perspectives upon the fantastic as a mode of discovery and as a touchstone for the analytical critic, the case is not capped by the persuasive evaluation of some candidates for greatness in the writing of fantasy. This may be beyond Rabkin's brief, but the greatest obstacle that modern fantasy has to face in order to become something more than material for the science of criticism is doubt as to its literary worth and achievement: some may chafe at spending pages in the company of Agatha Christie, Ellery Queen, not to mention *Sex Sorceress,* when Mervyn Peake appears not to warrant a mention and when the author seems rather shaky about his knowledge of Dickens (Jarndyce does *not* marry Esther at the end of *Bleak House* [p. 12]). Nevertheless, *The Fantastic in Literature* is a responsible, stimulating and often entertaining study which will be indispensable for future theorists and critics of the fantastic and fantasy.

Saint David's University College, Lampeter   PETER MILES